Majestic Indolence

. . . his life of hope
And hazard, and hard labour interchanged
With that majestic indolence so dear
To native man.
Wordsworth, *The Prelude,* bk 8, ll. 387–90

. . . art only flourishes in leisure time, I guess . . .
Elizabeth Bishop, letter to
Dr. Anny Baumann, July 28, 1952

Majestic Indolence

English Romantic Poetry
and the Work of Art

WILLARD SPIEGELMAN

New York   Oxford
OXFORD UNIVERSITY PRESS
1995

Oxford University Press

Oxford   New York
Athens   Auckland   Bangkok   Bombay
Calcutta   Cape Town   Dar es Salaam   Delhi
Florence   Hong Kong   Istanbul   Karachi
Kuala Lampur   Madras   Madrid   Melbourne
Mexico City   Nairobi   Paris   Singapore
Taipei   Tokyo   Toronto

and associated companies in
Berlin   Ibadan

Copyright © 1995 by Willard Spiegelman

Published by Oxford University Press, Inc.,
200 Madison Avenue, New York, New York 10016

Oxford is a registered trademark of Oxford University Press

All rights reserved. No part of this publication may be reproduced,
stored in a retrieval system, or transmitted, in any form or by any means,
electronic, mechanical, photocopying, recording, or otherwise,
without the prior permission of Oxford University Press.

Library of Congress Cataloging-in-Publication Data
Spiegelman, Willard.
Majestic indolence : English romantic poetry
and the work of art/Willard Spiegelman.
p. cm.   Includes index.
ISBN 0–19–509356–9
1. English poetry—19th century—History and criticism.
2. Art and literature—Great Britain—History—19th century.
3. Aesthetics, British—19th century.
4. Romanticism—Great Britain.
I. Title.   PR590.S66 1995   821'.709—dc   94–33158

Excerpts from *One Art* by Elizabeth Bishop, edited by Robert Giroux.
Copyright © 1994 by Alice Helen Methfessel.
Reprinted by permission of Farrar, Straus & Giroux, Inc.

Excerpts from "The End of March," "Filling Station" and "Poem,"
in *The Complete Poems, 1927–1979* by Elizabeth Bishop.
Copyright © 1979, 1983 by Alice Helen Methfessel.
Reprinted by permission of Farrar, Straus & Giroux, Inc.

I am grateful to Margaret Nemerov for permission to reprint "The Metaphysical Automobile,"
in *The Collected Poems of Howard Nemerov* (Chicago: University of Chicago Press, 1977).

"The Silken Tent," from *The Poetry of Robert Frost,* edited by Edward Connery Lathem.
Copyright 1942 by Robert Frost. Copyright © 1969 by Henry Holt and Co., Inc.
Copyright © 1970 by Lesley Frost Ballantine. Reprinted by permission of Henry Holt and Co., Inc

1 3 5 7 9 8 6 4 2

Printed in the United States of America
on acid-free paper

PR
590
.S66
1995

For Charles Rowan Beye

Καὶ οἱ συνιέντες φανοῦσιν ὡς φωστῆρες τοῦ οὐρανοῦ

Qui autem docti fuerint fulgebunt quasi splendor firmamenti.

And they that be wise shall shine as the brightness of the firmament.

Daniel 12:3

Acknowledgements

An academic who claims to be working on indolence elicits a predictable assortment of quips, wisecracks, and know-it-all glances from colleagues and nonacademic friends. Jokes about narcolepsy, hammocks, lazy afternoons, and unfinished tasks abound. The image of the professor who hardly works at all is exaggerated, though hardly groundless. The American university, the contemporary institutional Maecenas for artists and scholars alike, provides the closest thing to a pastoral *locus amoenus* in our late-industrial world. (In his fable *The Parasite* Michel Serres has termed his titular character "sometimes professorial, sometimes pastoral.") And college teachers are practically the only workers who can routinely count on extended temporal grace, whether in the form of sabbatical leaves or of summer respite, as a dividend by which to accomplish a different kind of "work." I recognize such time as anyone's greatest gift, the means by which we transform the pastoral into the georgic.

Nowhere has the passage of time seemed so powerful or frightening as in my realization that I first read a book of literary criticism in 1962 as a college freshman. That book—for a course in nineteenth-century French literature—was Irving Babbitt's *Rousseau and Romanticism,* a work antiquated even then. Perhaps I needed the three intervening decades to come to grips with my first exposure to Romanticism and its detractors as well as its advocates.

My professional debts are institutional and personal, the former often serving as an occasion for the latter. The National Endowment for the Humanities provided me with a series of awards, extending from a summer grant in 1984 to a yearlong fellowship (1990–91), which allowed me the time to begin and finally to complete this project. In 1989, at an NEH-sponsored seminar entitled "The Lyric and History," intended for college teachers and held in New Haven, I first tried out some of my speculations before an audience under the patient guidance of Paul Fry. Two years later, at Harvard University's Center for Literary and Cultural Studies, I further elaborated on my ideas at a regular meeting of the Romanticism study group. The probing questions and criticisms of John Hodgson, William Keach, David Perkins, Alan Richardson, Charles Rzepka, and Vernon Shetley forced me to clarify my focus and to expand my scope. As usual, I am grateful to the deans of Dedman College at Southern Methodist University for their continuing encouragement and support of my scholarly endeavors.

Others who have contributed in different ways to my thinking about, and grapplings with, indolence may not remember their advice or recognize their ideas as I have absorbed and transformed them in the following pages. These people include David Bromwich, Paul Cantor, Bonnie Costello, Roger Gilbert, Sander Gilman, John Hollander, J. D. McClatchy, and Anya Taylor. Barbara Charlesworth Gelpi, the press reader of my manuscript, made invaluable recommendations and steered me away from some flagrant errors. At Oxford University Press, Elizabeth Maguire and Henry Krawitz proved themselves models of editorial generosity and kindness. Amanda Heller performed the copy editing with a light but steady hand.

Three other friends variously supported my indolence and shared my labors. Kenneth Bleeth read successive versions of the manuscript and aided me in honing and expanding it where necessary. Stephen Orgel steered the book to its final destination at Oxford. Charles Rowan Beye provided me with a haven in Cambridge during the year of the book's writing; he taught me Greek a long time ago and, subsequently, much else about life and literature. I happily dedicate this book—about modern transformations of pastoral—to a classicist who has himself negotiated the straits of *otium* and *labor* and come back to port smiling.

Contents

A Note on Editions
and Abbreviations

Unless otherwise noted, I have used the following editions:

The Complete Poetical Works of Samuel Taylor Coleridge, ed. E. H. Coleridge (Oxford: Clarendon Press, 1912). Hereafter *CP.*

The Poetry of Robert Frost, ed. Edward Connery Lathem (New York: Henry Holt, 1969).

The Poems of John Keats, ed. Jack Stillinger (Cambridge, Mass.: Harvard University Press, 1978).

Shelley's Poetry and Prose, ed. Donald H. Reiman and Sharon B. Powers (New York: Norton, 1977).

Walt Whitman, *Complete Poetry and Collected Prose* (New York: Library of America, 1982).

William Wordsworth, *Lyrical Ballads, and Other Poems, 1797–1800,* ed. James Butler and Karen Green (Ithaca, N.Y.: Cornell University Press, 1992).

———, *Poems, in Two Volumes, and Other Poems, 1800–1807,* ed. Jared Curtis (Ithaca, N.Y.: Cornell University Press, 1983).

———, *The Prelude, 1799, 1805, 1850,* ed. Jonathan Wordsworth, M. H. Abrams, and Stephen Gill (New York: Norton, 1979). Unless otherwise noted, all references are to the 1805 version.

The following works are referred to throughout the text:

Samuel Taylor Coleridge, *Biographia Literaria,* 2 vols., ed. James Engell and W. Jackson Bate, in *The Collected Works of Samuel Taylor Coleridge,* ed. Kathleen Coburn (Princeton, N.J.: Princeton University Press, 1983). Hereafter *BL.*

————, *Collected Letters,* ed. Earl Leslie Griggs (Oxford: Clarendon Press, 1956–71). Hereafter *CL.*

————, *The Notebooks of Samuel Taylor Coleridge,* 3 vols., ed. Kathleen Coburn (Princeton, N.J.: Princeton University Press, 1957–73). Hereafter *Notebooks.*

John Keats, *The Letters of John Keats,* 2 vols., ed. Hyder E. Rollins (Cambridge, Mass.: Harvard University Press, 1958). Hereafter *Letters.*

William Wordsworth, *The Letters of William and Dorothy Wordsworth,* 2nd ed., ed. Ernest de Selincourt, rev. Chester L. Shaver. Vol. 1: *The Early Years, 1787–1805* (Oxford: Clarendon Press, 1967). Hereafter *EY.*

————, *The Letters of William and Dorothy Wordsworth,* 2nd ed., ed. Ernest de Selincourt, rev. Mary Moorman. Vol. 2: *The Middle Years, Part 1, 1806–11* (Oxford: Clarendon Press, 1969). Hereafter *MY.*

————, *Prose Works of William Wordsworth,* ed. W. J. B. Owen and Jane Worthington Smyser (Oxford: Clarendon Press, 1974). Hereafter *PrW.*

Majestic Indolence

1

"Majestic Indolence":
The Progress of a Trope

The New Historicism has cast much in doubt. This latest avatar of Marxist criticism has proved to have a stern side in spite of its debts to Mikhail Bakhtin's "carnivalism." Many of its practitioners take a skeptical, even disapproving, stance toward "high" canonical culture, which they define as the result and reflection of a hierarchical, class-bound structure, and toward aesthetics, which they consider a misguided intellectual exercise in bad faith.[1] This book is an attempt to salvage aesthetics—and literary formalism in general—by examining one kind of poetry which for want of a more specific word I label "pastoral," and the psychological and physical phenomenon of indolence, which I shall deal with in both its negative manifestations (sloth, torpor, and paralyzing dejection) and its positive ones (leisure and "wise passiveness"), focusing on a specific literary and cultural setting, namely, Romantic England from the publication of *Lyrical Ballads* (1798) to the death of Shelley (1822).

This study will follow several paths. I am interested, first, in the way indolence as a human condition underwent a revaluation during this period; second, in the historical and economic conditions that made such a revaluation possible; and third and most important, in the effects, manifestations, and even causes of these changes in the work of the Romantic poets. I shall discuss variations on my central theme, focusing on different representations of indolence. For Wordsworth, the overlapping of and distinctions between work and play are crucial to the great poetry written between 1798 and 1805. For Coleridge, I have devised a close reading of "Dejection: An Ode" that connects the theme of paralyzing torpor to the

3

rhetorical device known as chiasmus, which Coleridge used habitually throughout his poetry. With Keats, I consider indolence not only as the subject of what has been thought the weakest of his great odes but also as the condition he figures in his characterizations of Melancholy and Autumn. Not politics or class (as Marxist critics would have it) but physiology and aesthetics seem to me the proper measures of such figuration. With respect to Shelley, I examine the most important experiments since Milton in pastoral poetry: that aristocratic—or, in Shelley's case, quasi-aristocratic—genre that continually converts the world into an arena for aesthetic wonder and contemplation. Finally, I make an Atlantic crossing to examine the transformation of the English Romantics' sensibility at the hands of their American successors, Whitman and Frost.

Above all, I hope to retrieve for contemplation the category of "the aesthetic," which has taken some hard knocks lately from apostles of both the political right and left.[2] Beginning with so temperate a thinker as Raymond Williams, the new sociologists of literature have deliberately undervalued the formal dimensions of art, preferring to view it primarily if not exclusively as a category of historical effect. As Williams writes, "[W]e cannot separate literature and art from other kinds of social practice, in such a way as to make them subject to quite special and distinct laws."[3] Another version of this idea has been stated by Jerome McGann, to whom so many of the new critics of Romanticism are indebted: "If literature is simply 'free play' and recreation, it faces a true crisis of its legitimacy."[4] This New Historicist speaks in a tone that we might label neopuritanical; we can hear in McGann's attitude something of Irving Babbitt's much earlier disapproval of Romanticism and what he regarded as its excesses.[5] "Recreation" and "free play" are, in fact, very much at the center of my interest here. I contend that indolence, as both the social and personal manifestation of recreative freedom, was transformed and elevated by the Romantic poets in their individual efforts to legitimate their innovations in poetic forms and genres. Grounded in freedom, the aesthetic impulse is one way in which we define our human condition. As Friedrich Schiller aphoristically put it in his fifteenth "Aesthetic Letter": "[M]an shall only *play* with Beauty, and shall play *only with Beauty*. . . . [M]an only plays, when . . . he *is* a man, and *he is only entirely a man when he plays*."[6]

It is true that everything exists within a context, but the important thing is one's choice of context. To insert art exclusively in a material or even a historical framework is to deny precisely what makes it "art" (the quotation marks suggest its currently embattled status) instead of mere propaganda.[7] A Marxist critic may prefer to think of art as social evidence no different in kind or form from other types of social evidence. Nevertheless, however entwined poetic texts may be in the material conditions of their composition and reception, and however programed an author may be by the ideological positions that he or she has deliberately or unintentionally taken or refused, we must not lose our focus on a poet's use of language, which alone will allow us to understand and evaluate artistic achievement.

By attempting to undo Kant's "aesthetic feeling," which has provided the basis of all modern aesthetics for roughly two centuries, McGann wishes to submerge poetry within a sociological matrix:

> [P]oetry deals in the communal experiences of human beings. But a poem stands to its materials in a certain way, with a specific set of interests and methods of self-presentation. As a consequence, a poem will either center or marginalize what it represents, and certain matters salient to the work will be left out of its accounting altogether. In this respect every poem is an action, and the text is its residual form. (p. 53)

Poets, however, perform these actions linguistically: words are materials, and prior texts are quasi-human models to emulate or avoid. Even if one does not wish to subscribe to Harold Bloom's portrayal of a vast Oedipal battlefield littered with the victors and victims of an internecine Anglo-American literary struggle, one may still assent to his claim that reading a poet means following the reading that he or she has performed on precursors. (Although feminist critics have scuttled many of Bloom's ideas as exclusively masculine in their bias and application, they have agreed to a separate but equal "history" of women's writing that takes its cue from the same premise, namely, that writers base their works on prior writers.)[8] I assume as a point of faith and as a methodological beginning the dictum from the late Hugh Sykes Davies that "the best commentary on a passage of Wordsworth is always another passage of Wordsworth." I also agree in principle with the suggestion made by the classicist W. R. Johnson that future observers may very well look back in wonder at the attempts made to appropriate literature to sociology and politics at the end of the twentieth century, and to ignore the pleasure principle at work behind acts of reading. Such old-fashioned words as "pleasure" and "beauty" inform Johnson's elegant treatment of Lucan.[9]

In this introductory chapter I briefly examine the conditions that made "indolence" possible—and even socially, medically, and philosophically fashionable—in order to arrive at a deeper understanding of those linguistic turns that enable us to understand the aesthetic (i.e., formal, mimetic, and expressive) achievements of several poets in some of their characteristic works. Thus, I deem it significant that variations on "indolence" and "indolent" appear frequently and positively in Wordsworth's poetry but almost always negatively in Coleridge's; in Byron's and Shelley's poems the words never appear at all.[10] Whereas, by the nineteenth century, "sloth" maintained its position in a fading hierarchy of ecclesiastical vices and "idleness" retained its primary connotations of vanity and emptiness, both "indolence" and "leisure" had gained a greater and more positive currency among the poets.[11] Social and economic conditions at large may be held responsible for the conditions that make leisure possible to one class of people, but we must grant to the poets the aesthetic power to enforce a revaluation of an abstraction through their figurative grapplings with it. When Wordsworth is able to think of indolence as alternately "tiresome," "pleasing," "voluptuous," and, in his most resonant predication, "majestic," we know as readers that the social and poetic realms are tightly connected in a Gordian knot of causality we cannot easily untie.

The changes that occurred within the European cultural and political milieu between the Renaissance and the nineteenth century had material and economic causes but also intellectual ones. Such a transformation might explain, and in turn be explained by, the difference between Montaigne's examination in his essay "On Idleness" and later renderings of the same psychological condition. The brain, says the Frenchman, is like land: rich, but left untilled it will teem with wild and useless plants, so we must master it in order to keep it serviceable. Not acknowledging the virtues of letting land lie fallow, Montaigne continues with the human application of his metaphor: "[I]f we do not occupy [our minds] with some definite subject which curbs and restrains them, they rush wildly to and fro in the ill-defined field of the imagination." Idleness per se is wild and ill-conceived, a frenzy rather than authentic leisure. "The mind that has no fixed aim loses itself, for, as they say, to be everywhere is to be nowhere." Although he hopes to rest in retirement and in self-contemplation, he finds, to the contrary, with Lucan (4.704), that "variam semper dant otia mentem." Many chimeras occupy the mind; he decides to write about them so that he might tame, purge, or even order them, and hence become ashamed of them. Only in this way will he be able to control the wild, unpredictable, and unstable flights of imagination, that faculty which threatens to undermine sanity and reason.[12]

From Montaigne's practical metaphor, which conceives of idleness as the negation of productivity, we can make an instructive leap to Rousseau, who in his *Reveries of the Solitary Walker* confesses:

> I would slip away and go throw myself alone into a boat that I rowed to the middle of the lake when the water was calm; and there, stretching myself out full-length in the boat, my eyes turned to heaven, I let myself slowly drift back and forth with the water, sometimes for several hours, plunged in a thousand confused, but delightful, reveries which, even without having any well-determined or constant object, were in my opinion a hundred times preferable to the sweetest things I had found in what are called the pleasures of life.[13]

Such a leap between texts from the Renaissance and the late eighteenth century would be facile were it not for the fact that the difference between Montaigne and Rousseau is similar to that between Locke or the more conventionally Christian Samuel Johnson and Coleridge or Shelley (as I describe them in chapters 3 and 5). Moving on to England after the first wave of Romanticism, we can see how George Eliot, that scrupulous reader of Wordsworth, inherited the aesthetic as well as the ideological force that we call Romanticism, in spite of her own stern morality. Here she describes the pleasures of fatigue and the abandonment of the will:

Maggie was hardly conscious of having said or done anything decisive. All yielding is attended with a less vivid consciousness than resistance; it is the partial sleep of thought; it is the submergence of our personality by another. Every influence tended to lull her into acquiescence: that dreamy gliding in the boat, which had lasted for four hours, and had brought some weariness and exhaustion—the recoil of her fatigued sensations from the impracticable difficulty of getting out of the boat at this unknown distance from home, and walking for long miles—all helped to bring her into more complete subjection to that strong mysterious charm which made a last parting from Stephen seem the death of all joy, and made the thought of wounding him like the first touch of the torturing iron before which resolution shrank. And then there was the present happiness of being with him, which was enough to absorb all her languid energy.[14]

In retrospect, of course, this passage reflects the tragic consequences of indolence and yielding, but it also demands of its reader at the time a sympathy with Maggie Tulliver's situation. In spite of her own awareness of the sexual dangers of acquiescence, Eliot has also absorbed the truth of Schlegel's aphorism in *Lucinde:* "Laziness is the one divine fragment of a godlike existence left to man from paradise."[15] Such a legacy, however fragmented, explains the Romantic reinvigoration of that genre of classical poetry most conducive to indolence, the pastoral, which I shall discuss in detail in chapters 2 and 5.[16]

Indolence has enjoyed its own linguistic as well as experiential history. We learn from the *OED* that two of its oldest meanings are now obsolete: "insensibility or indifference to pain" and "freedom from pain; state of mind in which neither pain nor pleasure is felt." Originally it was synonymous with Epicurean *apatheia* ("like the state of a sleeping man" [*OED* cites Thomas Stanley's 1656 *History of Philosophy*]), and only in the eighteenth century did it come to suggest both a more pathological state and a more genial one. Thus, "love of ease" and "laziness" become the more neutral counters to "slothfulness" and "sluggishness." In *Tatler,* no. 132 (February 11, 1710), Steele refers to "a good-natured indolent man" in an essay about the somnolent talk of old men around the fire at a club. The sense of leisurely, pleasurable inactivity seems to have gained the upper hand over either sinful lethargy, torpid senselessness, or mere indifference. By the middle of the eighteenth century cheerful, not to say enviable, indolence had come into its own.

Until 1200 sloth was primarily a monastic vice. Its transformation into good-natured indolence occurred during the six centuries between the High Middle Ages and the beginning of the modern industrial era. As early as 1545 an advice book for servants by Hugh Rhodes labels sloth "the governour of all vyce." This new, fairly atypical emphasis marks the start of a shift away from the conception of the disease as primarily a neglect of ecclesiastical duties, for as Morton Bloomfield and Siegfried Wenzel have noted, the sin of sloth (acedia or accidie) was originally a theological temptation formulated among the Alexandrian monastics.[17] Although Horace (*Epistles* 1.1.38) includes inertia among a list of vices, Christian acedia is clearly different from pagan listlessness. Psalm 118, in the Septuagint translation, uses "acedia" to refer to the sleep of the soul, which Wenzel suggests may be caused by "weariness from the prolonged assault of other temptations (mostly, fleshly thoughts) or by plain boredom" (p. 8). For the classic definition he cites the *Instituta* (A.D. 425) of Cassian, book 10:

> Our sixth combat is with what the Greeks call acedia, which we may term weariness or distress of heart. This is akin to dejection, and is especially trying to solitaries, and a dangerous and frequent foe to dwellers in the desert; and especially disturbing to a monk about the sixth hour, like some fever which seizes him at stated times, bringing the burning heat of its attacks on the sick man at usual and regular hours. Lastly, there are some of the elders who declare that this is the "midday demon" spoken of in the ninetieth Psalm. (p. 19)

As a salient consequence of the transformation of sloth, one sees that whereas the monks required the company of other monks—sometimes in a social, communal, or even a quasi-urban setting—to protect them from the *daemon meridianus* and the demons of unrelieved solitude, in the modern age it is the city itself and the ills of society that cause the malady, for which the best cure is escape *from* other people and *to* the relative isolation of the country.

By the time of Aquinas sloth is related to *tristitia,* an aversion from man's *spiritual* good, against divine good itself (Wenzel, p. 55). Its opposite is no longer stoic fortitude but *gaudium,* the spiritual joy that counters spiritual sorrow. More than religious dryness, what Saint Bernard called "sterilitas animae" (because the spiritually dry person theoretically knows and worries about his condition), sloth becomes what Dante (*Purgatorio* 17) calls a "lento amore," loving a great good with less intensity (*vigore* or *cura*) than it deserves. The meridian devils have retreated, to be replaced by simple weariness. Petrarch, the forerunner of all modern psychologists of indolence, combines bodily with spiritual inertia in his definition, and leaves behind the Thomistic "grief at some true evil" (which formed part of acedia in the *Summa Theologiae*) in favor of a lament, a sense of "disgust at surroundings that hinder concentration—not on prayer but on writing poetry, history, moral philosophy—, and weariness of a world which seems disgusting and contemptible, but which it is also a delight to fret about. Elizabethan melancholy and Romantic *Weltschmerz* are not too far away" (Wenzel, p. 162). Goethe's Werther and Chateaubriand's René, sufferers from both bodily and spiritual inertia, are Petrarch's descendants.[18]

Over the years, sloth changed places with its six siblings in traditional allegorical pageants.[19] So, for example, Chaucer's Parson, who describes it as a paralysis of will (it "forsloweth and forsluggeth"), places it midway between the sins of the spirit—pride, envy, and anger—and those of the flesh—avarice, gluttony, and lechery—as if it occupied a neutral space as an unclassifiable abridgment between the two categories. The one remedy, urges the Parson, is good works, however slight: "An ydel man is lyk to a place that hath no walles: the develes may entre on every syde." Since sloth is essentially the absence of a will to work, it is best cured by busyness, lest wanhope and somnolence lead toward negligence, laziness, and ultimately *tristitia. Fortitudo* and magnificence, in its literal sense of the doing of great deeds, will extirpate the sickness. In *The Faerie Queene* "sluggish Idlenesse" is the first of Lucifera's sage councillors in the House of Pride (1.4.18–20). Spenser has in one way given new prominence to the vice, but in another he has returned it to the older monastic paradigm. His figure is a monk who sleeps rather than reading his worn but little-used breviary. Spenser says that the man withdrew from worldly cares

> And greatly shunned manly exercise,
> From every work he challenged essoyne [pleaded exemption]
> For contemplation's sake: yet otherwise,
> His life he led in lawlesse riotise:
> By which he grew to grievous malady:
> For in his lustlesse limbs through evil guise
> A shaking fever raigned continually.[20]

It was left to Robert Burton in the next century to combine the spiritual and the psychological dimensions of "acedia" and to redefine, under the rubric of "melancholy," what was to become known for at least two centuries as the distinctive malady of the English. "Idleness," wrote its epic historian and taxonomist, "is the *malus genius* of our nation."[21] And idleness has its obvious cure:

> There is no greater cause of melancholy than idleness, "no better cure than business," as Rhasis holds: and howbeit *stultus labor est ineptiarum,* to be busy in toys is to small purpose, yet hear that divine Seneca, better *aliquid agere quam nihil,* better do to no end than nothing. I writ therefore, and busied myself in this playing labour, *otiosaque diligentia ut vitarem torporem feriandi,* with Vectius in Macrobius, *atque otium in utile verterem negotium.* ("Democritus to the Reader," 1:20–21)

Playing labour: in this gracefully paradoxical figure Burton has provided a clue to an understanding of the transition from the medieval and Renaissance views of indolence as slothful sin to the modern formulation that would allow for the invention of "health cures" and, more specifically, for the manifest indolence of the writer as a version of labor (hence, Wordsworth's "wise passiveness" as a psychological and vocational possibility). Leisurely employment ("otiosa diligentia") effects the conversion of *otium* to its useful opposite. As Ruth Fox, one of Burton's most astute readers, puts it: "The key that secures mankind in its melancholy condition is idleness, and idleness is the key that unbolts the door as well. For scholarship is idle—apparently useless—questioning, but it is also the epitome of purposeful work—method and composition."[22]

Burton's concluding advice—"Be not solitary, be not idle"—may very well strike some readers as "tinkling and inconsequential" (Fox, p. 248) after his enormously moving call for loving one's fellow men by loving God, except that, as Fox notes, Burton has constructed his entire treatise as a vast paean to human industry and its invariably "civilizing" force which redeems humanity from its "natural," that is, indolent and melancholy state. From such an argument to the economics of Smith and Ricardo, and later of Marx, seems an inevitable progress. If idleness can be construed as a social ill, curable by the sensible admonition to work, then even a literary critic who grinds no Marxist axe can sense some connection between the development of the modern industrial state and the transformation of a psychological condition from a religious sin into a blot on the social order. But if "playing labour" becomes the condition of the writer in the modern world, then we might observe that literary production, which normally takes place in solitude, will have a new justification. As it does, both the economics of publishing and the situation in which the writer performs his labor will change in order to glorify indolence, rendering it necessary as well as merely attractive. By the middle of the eighteenth century, indolence was coming of age.

Aldous Huxley has succinctly and elegantly traced the metamorphosis of acedia—from deadly sin to disease to lyric emotion—by looking first at the torpor of the desert monk, struck with disgust and lassitude; next at the analysis of Chaucer's Parson; and finally at the eighteenth century, when the disease became "a literary virtue, a spiritual mode . . . a mixture of boredom, sorrow and despair."[23] Although he does not cite him, Huxley follows Wordsworth by ascribing the new respectability of acedia to world events—specifically, the failures of the French Revolution and Napoleon, then the defilement of nature by industry, and the growth of great cities. In the wake of World War I, he laments: "With us it is not a sin or a disease of the hypochondries; it is a state of mind which fate has forced upon us" (p. 25). Idleness, in other words, has been historicized. Modern man is the victim of the social environment and his lassitude the result of his own willfulness. Huxley implies that acedia has now become a punishment for a failure of will rather than a disease that demands its own punishment. No disease, therefore no cure.

Two kinds of causes for the upward mobility of indolence—in its positive as well as its negative guises—may be inferred, the first social and economic, the second medical and philosophical. As J. H. Plumb and others have observed, the eighteenth century witnessed unprecedented growth in what we would now call the leisure industry. Among its several offspring money counts health, happiness, and also free time, which made possible holiday travel and therefore the construction of whole towns dedicated to the leisurely pursuit of health. In the 1740s a Dr. Russell Brighton decided that bathing in and drinking seawater were beneficial activities: hence the birth of the seaside resort.[24] In addition, by midcentury most of the people who went to spas such as Bath had ailments derived from overeating.[25] New wealth created the time and money for new activities such as casual shopping (for which eighteenth-century tradesmen devised the bow window and the display cabinet) and the development of paying audiences for sports. Not only did theater, music, and horse racing in their essentially modern forms develop between 1670 and 1770, but they also inspired festivals of leisure that brought these activities to country towns. Formerly private entertainments gave way to public ones. Private leisure took on public dimensions, as assembly rooms built by subscriptions in market towns sometimes held twice their capacity for Masonic meetings.

Plumb has suggested that the growing middle classes were willing to spend more on both "enjoyment and self-improvement." ("Commercialization of Leisure," p. 285). He thus combines, without explicitly saying so, the *dulce* and *utile* of traditional aesthetics. Consequently, sport and culture in general became less elitist and private, and more public. Such expansion contributed, as I shall argue later, both to the glorification of leisure in the works of the Romantic poets and in their turning away, for various reasons, from the public displays of such leisure activities. Most important for our purposes was the growth of reading as a leisure activity made possible by the expansion of the printing trade (a growth that would accelerate spectacularly after the invention of wood pulp paper in the mid–nineteenth century). Freedom of the press in the 1690s led to journalism in the eighteenth century, which in turn led to the development of newsrooms and circulating libraries, the publication of musical scores, and the new production of specialized children's books (in addition to clothes and toys). With all of this commercial activity came the advertising of leisure activities, which were associated in part with the possibility of self-improvement. Primers and other easily and cheaply available books gave mutual benefits to both seller and buyer. Commerce and education went hand in hand. "Leisure could be turned to profit," as Plumb puts it, ("Commercialization of Leisure, p. 267), and profit could be derived from leisure activity as knowledge, available through publishing, became less arcane. And with the new knowledge and the new leisure came the new refinement. Norbert Elias and other sociologists have noted that the civilizing of game contests developed first in England among the aristocracy and gentry of the eighteenth century. "Civility" (Erasmus' term) came to include, as more than an ideal to be paid lip service, temperance and the avoidance of indulgence and self-castigation. "Sociability as a basic element of leisure plays a part in most if not in all leisure activities," at least according to a sociologist's view.[26]

It is not my purpose to speculate on the deeper connections between social–economic causation and medical–psychological diagnostics except to allow for their—at least—parallel paths. As leisure became widespread, economically feasible, and morally defensible, indolence also became, if not yet socially respectable, at least medically tolerated. A rapid survey of the early psychiatric literature suggests a subtle but discernible upward re-valuation of leisure in its personal and social forms. In the Renaissance melancholy was a symptom of and therefore a synonym for madness; its manifestations included delusions as well as depression. For these at least one Elizabethan writer advised the curative potential of rural life: "[L]et them ryde or walke by places pleasant and greene, or use sailing on wa-ter."[27] Relaxation came to be understood as a vital part of the treatment for melancholia (of which indolence had previously been considered a symp-tom). For example, Thomas Wallis, in *An Essay of the Pathology of the Brain and Nervous Stock* (1681), recommends "pleasant talk or jesting, Singing, Musick, Pictures, Dancing, Hunting, Fishing and other pleasant Exer-cises." His pastoral program was repeated by the cardinal rule in Richard Baxter's *Signs and Causes of Melancholy* (1716), to "put [the patients] in a pleased condition," which was the opposite of standard earlier treatments that included the administering of pain or shock, and which involved a proto-version of group therapy, encouraging patients both to help those worse than they and to find an outlet for own their anger (the emotion Freud later acknowledged as the obverse of melancholia).[28] Throughout the eighteenth century, in fact, melancholy was no longer synonymous with madness but with depression; thus, it came to assume its modern meaning. And it remained, specifically, an English malady, climate-related.[29]

The English malady (*morbus anglicus*) had no keener observer or sufferer in the eighteenth century than Samuel Johnson, whose comments echo those of Montaigne which I cited earlier.[30] In chapter 44 of *Rasselas*, "The Dangerous Prevalence of Imagination," he observes that "all power of fancy over reason is a degree of insanity," and goes on to trace a pattern of causation that begins with solitude and moves through idleness and the cessation of inquiry:

> He who has nothing external that can divert him, must find pleasure in his own thoughts, and must conceive himself what he is not: for who is pleased with what he is? He then expatiates in boundless futurity, and culls from all imaginable conditions that which for the present moment he should most desire.

Eventually, through the despotic reign of fancy, the mind is fed on false-hoods, "and life passes in dreams of rapture or of anguish." The eruption to kaleidoscopic madness begins in simple stasis. Like nature, the mind abhors a vacuum; vacancy demands reparative filling; and inactivity leads to an explosive parody of activity.

The dread of sloth, and of its consequences, still held a powerful sway over Christian souls. Doubtless Dr. Johnson spoke for many who shared his phobia about idleness when he wrote in a diary entry for April 21, 1764: "My indolence, since my last reception of the Sacrament, has sunk into grosser sluggishness . . . my appetites have predominated over my reason. A kind of strange oblivion has overspread me, so that I know not what has become of the last year."[31] As early as 1729 Johnson heroically attempted to defend himself against what was to become a lifelong assailant: "I bid farewell to Sloth, being resolved henceforth not to listen to her siren strains" (*Diaries,* p. 26). That his enemy is gendered adds something to our understanding of the particular fears of Johnson himself: idleness is associated specifically with the fear of unmanliness, of being unmanned, seduced into a passionate torpor, which itself creates a circle from which there is no apparent escape except through a heroic act of will. As he claims (echoing Virgil's "facilis descensus Averno . . . sed revocare gradum") in a *Rambler* essay:

> Indolence is therefore one of the vices from which those whom it once infects are seldom reformed. . . . To do nothing is in every man's power; we can never want an opportunity of omitting duties. The lapse to indolence is soft and imperceptible, because it is only a mere cessation of activity; but the return to diligence is difficult, because it implies a change from rest to motion, from privation to reality.[32]

Precisely because Johnson's specific kind of indolence, and his accompanying fear of it, mixes conventional Christianity with a Lockean distrust of the dangers of unbridled imagination, it stands as a pivot between the medieval theological status of sloth and its location as a mental infirmity described by proto-psychiatrists from the Renaissance onward.[33]

Ultimately the treatments for melancholy suggested by seventeenth-century experts would lead to the Mitchell–Playfair cure of enforced relaxation, one that delicately balances rest with physical and mental activity, both of which are intended to relax and stimulate the patient. Such a balance came through the additional filter of Romantic poetry. S. Weir Mitchell himself (whose late Romantic poetry I cite in chapter 6), acknowledging the salubrious effects of outdoor exercise, also seemed to think that the American climate was too despotic to allow for the kind of healthful walking that the English delighted in, but nevertheless recommended rural life for both nationalities, as well as both sexes. Our cares, he wrote, disappear in the country: "At home, in cities, they seem so large; here, in the gentle company of constant sky and lake and stream, they seem trivial, and we cast them away as easily as we throw aside some piece of worn-out and useless raiment."[34] The cure is the virtually automatic product of both exercise and the leisurely perusal of books: "Read," advises the good doctor, "as you lie in a birch canoe or seated on a stump in the woods." Read what? Ruskin and Wordsworth are, unsurprisingly, two favorites. As both Wordsworth and (still earlier) Rousseau realized, idleness may stimulate healthful activity rather than subduing or parodying it.[35]

Roy Porter has shown why it made sense in post-Cartesian England to regard mental disorders as bodily in nature—hence organic and mechanical—rather than spiritual. In so doing, philosophers and physicians alike managed to deal with mental problems without involving the eternal soul or the threat of satanic possession.[36] He has convincingly disputed Michel Foucault's claim in *Madness and Civilization* that "madness was perceived through the condemnation of idleness."[37] Confinement for madness was less general in England than in France during the eighteenth century; this suggests that the English dealt with both sloth in particular and mental illness in general differently from the French. In addition, asylum life was in fact characterized by idleness (indolence was conceived as a treatment rather than a symptom of disease) or by token occupational therapy such as recreational gardening. Above all, Porter remarks the great number of complaints by eighteenth-century writers on the subject connecting "the English vice" not just with climate and food but with wealth in general. He cites George Cheyne on "the Inactivity and Sedentary Occupations of the better Sort (among whom this Evil mostly rages) and the Humours of living in great, populous and consequently unhealthy Towns" (Porter, *Mind-Forg'd Manacles*, p. 83).

There is an inevitable, logical connection between such antiurban sentiments and Wordsworth's condemnation, in the Preface to *Lyrical Ballads,* of the "multitude of causes" that are blunting "the discriminating powers of the mind, and unfitting it for all voluntary exertion to reduce it to a state of almost savage torpor" (*PrW,* 1:128). Sloth, conceived negatively, and leisure, its beneficial opposite, went hand in hand as the price of progress. Both are marks of distinction: according to Porter "being ill could be symptomatic of well-being," just as having a suntan became the enviable mark of a life of leisure once Coco Chanel redefined the parameters of beauty on the Riviera in the 1920s. Like vice, madness was tied to the increase in wealth, luxury, and "unrestrained liberty," declared Dr. William Rowley (1788). From this standpoint it is no surprise that, in the minds of many authorities, the noble savage never had to worry about mental disease.[38]

Once acedia became known as an urban disease that spared both the lower orders and the rural ones, an obvious remedy for it was country living, the regimen of recreation, exercise, and simple diet on some early equivalent of a modern health farm. Cheyne's health cure led to the belief in the salubriousness of "taking the waters."[39] Here, of course, two kinds of recommendations diverged from each other. To the extent that the spa, and spa life, became a staple of the Georgian rest cure, it was a social experience, leading eventually to the urbane European tradition of moving seasonally from one spot to another. And it inspired a wide variety of novelistic treatments, from Jane Austen to Thomas Mann. Even Coleridge ventured an observation on the fashion of sea bathing: "Fashion's pining sons and daughters, / That seek the crowd they seem to fly, / Trembling they approach thy waters, / And what cares Nature, if they die?"[40] But since solitude was considered an antidote to the overstimulation of urban pressures, a solitary life would enable the distressed individual to calm his or her nerves, not merely restoring the rule of reason to overwrought passions (according to the older model) but also (according to the newer one) allowing himself or herself to eradicate the effects of the misassociation of ideas in a state of nervous excitement. The increase of wealth and leisure led to the establishment of social life in the country, the growth of "modern" urban tension to the need for rustication as a means of restoring jangled nerves. Although historians such as Plumb emphasize the bourgeois, upper–middle-class nature of much of the new entertainment and leisure at the end of the eighteenth century, the contemporary fashion for walking tours had strong democratic overtones. On one such tour Coleridge and Southey devised their scheme for a Pantisocracy; a recent biographer of Coleridge stresses the bohemianism of their leisure: "Young men from the universities dressed as tramps and wandered over the countryside, staying at local inns, talking enthusiastically with 'the common people,' hill-climbing, swimming, star-gazing and communing with nature."[41]

All the early authorities seem to agree, foreshadowing Freud's *Civilization and Its Discontents,* that "insanity increases with civilization"[42] and may be attributed to capitalist economic dislocation, industrialization, and modern life in general. Roy Porter offers evidence that migration to factory towns *renewed* social solidarity rather than abolishing it, but it seems nevertheless to be a point of faith, if not of evidence, among contemporary nineteenth-century physicians and philosophers that the pace of urban life has alienating effects on members of all social classes. Indolence and torpor, replacing the older sin of sloth, became paradoxically a symptom of the disease of modern life at the same time that leisure, recreation, and rural retreat were viewed as having curative powers to assuage the emotional, psychological, and physical strains of that life. It is at the pivotal point between these two extremes that I would locate the Romantic poets and their tropings of indolence.

A belief in the salubrious effects of country life (instead of what Marx dismissed as its "idiocies") coincided with the establishment of "the picturesque" as an aesthetic and psychological category, which itself resulted from—or at least was contemporaneous with—the new wealth in Georgian England. Raymond Williams makes the most pithy connection between art and economy: "[T]he picturesque journeys—and the topographical poems, journals, paintings and engravings which promoted and commemorated them—came from the profits of an improving agriculture and from trade."[43] Art historians and other students of landscape have recently observed the way in which the repose celebrated by landscape art was an implicit recognition of work performed by others.[44] As such, both the land and the landscapes that depict it became objects carrying economic as well as aesthetic values. Especially in eighteenth-century England, the upper classes began to see the landscape, like the land, as a cultural and aesthetic talisman. Ann Bermingham makes the cogent point that

> this coincidence of a social transformation of the countryside with the rise of a cultural–aesthetic ideal of the countryside repeats a familiar pattern of actual loss and imaginative recovery. Precisely when the countryside—or at least

large portions of it—was becoming unrecognizable, and dramatically marked by historical change, it was offered as the image of the homely, the stable, the ahistorical.[45]

At the end of the eighteenth century, the topos of repose, a staple of the pastoral from Virgil through the pictorial equivalent of Virgilian Eclogues in the landscape painting of Claude and Poussin, was supplemented by pictures that displayed both labor *and* Virgilian *otium;* by the 1780s those depicted laborers constituted a new class, the rural poor. By the time of Constable, the figures at leisure in the paintings "in most cases are other than workmen."[46]

Alan Liu has argued that the development of "the picturesque" was a visual means of controlling a landscape comparable to the actual land enclosures taking place in England throughout the century.[47] From the Claude glass to twentieth-century tourist guides that label actual spots or occasions as "photo opportunities," what Wordsworth referred to as the despotism of the bodily eye has permitted, indeed encouraged, the leisured viewer–tourist to appropriate and enjoy that which he cannot possess.[48] Liu makes the Foucauldian point that "the object of the picturesque was 'command,' which, first of all, required the regimentation of the viewer" (*Wordsworth,* p. 95). Command is but half the story; what the viewer requires in the picturesque experience, as in the experience we usually label "the sublime," is the elimination of his or her own will so that judgment can be suspended along with consciousness and the will or authority of others may take charge.[49] The tourist relinquishes will in order to achieve an "aesthetic" response. And, as Coleridge was among the first to note, the experience of the picturesque, like that of tourism in general, frequently requires the submission of the viewer to literature. From early on the picturesque involved a willing abandonment of the eye that sees to the eye that reads, as Coleridge's laughter at tourists with guidebooks reminds us: "Ladies reading Gilpin's etc while passing by the very places instead of looking at the places."[50] Seeing was replaced and superseded by reading; pleasure and instruction, as Plumb's studies of the eighteenth-century middle classes prove, neatly coincided. Travel came to depend on travel literature, and tourists to require literary guidebooks as well as actual ciceroni. Travel literature may perhaps even be said to have replaced, as well as stimulated, the travel it was meant to encourage. In addition, a viewer's sense of place, especially that of an English tourist in Italy, quickly became inseparable from the traditional depictions of that place and the accumulated pressures brought to bear especially on a traveling writer.

Aesthetic enjoyment, appreciation, and indeed experience demand the suspension of the will; the honeyed bliss of the aesthete is passiveness in its positive guise. The greed of the eye for sensuous pleasure takes over during those moments when the mind, in Wallace Stevens's words,

lays by its trouble and considers.
The fidgets of remembrance come to this.

This is the last day of a certain year
Beyond which there is nothing left of time.
It comes to this and the imagination's life.
                    ("Credences of Summer")[51]

The state of indolence engenders a reverie during which any rural land-scape can enter the mind and settle there for future restoration. Wordsworth may well have been rebelling against the excessively "visual" orientation of theorists of the picturesque, preferring to contemplate and to *use* landscape in both its essential nakedness (especially in the characteristic Lake District scenes among which he lived) and in its relation to human feeling. Still, learning begins with the laying asleep of the bodily eye, as he announces in "Tintern Abbey," so that true vision may occur. There exists a crucial balance between what an older critical vocabulary would label "seeing" and "vision," passivity and activity, sense and imagination. Will and indolence start to function as aspects of investment and capital formation. The New Historicists have correctly encouraged us to understand how aesthetic appreciation appropriates the language of economics. It is of considerable importance, apart from the autobiographical truthfulness of the experience that Dorothy Wordsworth reports in her Grasmere journal, that Wordsworth found "a host of *golden* daffodills," rather than any other flower, on his walk around the lake on April 15, 1802.[52] The anthropomorphized performers become, within the psychic economy of Wordsworth's imagination, the equivalent of money in the bank, capital stored away for the interest that will accrue later on. Not knowing at the time "what *wealth* to me the show had brought," Wordsworth reaps the rewards of his capital investment only later, when he replicates his earlier passivity, indolently lying about in "pensive mood"; the accumulated interest of his capital returns to him in a flash, unexpected and unsought, like a magical bequest in a fairy tale. In addition, the theatricality of the scene corresponds to the scenery of the River Wye, which to early theorists of the picturesque is better seen by boat than on a jolting carriage because the two sides recede, converge, rise, and sink, thereby changing the background destination, which sometimes disappears from view.[53]

Most significantly, in the last stanza of "I Wandered Lonely as a Cloud," which repeats in miniaturized form the actions contained within the previous three stanzas, the dreamer–investor achieves the personal union with those flowers which he was denied at the time of the actual experience: "And *then* my heart with pleasure fills, / And dances *with* the daffodils" (emphasis added). Surely this is a capitalist's dream come true: pleasure, like money, develops silently within the banked recesses of the imagination, either to be withdrawn at will or to force itself upward and outward as it overflows its confines. The "spontaneous overflow of powerful feelings," Wordsworth's aphoristic 1800 definition of poetry, describes as well the growth of psychic capital from which he created his own most charac teristic poetry. It is not so much that the observant poet *makes* his own investments, however; rather, they are made for him as he wanders thoughtlessly and will-lessly, the passive and indolent recipient of action foisted upon him. Like Raisley Calvert's surprising and generous bequest that freed Wordsworth in 1795 to become a poet, symbolic money comes unknown to the wanderer, who realizes his wealth only ex post facto. An openness to such experience is the only guarantee of future rewards. When opportunity knocks, as he announces at the end of *The Prelude,* the "higher" mind knows how to take advantage of it: "willing to work and to be wrought upon."[54]

In the joint effort of working and being wrought upon, of action and will on the one hand and, on the other, the receptivity that is most potent when it stems from indolence, Wordsworth and the other Romantic poets developed a program for both spiritual and aesthetic sensitivity. Training the eye first to *value* and then to evaluate—the requirements of modern artistic connoisseurship—depends on the leisure to witness the scenery, whether natural or depicted. Another word for this leisure is freedom, and it is significant that the central premise of Kant's *Critique of Aesthetic Judgement,* which formed the philosophical core of Coleridge's aesthetics and the shared assumptions of all the major Romantics, should rely heavily on the many senses of that word. Freedom, in the sense of disinterest, is a prerequisite for taste, "the faculty of estimating an object or a mode of representation by means of a delight or aversion apart from any interest." And freedom, in the sense of leisure, achieves a necessary as well as an ontological status in the estimate of "aesthetic finality" as "the conformity to law of judgement in its *freedom."*[55] Kant unites "the aesthetic," that is, what he labels taste, with leisure, which he labels freedom. A feeling for the beautiful (as opposed to that for its standard eighteenth-century opposite, the sublime) "presupposes that the mind is in restful contemplation, and preserves it in this state" (p. 94).

Kant's multiple pairings always tend to include one "free" element and one that is restricted, confined, or otherwise contingent. So "art," as opposed to "craft," may be defined on the basis of its freedom and playfulness. Craft, the lesser of the pair, is mere labor or business (what Virgil, for example, would distinguish as *negotium* from the classical *otium* of his Eclogues), whereas we call art that which "could only prove final (be a success) as play, that is, an occupation which is agreeable on its own account" (p. 164). Likewise, Kant distinguishes between, but also makes a synthesis of, the twinned arts of speech: rhetoric, "the art of transacting a serious business of the understanding as if it were a free play of the imagination," and poetry, which consists of "conducting a free play of the imagination as if it were a serious business of the understanding" (p. 184). Poetry gives freedom to the imagination, but it also develops *from* the freedom of leisure.

We might even apply Kant's definition of instances of beauty as "purposiveness without the idea of purpose" to all poetry, and especially to pastoral, the genre that treats of action without the appearance of action, or "workability" without the onus or obligation of work. If "beauty is the form of *finality* in an object, so far as perceived in it *apart from the representation of an end*" (p. 80), we have not only the ground, as Jerome McGann and other recent critics of Romanticism argue, for Romantic aesthetics, but also the only possible warrant for "the aesthetic" as a distinct category. Aesthetics has always and not just recently been, it seems, the Cinderella of philosophy, fated to serve the needs of her more arrogant sisters. As long ago as 1955 a Kantian philosopher could lament his field's loss of dignity: "[I]n view of the general decline of interest in aesthetics, courage is no longer needed for the expression of any particular aesthetic view. Perhaps it is needed by those who still profess an unfashionable concern with aesthetics at all, as a philosophical subject."[56]

Just as the theatrical performance of Wordsworth's daffodills generates unlooked-for creative interest (money in the mind's bank), so poetry, which for Kant is the synecdoche for the category of "the aesthetic," presupposes a leisure that then occasions both liberation and enrichment. Poetry, for Kant, gives freedom to the imagination by offering up to us a single form of any concept, "which couples with the presentation of the concept *a wealth of* thought to which no verbal expression is completely adequate . . . thus rising aesthetically to ideas" (p. 191).

The relationships among the manifold meanings of freedom, leisure, and indolence might spark a lively debate among historians, philosophers, sociologists, and literary critics. And yet economic language and considerations are necessary but hardly sufficient to explain the aesthetic impulse, which remains (as I shall show in the next chapter) more related to the useless play of childhood than to adult labor. Elizabeth Bishop, a careful student of her Romantic precursors, once remarked in a letter: "[W]hat one seems to want in art, in experiencing it, is the same thing that is necessary for its creation, a self-forgetful, perfectly useless concentration." That same uselessness recurs as a motif in her great, late lyric, simply titled "Poem," about the perfectly "useless and free" painting left by her great uncle as a "minor family relic / handed along collaterally" among family members, a legacy important to some, unnoticed by others. The painting—not merely a legacy but also "about the size of an old-style dollar bill"—inspires an aesthetic revelation in the poet, who, recognizing a familiar landscape in the picture, senses that life and its depicted representation are only "the little that we get for free, / the little of our earthly trust. Not much."[57] Not much; but neither, I would argue, merely irrelevant or luxurious. The chance to create or appreciate art depends on leisure, but such leisure, especially in the modern age, is hardly restricted to a single class. Uselessness may look more like a synonym for necessity than its opposite.

I take it as a symbolically appropriate fact that the earliest surviving letter from Wordsworth mingles almost instinctively many of the themes I have been rehearsing here. Writing to Dorothy on September 6, 1790, Wordsworth describes his summer vacation in France, events better known to us through his later treatment of them in book 6 of *The Prelude*. Money, travel, leisure, and learning intermingle in tones appropriate to the concerns of any middle-class college student of the past two centuries:

> [O]ur united expenses since we quitted Calais which was on the evening of the 14th of July have not amounted to more than twelve pounds. Never was there a more excellent school for frugality than that in which we are receiving instruction at present. I am half afraid of getting a slight touch of avarice from it. It is the end of travelling by communicating Ideas to enlarge the mind; God forbid that I should stamp upon mine the strongest proof of a contracted spirit. (*EY,* p. 32)

Wordsworth's frugality enlarged both pocketbook and mind, and even though the former was the necessary condition for the latter, it was not in itself sufficient to guarantee an ample spirit. The son of the agent for a Tory landowner, Wordsworth himself would return to the social and political class whence he sprang, but in his brief radical youth he profited in all senses from the conditions that made possible his appearance in France in the "golden" days after the first year of the Revolution. How the leisure—for travel, for contemplation, for appreciation—I have described came to be is a subject for social and economic historians. The way it affected the poetry of the English Romantics, and in turn was affected by it, is the subject to which I now turn.

2

Wordsworth at Work and Play

Shakespeare's Prince Hal, that self-serving Machiavel, uses a puritanical distinction to exculpate his own dissipation and to prepare his audience for his future renovation:

> If all the year were playing holidays,
> To sport would be as tedious as to work;
> But when they seldom come, they wished-for come,
> And nothing pleaseth but rare accidents.
>
> *(1 Henry IV* 1.2.192–95)

The young gadabout bases all human behavior on an economic model: paying the debt he never promised, he claims that he will prove his moral worth by reforming himself into the very image of princely authority that his father claims he has lacked. Redeeming himself by redeeming time, Prince Hal will abandon "playing holidays" in favor of monarchic work.

At the same time, Hal speaks for the world of carnivalism identified by Mikhail Bakhtin and C. L. Barber, that mirror image of, and opposite to, the divinely ordained cosmic and social order that holiday misrule temporarily turns topsy-turvy. Freedom, holiday, misrule, and "rare accidents" are deliberately built into a social scheme as safety valves, allowing the individual and (on a grander scale) the mob sufficient release from worldly cares to ensure their greater subservience to them. "During carnival time life is subject only to its laws, the laws of its own freedom," says Bakhtin, thereby uniting through his language the very conditions one might normally expect custom to separate.[1] To claim a law for anarchy is to make a social and political point about the co-optation of potentially disruptive forces by the dominant order, whether a political or a psychological one. Pleasure, we might say, has claims to its own business: *otium* may signify the epitome rather than the opposite of *negotium*.

These Renaissance concerns permit us to see Wordsworthian indolence as both a result of and a change from earlier incarnations. There is much virtue in Prince Hal's "if," for he knows as well as Shakespeare's Globe audience that all the year is decidedly *not* playing holidays. The same conditional mood obtains at the beginning of a famous Wordsworthian crisis moment, when the wandering poet affirms his essential leisure up until this point: "My whole life I have liv'd in pleasant thought, / *As if* life's business were a summer mood" ("Resolution and Independence," ll. 36–37; emphasis added). This poem asks us to consider nothing less than the relationship between play and work, summer moods and life's business, pastoral *otium* and *negotium*, indolence and (to cite his famous formulation from *The Prelude*, book 6) "effort and expectation and desire," distinctions at the heart of Wordsworth's greatest poetry. As it turns out, within "Resolution and Independence" and Wordsworth's other major lyrics, and in the early books of *The Prelude*, "life's business" *is* to be found in the moods or credences of summer.[2] Anatomies of happiness are seldom as conventional or automatic as anatomies of distress, but Wordsworthian *pleasantness* is a condition we need to understand.

The opening seven stanzas of "Resolution and Independence" depict a wandering poet who undergoes a manic-depressive episode, and succumbs to a temporary anxiety by falling out of a mood of thoughtless happiness before being reinvigorated by his meeting with the resolute leech gatherer. "Happy as a Boy" (l. 18), mounted "high . . . in delight" (l. 24), the poet sinks into a dejection in which "fears, and fancies, thick upon me came; / Dim sadness, and blind thoughts I knew not nor could name" (ll. 27–28). Beset by nameless terrors, the poet experiences not just a momentary crisis of feeling but a crisis of representation: what occurs has never happened before; he can neither see nor diagnose his "blind thoughts." Melancholy defies troping, but a subsequent self-analysis reminds the self-proclaimed "happy Child of earth," who is at home with the surrounding "blissful Creatures," that the future may tell another story. As soon as he places himself *in* time, Wordsworth prepares himself for the anxieties of self-consciousness. Thinking in time means thinking *of* time, and the holiday mood disappears: "But there may come another day to me, / Solitude, pain of heart, distress, and poverty" (ll. 34–35). It is a curious fact that the poet who, in the Preface to *Lyrical Ballads*, consciously abjured the use of "personifications of abstract ideas" (*PrW*, 1:130), should display what another poet (say, Spenser or even Keats) might use as materials for an allegorical pageant, a list of nominal conditions in which naked nouns, unembellished by predicates, undefined by self-analysis, stand so boldly as a cold threat to the speaker's sense of his own carelessness.

The stanza that follows, listing the poet's fears, is a virtual study in the economic planning of a poetic life:

> My whole life I have liv'd in pleasant thought,
> As if life's business were a summer mood;
> As if all needful things would come unsought
> To genial faith, still rich in genial good;
> But how can He expect that others should
> Build for him, sow for him, and at his call
> Love him, who for himself will take no heed at all?
>
> (ll. 36–42)[3]

On the one hand, it is tempting to interpret the poem as a dialectical meeting between the self-delighting, thoughtless indolence of the Wordsworth figure and the self-ennobling, arduous labor of the leech gatherer. The old man corrects the self-induced, neurotic "dim sadness" of the poet by providing him with a model of real resolution in the face of genuine economic hardship. On the other hand, the very fact that the poet has prepared himself for the encounter with his momentary crisis of consciousness allows him to be schooled by the old man's stoicism. Something he needs, in other words, has in fact come to him unsought, thereby validating rather than undercutting the "pleasant thoughts" of his only apparently self-deceiving indolence. As he announces at the sight of the old man (ll. 50–51), the unexpected vision arrives "by peculiar grace, / A leading from above, a something given." The something given, that which has come unsought, not only admonishes and strengthens but also confirms the rightness of the poet's apparent laziness.[4]

Wordsworth's greatest original work is his defense of play: business and leisure turn out to be pretty much the same thing. In book 8 of *The Prelude* he takes a retrospective look at the earlier chapters and attempts to prove his central premise: that "love of nature leads to love of man." The book opens, significantly, with a depiction of a rural fair in Grasmere, a fair that responds to the hellish chaos of London, and especially of Bartholomew Fair as Wordsworth presents it in book 7. Unlike the "blank confusion" of the urban arena, the Grasmere Fair, a meeting of friends and neighbors, combines business and gaiety in which all share.[5] Later in the book, while describing the lives of the "real" shepherds who became exemplars of a new pastoral, Wordsworth inadvertently offers a description that I take as his ideal for himself (or any working poet) as well as for his nominal subjects:

> He feels himself
> In those vast regions where his service is
> A freeman, wedded to his life of hope
> And hazard, and hard labour interchanged
> With that majestic indolence so dear
> To native man.
>
> (8.385–90)

Where labor is hard, indolence is equally majestic, to match and finally to supersede life's hazards, or so a hopeful Wordsworth wants to believe.

In this chapter I will examine some of Wordsworth's characteristic ways of defining and defending various states of indolence, in both its negative and positive guises, and in both individual and social manifestations. Whereas Keats typically invokes the work of art, in the form of the Grecian urn, as a material aesthetic object, Wordsworth examines the labor that produces art. From Keats's opening line of *Endymion*—"A thing of beauty is a joy forever"—at least through Yeats's opening of "Nineteen Hundred and Nineteen"—"Many ingenious, lovely things are gone / That seemed sheer miracle to the multitude"—a major strain of Romanticism was the glorification of the art object. In addition, one might say that Yeats was responding to a complementary Wordsworthian strain when he claimed that

> to articulate sweet sounds together
> Is to work harder than all these, and yet
> Be thought an idler by the noisy set
> Of bankers, schoolmasters, and clergymen
> The martyrs call the world.
>
> ("Adam's Curse")

We must, in the words of Yeats's woman, "labor to be beautiful" and to make beauty: such is the crisis of art, especially from a Marxist perspective, in the modern world. For some Marxists a piano maker is a laborer, but a piano player (from, for example, a bourgeois household) is not. A product of the professional middle classes, Wordsworth was sensitive to such possible charges well before either Marx or Yeats. For him the work of art involves nothing less than a consideration and an enactment of those processes of labor and leisure that define not only the alternating rhythms of workday and holiday time but also their virtual identity.

Such rhythms have an obvious origin in classical versions of pastoral, and they also constitute a legacy from Wordsworth to many of his contemporaries and successors. A charming essay by Hazlitt, "On a Sun-Dial," which appeared in the *New Monthly Magazine* in October 1827, takes its inspiration from a sundial seen at a monastery near Venice, inscribed with a motto from Horace: "Horas non numero nisi serenas." The lessons Hazlitt learns from his deliberations here are, strictly speaking, Wordsworthian more than Italian, monastic, or classical. He blithely turns from "the common art of self-tormenting"; instead, he claims, we should "take no note of time but by its benefits, to watch only for the smiles and neglect the frowns of fate, to compose our lives of bright and gentle moments, turning always to the sunny side of things." From "the region of pure and blissful abstraction" into which he floats, Hazlitt then constructs a vision of a loitering monk who, taking his cue from the fruit ripening in silence, decided "to efface that little from his thoughts or to draw a veil over it, making of his life one long dream of quiet!" From nature and from mind comes the inspiration to dream, to be happy, to be indolent—and to construct the sundial: "Out of some such mood of mind, indolent, elegant, thoughtful, this exquisite device (speaking volumes) must have originated." And from such a reverie Hazlitt proceeds to consider his own lot. He would prefer to ignore time, to "lie whole mornings on a sunny bank on Salisbury Plain, without any object before me, neither knowing nor caring how time passes, and thus 'with light-winged toys of feathered Idleness' to melt down hours to moments."[6]

A day spent "killing time with thought, nay even without thinking": such is the goal of the modern loiterer, the dreamer, the flaneur. It is also the condition of the Wordsworthian poet. "Stanzas Written in My Pocket-Copy of Thomson's Castle of Indolence" (1802) depicts an indolent poet—or, rather, two poets—whose "business" is equivalent to his "delight." This grab bag of Wordsworthian commonplaces is contemporaneous with "Resolution and Independence" (to which it has stylistic resemblances, most notably a terminal alexandrine in each stanza) and offers not one but two versions of Wordsworthian indolence, in the doubled portraits of Coleridge and Wordsworth contained therein. In both cases, as Lucy Newlyn has shown, Wordsworth has tried to exempt the indolent men from charges of wasting time.[7] Such an effort characterizes all of his best poetry during his creative maturity. From his letters, from what else we learn of his daily life from his sister's writing, and from his thematic negotiations of the problems of work and nonwork, *negotium* and *otium*, we get a sense of Wordsworth's position as a poet in the modern world.

To start, I propose a careful look at one section of a canonical poem. "Nutting," the spot-of-time that might have appeared in the opening books of *The Prelude* but found its separate way into the 1800 *Lyrical Ballads*, is rightly seen as a depiction of a young boy's rapaciously active engagement with nature. Beginning with a twenty-line preparation that readies the young, bohemian, quasi-chivalric adventurer for a day in the woods, where he discovers a Miltonic, virginal Eden, "Nutting" concludes with the destruction of the bower by the violent molester and with the sense of guilt that overwhelms him virtually immediately. A brief afterword in the form of a deliberately anticlimactic moral tag concludes the poem. The longest, and central, section of the poem, however, is the one that most critics tend to pass over. These lines of contemplative leisure, settling the child within a pastoral landscape and within the idling luxuriance of his own mind, dramatize the beauties and threats of the Wordsworthian indolent moment:

> —A little while I stood,
> Breathing with such suppresion of the heart
> As joy delights in; and with wise restraint
> Voluptuous, fearless of a rival, eyed

The banquet, or beneath the trees I sate
Among the flowers, and with the flowers I play'd;
A temper known to those, who, after long
And weary expectation, have been bless'd
With sudden happiness beyond all hope.—
—Perhaps it was a bower beneath whose leaves
The violets of five seasons reappear
And fade, unseen by any human eye,
Where fairy water-breaks do murmur on
For ever, and I saw the sparkling foam,
And with my cheek on one of those green stones
That, fleec'd with moss, beneath the shady trees,
Lay round me scatter'd like a flock of sheep,
I heard the murmur and the murmuring sound,
In that sweet mood when pleasure loves to play
Tribute to ease, and, of its joy secure
The heart luxuriates with indifferent things,
Wasting its kindliness on stocks and stones,
And on the vacant air.—Then up I rose. . . .

                                        (ll. 20–42)

These lines are bracketed by the two sections of action—the boy's setting out and his destruction of the bower—but we may also understand this separate moment of suspension as the central point (and not just structurally) of the experience. Joy and sadism are intertwined in what is clearly a rendering of a young, aggressive male's capacity for aesthetic contemplation.

The sections that precede and follow this one are filled with simple transitive verbs which, when listed, make a miniaturized outline of the entire experience: first, "I sallied forth," "I turn'd my steps," "I forc'd my way," and "Then up I rose, / And dragg'd to earth," "I turn'd away," "I felt a sense of pain." What happens in the poem is what the boy *does*. But in the middle he "stood," "sate," "play'd," "saw," "lay," and "heard." He poses (in both senses), or reposes, stationing himself for an aesthetic experience that derives from the certainty of his mastery. Like Browning's Duke of Ferrara, he alone controls the scene that he views. This is the leisured moment of a workingman who relishes his hesitation before returning to the work he is determined to accomplish. It is a reward, a blessing, or (in the words of "Resolution and Independence") a "something given," making him falsely, inflatedly generous, "wasting [his] kindliness" on vacancy. It is also, I infer, the necessary condition for the subsequent destruction. So conscious a hedonism aggravates the violence of the rape. Aestheticized savagery is rare in Wordsworth's poetry. "Nutting" stands out for its implicit suggestion that only a man capable of a restrained yet self-indulgent aestheticism can become the brutal ravager of the patient mossy bower.

The Edenic condition of the bower encourages a reconsideration of

Wordsworth's deliberate use of the pastoral in connection with the twinned motifs of work and leisure (a reconsideration I shall pursue later in a discussion of "The Idle-Shepherd Boys" and "Michael"). The bower is both a classic *locus amoenus* and a parody of one.[8] Expected components—trees, flowers, water—are present, as is a symbolic flock of sheep among the scattered mossy stones. The condition of *otium* is the more valued by virtue of the release from labor and the preparation for even greater labor that follows. Relaxation in the pastoral world always represents an escape from both georgic toil and the natural threats of the noonday sun. But Wordsworth introduces potential discordances by injecting the sinister note of jealous control that no earlier pastoral observer maintained, and by construing a "pleasance" that is positively unreal rather than merely conventional (the uncertain "Perhaps it was" and "fairy water-breaks"). Above all there is the strange abstraction (Wordsworth's way, as I have mentioned, of replacing those "personifications" he claims to abjure) in the doubled "murmur and the murmuring sound," which requires us to imagine a reflection of a sound (a symphony of echoing without clear origin), or a sound in both its empirical and ideal forms. The passage has moved from simple sensory reminiscence ("A little while I stood") to a strangely generalizing, depersonalized self-defense ("in that [mood] pleasure pay[s] tribute to ease . . . the heart luxuriates"). Just as the physical setting becomes more opaque, less conventionally pastoral, so does the poet's self-depiction extend from simple acts of leisurely observation to hiding the self in the language of what Wordsworth refers to in "The Old Cumberland Beggar" as the "one human heart." The conditions of leisure, aesthetic contemplation, and relaxation here not only precede but actually seem to engender larger philosophical generalizations. This is also how Wordsworth controls the major revelations of "Tintern Abbey," moving from empirical data to capacious conclusions.[9] "Nutting," however, does something more: it forces us to consider contemplative or voluptuous leisure as the (narrative) cause of violent action and the (formal) cause of philosophical abstraction. Pastoral and play occupy the central space in the poet's rendition of rape and education.

The "play" element in this scene creates a mock-heroic, and thereby a mock-tragic, event out of an ordinary but immortal childhood recollection. No poet before Wordsworth was so sensitive to the serious dimensions of childhood activity: the powerful enjambment and the Miltonic construction in "wise restraint / Voluptuous" (where we might expect something like "wise restraint / Contemplative"), along with the description of the bower, alert us to the tensions implicit in rendering a scene both innocent and guilty.

Neither was any poet so aware of the inevitable necessity of childlike play to sane adulthood. In discussing *Lyrical Ballads,* which he labels "experiments in expressing glee and or investigations of that state," Donald Davie has invoked the model of the Nietzschean Dionysus, the healthy temperament reveling in morbidity.[10] All critics are compelled to make some com-

mentary on the peculiar relationship between morbidity, grief, and madness and gaiety, playfulness, and community which informs such (to contemporary tastes) strange poems as "Peter Bell" and "The Idiot Boy."[11] At
least one critic has usefully applied the theories of the psychologist D. W.
Winnicott to these poems; and it is the principle of *free play,* the heart of
Winnicott's theory of a child's "re-creation of the real world in order to feel
really at home in it," that defines the difference between the healthy fancies
of Wordsworth's children or childlike characters and the superstitious,
obsessive anxieties of his neurotic or tragic ones.[12]

The element of play, in which a child imaginatively reinvents an already
known world, sits squarely at the center of Wordsworth's universe,
whether in characters such as the Boy of Winander, the hero of "Nutting,"
and other autobiographical representations, or in the dialectic structure of
the adult conversation poems in *Lyrical Ballads,* in which the dialogue
represents the play element in human discourse.[13] The indolence, whether
bodily (mere relaxation) or spiritual (a suspension of will), demanded
for such conversation may be considered the highest value in Wordsworth's world.[14] The parallel to a cardinal element in Schiller's *Aesthetic
Letters* (which I discussed in the previous chapter) is too clear to evade:
"[M]an shall only *play* with Beauty, and shall play *only with Beauty.*
. . .[M]an only plays, when . . . he *is* a man, and *he is only entirely a man
when he plays.*" By transforming their Olympian deities into ever-happy,
nonworking, removed creatures, the Greeks "made *indolence* and *indifference* the enviable lot of divinity; a merely human name for the freest and
noblest existence."[15]

Although he at least sometimes harbored deep suspicions of leisure
and play—his own puritanism rising to the surface against his will—
Wordsworth brought to earth these divinities, embodying their principles
of freedom, leisure, and play in his human characters. In so doing he
provided a new justification for what became in our own century those
aesthetic principles of Auden and Eliot that stem from the Romantic notion of the work of art as an autonomous, self-contained organism.[16] The
origin of such a relation between human freedom and aesthetic principles
may also be traced back to Schiller's theory of a universal phenomenon "in
all races who have arisen from the slavery of the animal condition—delight
in *show,* inclination for *ornament* and for *play*" (Letter no. 26, p. 130).
Aesthetics, like leisure, is hardly an invention of the Enlightenment or of
bourgeois industrial society. It reaches still farther back to Plato (*Laws*
7.803: "Life must be lived as play, playing certain games . . . and then a
man will be able to propitiate the gods") and Aristotle (especially on
music; see *Politics* 8.1337B and 1399A).[17] As it was for the Greeks, so it
was for the German and English Romantics: nature, as Aristotle says,
requires not only that we work well but also that we be able to idle well.
Leisure and play, those universal categories, are the telos of all work.
The Greek *schole,* origin of our "scholarship," was the equivalent of free
time.

Play, show, and ornament (even its Derridean sense of "the supplement") define the *work* of art in its nominal and its active status: art as a self-sustaining unit and as a process that retains a close proximity to the activities of children and gods, who are alike in their freedom.[18] Such freedom derives from idleness, however momentary, since idle moments provide Wordsworth with the ontological condition necessary for pastoral contemplation in both its serious and its holiday moods. Wordsworth is well aware of the potential charges of solipsism that may be put to an indolent version of himself in "Expostulation and Reply," the first of the dialogic poems in *Lyrical Ballads*. Not only solipsism but also the ease of primogeniture informs Matthew's charge to the dreaming poet, who refuses to nourish himself by reading:

> "You look round on your mother earth,
> As if she for no purpose bore you;
> As if you were her first-born birth,
> And none had lived before you!"
>
> (ll. 9–12)

Passivity, threatened by charges of hybris, has a wisdom of its own, which denies the will but elevates the senses ("The eye it cannot chuse but see, / We cannot bid the ear be still; / Our bodies feel, where'er they be, / Against, or with our will" [ll. 17–20]). The body-centered consciousness here feeds the supposed idler and keeps him active even when he appears not to be. Matthew accuses William of arrogance, purposelessness, and solipsism, but the young man deftly turns the accusations to his own advantage, defeating his interlocutor on his own terms. The "light bequeathed" by books (ll. 5–6) *he* gets by his thoughtless seeing; the apparent renunciation of past wisdom is converted by the self-contained organism that wisely, passively feeds itself.

As the resounding conclusion to his own response, William matches Matthew's questions with one of his own:

> "Think you, mid all this mighty sum
> Of things for ever speaking,
> That nothing of itself will come,
> But we must still be seeking?"
>
> (ll. 25–28)

His question remains unanswered because of its paradoxical nature. *Something* will come of itself, ex nihilo, without our actively pursuing it. As in "Resolution and Independence," needful things come, in fact, unsought, just as Wordsworth's inheritance from Raisley Calvert partly laid to rest his own, and his family's, fears for his professional life.[19] Wordsworth was well aware of his status as a second-born son, especially within a family whose patrimony was denied until years after the completion of *Lyrical Ballads;* the conclusion to his argument literally *borrows* the words of Matthew's opening demand and aims them backward at their origin:

> "—Then ask not wherefore, here, alone,
> Conversing as I may,
> I sit upon this old grey stone,
> And dream my time away."
>
> (ll. 29–32)

Dreaming signifies waste to the older man but generative activity to the younger one. With a heart that unconsciously "watches and receives" (his phrase from the pendant poem, "The Tables Turned"), the young Wordsworth has delicately put down the spokesman for the older, puritanical dispensation that posits work, or activity in general, as the source of moral and economic value, not by refusing the terms of the argument but by appropriating them.

The deliberate holiday spirit of these dialogues is decidedly not that of Renaissance Maying poems. It is significant that the invitation "It is the first mild day of March," with its reminder that the "hour of feeling" will create a "living Calendar," and with its hope that speaker, sister, and Edward will give one day "to idleness," bookless and footloose in the woods, comes not in May but in the still barren, leafless earlier month. Both eroticism and the green world are forsworn in favor of an enrichment that derives from early bareness. One day of idleness, of resigning one's "morning task," will tune their souls "to love."

In both "The Two April Mornings" and "The Fountain," added to the 1800 volume, Wordsworth continues to investigate the relationship, both in opposition and in resemblance, of work and idleness, just as he conflates joy and sadness. In the first poem, with its complicated time scheme in which one layer of memory replaces a later one as Matthew realizes that what is dead (his daughter) can never be replaced even by what most resembles it (another "blooming girl"), the "blithe" man traveling "merrily" suddenly succumbs to a sigh of sadness, just as the speaker refers to their "spring holiday" (l. 8) as "our work" (l. 13). "The Fountain" maintains the same tension. William sings "idle songs" and invites Matthew to sing some "half-mad thing of witty rhymes" from a previous April rendezvous. To this invitation to gaiety "the grey-haired Man of glee," whose "heart is idly stirred," delivers his sober series of reflections on the inevitable depredations of time, his sense of what William Empson referred to as the impoverishment even of a life rich in intimacy.[20] His summary of the human condition (ll. 21–56), surely among the most movingly simple in all of Wordsworth's poetry, is met by the somewhat addled William with the blitheness that comes from either callow ignorance or lack of attention:

> "Now both himself and me he wrongs,
> The man who thus complains!
> I live and sing my idle songs
> Upon these happy plains,

> And, Matthew, for thy Children dead
> I'll be a son to thee!"
> At this he grasp'd his hands, and said,
> "Alas! that cannot be."
>
> (ll. 57–64)

The young Wordsworth does not understand the principles of nonreplacement and nonsubstitution that underlie Matthew's sense of the economy in human relationships. As a poet, perhaps, he feels that metaphor (resemblance) sanctions metonymy (replacement), but Matthew knows better. "Many love me, but by none / Am I enough belov'd" (ll. 55–56) suggests that there is no such thing as *too much* love—whether from a single source or many is unclear—and that only an overwhelming inundation will suffice. (This is what Blake means in the "Proverbs of Hell" when he remarks that nothing less than all will satisfy.)

In one way Matthew's denial (l. 64) constitutes a final word: this last piece of spoken dialogue in the poem somberly ends the discussion. But in another way, the Wordsworth figure has the last word, as he reports the pair's subsequent activity:

> We rose up from the fountain-side,
> And down the smooth descent
> Of the green sheep-track did we glide,
> And through the wood we went,
>
> And, ere we came to Leonard's Rock,
> He sang those witty rhymes
> About the crazy old Church-clock
> And the bewilder'd chimes.
>
> (ll. 65–72)[21]

He reestablishes gaiety through indirect discourse. We are told of, but we never hear, those witty rhymes about the crazy old clock. The clear implication is that wit, madness, idleness, gaiety, everything that defines youth and that the gray-haired old man can share at his will, can never be repeated but only reported. The undervoice here—Wordsworth's slightly heard but evidently deeply felt disapproval of idleness—is equivalent to Keats's failure ever to depict indolence in his ode about it. "The Fountain" exposes the credulity of youth, and then proceeds to sound the notes of ardent giddiness, although at this point they must ring a little hollow in our ears.

The major stance of *Lyrical Ballads* is one of approval toward holiday and gaiety, but the undertone of suspicion rises occasionally to a tone more fully voiced, as here, or as in Wordsworth's note on "The Thorn," which describes the speaker as a retired sea captain with moderate income: "Such men having little to do become credulous and talkative from indolence; and from the same cause, and other predisposing causes by which it is probable that such men may have been affected, they are prone to superstition." Here Wordsworth reminds us of the reverse of an idleness construed as freedom or leisure. On the one hand, we have "wise passiveness" that will generate something out of nothing active; on the other, credulity, loquacity, and superstition. Indolence may represent nothing more than a failure to exercise one's will in doing one's duty, as Wordsworth suggests in the Preface to *Lyrical Ballads* when he asks to be "protected from the most dishonourable accusation which can be brought against an Author, namely, that of an indolence which prevents him from endeavouring to ascertain what is his duty, or, when his duty is ascertained, prevents him from performing it" (*PrW*, 1:122).

Implicit in these dialogue poems is the spirit of Blake's *Songs of Innocence and Experience,* which demands a double view of those twinned states of the human soul. Like Blake, Wordsworth does not privilege one state over the other but gives voice to the claims of both. Such a dialectic has its origin in Virgil: beginning with the first Eclogue, pastoral rehearses but seldom resolves certain debates.[22] In *Lyrical Ballads* (and, as I shall show, in *The Prelude*), the voices in the argument center around the poles of work and play, matters very much on Wordsworth's mind as he settled squarely into adult responsibilities. The dialectic appears in nonlyrical poems such as "A Narrow Girdle of Rough Stones," one of the "Poems on the Naming of Places" added to the 1800 volume. The blank verse accords a seriousness to this group, which thereby *seems* more sober in mood; but the poems in fact treat the same philosophical and psychological dilemmas that the more "lyrical" ballads had. In this case three walkers around Grasmere Lake,

> One calm September morning, ere the mist
> Had altogether yielded to the sun,
> Saunter'd on this retir'd and difficult way.
> —Ill suits the road with one in haste, but we
> Play'd with our time; and, as we stroll'd along,
> It was our occupation to observe
> Such objects as the wave had toss'd ashore.
>
> (ll. 7–13)

We find here the deliberate pairing of holiday leisure ("saunter'd," "play'd with our time") with something approaching the hardship of work ("difficult way," "occupation").

The poem is an epistemological fable: the walkers see, and misinterpret, a piece of empirical data; they are corrected; and their final legacy is the name given to the spot where the correction occurs. This trio discovers a fisherman, a prototypical Wordsworthian border figure, whom they mistakenly identify as "an idle man, who thus could lose a day / Of the midharvest, when the labourer's hire / Is ample" (ll. 57–59).[23] Like the leech gatherer, the Old Cumberland Beggar, the discharged soldier in *Prelude*, book 4, or the blind beggar in book 7, the spectral figure unintentionally serves an angelic function by embodying stoic control and correcting the insensitive first impressions of the holiday strollers. The poem dramatizes the matter of *who,* exactly, has been idling, and what, in fact, idling means.[24] Wordsworth could at times issue stern denunciations of human indolence, as he does in "Gipsies" (1807), with its wonderment at a tribe incapable of even aesthetic contemplation (the moon looks at them but "they / Regard not her"), and with its naked conclusion suggesting a clear moral: "The silent Heavens have goings on; / The stars have tasks—but these have none."

Beyond such simple rectification and moralizing, however, lies a more complicated response to the figure of the Grasmere fisherman:

> The man was using his best skill to gain
> A pittance from the dead unfeeling lake
> That knew not of his wants. I will not say
> What thoughts immediately were ours, nor how
> The happy idleness of that sweet morn,
> With all its lovely images, was chang'd
> To serious musing and to self-reproach.
> Nor did we fail to see within ourselves
> What need there is to be reserv'd in speech,
> And temper all our thoughts with charity.
>
> (ll. 70–79)

In self-admonition, the strollers dub the spot "Point Rash-Judgment," but the overt lesson tells only part of the story. Just as Wordsworth concluded "The Fountain" by referring to, but refusing to quote, the mad old songs he and Matthew resumed, so here he tantalizes us with a significant absence in the tale. Why will he *not* tell us what thoughts immediately were his? Because he dare not? Cannot? Do they lie too deep for tears, or for words? The fact that the "happy idleness of that sweet morn" is suddenly transformed to "serious musing" is apparent, but the process (*how* it occurred) is deliberately scanted. Evasion comes as easily to Wordsworth as moralizing: we must take his refusal to "say" as a variant of the rhetorical gambit called *occupatio* (in one way his refusal constitutes an acknowledgment of what he has denied), and also as a deeply mysterious temptation to his readers to speculate on those matters he leaves half articulated.

Paradoxically, such lacunae occupy almost palpable space in *Lyrical Ballads*.[25] Those I have mentioned suggest, I think, that Wordsworth was comfortable with neither easy epicureanism nor self-correcting admonishings. His sense of his poetic "occupation" is riddled with the doubts that appear in his figurations of indolence and labor. The strongest proof of these self-doubts may be seen in a hazily but deliberately ambiguous reference in "A Poet's Epitaph," Wordsworth's strained effort at public satire. Nine quatrains address and dismiss various professional types (statesman, lawyer, preacher, soldier, physician, moralist). The voice is that of the epitaph, speaking from the stone and from beyond the grave.[26] But it is also the questioning voice of the living poet, wondering about his own place within a society that he feels resists or ignores his presence. Not only

the satirizing mood but also the epigrammatic mode of the poem changes
at line 37, when a different kind of person, anonymous and without an
occupation, approaches the grave. This person, first described and only
afterwards addressed, is the poet's double, who is bidden to step forward
after the poem has fleshed him out as a composite Wordsworthian type:
modest, homely, isolated, quiet, weak, and murmuring sweet music. But
the poem's voice expands to include someone else (but who?) in the drama
of description and invitation:

> He is retired as noontide dew,
> Or fountain in a noonday grove;
> And you must love him, ere to you
> He will seem worthy of your love.
>
> (ll. 41–44)

Every previous second-person pronoun addressed one of the types who
appeared and were dismissed. But to whom are these lines spoken? Not to
the youth, surely. Perhaps to the as yet unaddressed reader? To the speaker
himself? This would still be shocking in a poem whose apostrophes have
thus far all been directed to named individuals.

The concluding stanzas offer a possible key to the dilemma, but whether
this key will open an entry or lock it more firmly is a delicate question:

> But he is weak, both man and boy,
> Hath been an idler in the land,
> Contented if he might enjoy
> The things which others understand.
>
> —Come hither in thy hour of strength,
> Come, weak as is a breaking wave!
> Here stretch thy body at full length;
> Or build thy house upon this grave.—
>
> (ll. 53–60)

A rhetoric of antithesis mingles perilously with a rhetoric of parallelism
here. "Man and boy": is this a simplified version of "The Child is Father of
the Man"? Is the individual double or unitary? His enjoyment opposes the
understanding of "others," but Wordsworth has previously (ll. 49–50)
announced that the poet figure can also impart "random truths" "in
common things." Strength and/or weakness: are they simultaneous or alternating conditions? Finally, the address to lie down on, or ultimately
within, the grave: is it an invitation to pastoral *otium*, or a more ghoulish
seduction to suicide? Wordsworth is so sensitive to the very idea of being
"an idler in the land" that he must both praise and bury his mirror image in
the poem. The epitaph, which begins by seeming to come from a disembodied satiric voice, ends by including within its apostrophic reach the
universalized reader (the "you" of ll. 43–44), and the poet–youth who is
absorbed into the speaker as he is enjoined to build his own house, to make

his dwelling place (i.e., to perform his own work) upon the charnel house beneath.

Wordsworth's heeding the demands of work and the attractions of indolence is epitomized by the fact that two of the poems he specifically labels "pastorals"—"Michael" and "The Idle Shepherd-Boys"—thematize work as a central issue.[27] It is also exemplified by the pseudo-Virgilian epigraph chosen for the 1807 *Poems, in Two Volumes*: "Posterius graviore sono tibi Musa loquetur / Nostra: dabunt cum securos mihi tempora fructus." (Afterwards, our Muse will speak to you in a graver tone; when the seasons grant me their fruits in peace.) Here, Wordsworth suggestively equates a harder or graver (perhaps georgic) poetry with the blessings of pastoral ease. Such an equation had been in his mind at least since the second edition of *Lyrical Ballads* seven years earlier. "Michael" has the grandeur and simplicity of Wordsworth's blank verse. "The Idle Shepherd-Boys" is written in the stanzaic pattern of "The Thorn": nine octosyllabic lines with two hexasyllabic ones, in stanzas with an opening quatrain (*a b x b*) followed by a unit of *c d e e d f f* or *c d e e f c c* (every stanza has unrhymed nonce lines).[28] The apparent playfulness in Wordsworth's stylized stanzas disguises, I think, the same kind of doubts that problems of voice had indicated in "A Poet's Epitaph."

This antipastoral Sunday school lesson (Wordsworth is the master of the lighthearted sermon) begins with a three-stanza pastiche of commonplaces from "Expostulation and Reply" and elsewhere, which also predicts "Resolution and Independence" and the Intimations Ode, yet to come. The boys have given up work ("It seems they have no work to do / Or that their work is done"); they "wear the time away." Settling his lads within a naturally mirthful setting, where "both earth and sky / Keep jubilee," Wordsworth prepares them (and us) for a crisis similar to that which overtakes the poet in both of the later poems I mentioned previously. One difference, of course, is that "The Idle Shepherd-Boys" presents that crisis in a more jocular way than either of the first-person poems; another is that here alone the fate of another creature (in this case a stray lamb) is at stake. Impervious to the "plaintive cry" of the lost animal, the boys indulge in youthful heroics—a race and an effort to cross a lofty waterfall at Dungeon-Gill. In the middle of the cataract below swims the fallen lamb, whose mother bleats for him on the rocks above.

The depiction of the discovery suggests the depth of feeling Wordsworth associates with the potential tragedy that stems from an abnegation of work:

> With staff in hand across the cleft
> The Challenger began his march:
> And now, all eyes and feet, hath gain'd
> The middle of the arch.
> When list! he hears a piteous moan—
> Again! his heart within him dies—

His pulse is stopp'd, his breath is lost,
He totters, pale as any ghost,
And, looking down, he spies
A Lamb, that in the pool is pent
Within that black and frightful rent.

(ll. 56–66)

When, in the Preface to *Lyrical Ballads,* Wordsworth attested to the novelty of his poems by saying that the "feeling therein developed gives importance to the action and situation and not the action and situation to the feeling" (*PrW,* 1:128), he encouraged his readers to feel the oddity of making much ado about little. But he also tossed them a red herring: the boys respond with a fervor that virtually parodies, or at least approaches, those other moments throughout Wordsworth's poetry that we label apocalyptic. Having ignored their responsibility, they have responded legitimately to the call to come out into the light of things and enjoy the pastoral holiday.

Even more indicative of Wordsworth's double sense of the appeal and the delusions of heeding the holiday call is his transparently self-serving and too easy solution to the potentially tragic event:

When he had learnt, what thing it was,
That sent this rueful cry; I ween,
The Boy recover'd heart, and told
The sight which he had seen.
Both glady now deferr'd their task;
Nor was there wanting other aid—
A Poet, one who loves the brooks
Far better than the sages' books,
By chance had thither stray'd;
And there the helpless Lamb he found
By those huge rocks encompass'd round.

(ll. 78–88)

In the topsy-turvy world of youthful bravado, the boys' play is now described as their "task," which they abandon in favor of their former responsibilities. Most conveniently, a poet himself effects the saving of the lamb and also of the negligent boys. Exactly why he shows up is mysterious, of course, but no more mysterious than the appearance of the leech gatherer just at the moment when the poet in "Resolution and Independence" is looking for something needful that comes, as always in Wordsworth, unsought. The poet lends a helping hand immediately after he is described as "stray[ing]" himself, wandering lonely, thoughtless, will-less, and passive in his own (presumably) holiday mood. Wordsworth has lit upon a convenient solution to justify his joint need for pastoral indolence and pastoral care. And, as in "Nutting," he can end with a moral tag ("And gently did the Bard / Those idle Shepherd-boys upbraid, / And bade them better mind their trade") which seems like Sunday school moralizing but in fact betrays the deepest anxieties that Wordsworth himself must have felt in 1800 about the nature of work and play.

In her convincing reading of "Michael," the major 1800 "pastoral," Marjorie Levinson somewhat nostalgically holds up Michael as a model of unalienated labor, a man whose work equals his pleasure, and whose economy is a self-sustaining one based on use rather than exchange value. In a note, however, Levinson undermines the credibility of the materialist bias of much of the New Historicism in an unintentionally condescending remark: by converting ballad into lyric, "the private, self-reflexive utterance of a privileged class, one with the leisure to explore the inner life . . . Wordsworth's formal procedures enact social ones that cut both ways."[29] By denying self-consciousness to the poor, Levinson also denies them the pleasure, and the leisure, to enjoy the kind of art normally labeled "high" instead of "low" or "folk," limiting their occasional literary forays to traditional balladry. But Wordsworth's choice of his own version of Miltonic blank verse—partly grand, partly conversational, partly Old Testament in tonality—confers on "Michael" an aesthetic as well as a socioeconomic grandeur on behalf of its characters. One might even use the Marxist standard to defend traditional aesthetic values: no one ever *needed* a poem, and certainly any propagandistic or ideological need may be served equally well by a bad poem as a good one. Poetry, as a synecdoche for all art, produces unmediated pleasure, as does the unalienated labor performed by Michael in the glory days of his self-sufficiency. Therefore, art is necessary rather than symbolic: it cannot substitute for anything else. From Wordsworth's critical principles we might even infer that since poetry is emotion recollected in tranquillity, it requires a slowly inflationary psychic and creative economy to grow properly after it has been stored away in the bank of the mind.

"Michael" offers a more serious treatment of labor and leisure than "The Idle Shepherd-Boys." The unfinished sheepfold which symbolizes the covenantal bond between father and son also epitomizes a different *kind* of work from the shepherd's daily chores. It is both necessary and contingent, a utilitarian object and a visible reminder of the absent son who has gone to the city to save the patrimonial lands. Significantly, it is a kind of after-hours project for the aged shepherd: "Sometimes when he could find a leisure hour / He to that valley took his way, and there / Wrought at the sheep-fold" (ll. 449–51). Whereas Michael implicitly understands the proper relationship between work and leisure that are *essentially* the same thing, Luke has grown slack in the city, pursuing dissolute habits, losing both work and productive leisure, and consequently failing in his economic and filial responsibilities. The antithetical conditions are presented simultaneously: Michael works at the sheepfold (l. 451), while "[m]eantime Luke began / To slacken in his duty" (ll. 451–52).

The poem's denouement succeeds rapidly, but with an ambiguous, feinting narrative gesture. After all that we have learned of Michael, his wife,

their cottage, and their industry, it comes as something of a shock to note
that the narrator now retreats to both vagueness and hearsay:

> And to that hollow Dell from time to time
> Did he repair, to build the Fold of which
> His flock had need. 'Tis not forgotten yet
> The pity which was then in every heart
> For the Old Man—and 'tis believ'd by all
> That many and many a day he thither went,
> And never lifted up a single stone.
>
> There, by the Sheep-fold, sometimes was he seen
> Sitting alone, with that his faithful Dog,
> Then old, beside him, lying at his feet.
> The length of full seven years from time to time
> He at the building of this sheep-fold wrought,
> And left the work unfinished when he died.
>
> (ll. 469–81)

The passive generalizations ("'Tis not forgotten," "'tis believed") and the
deliberate uncertainty ("sometimes was he seen") distance narrator and
reader alike from a hero who seems to turn to sculpture—Old Shepherd
with Faithful Dog—but who occasionally is reanimated in his wonted
tasks. The most touching refusal is Wordsworth's unwillingness, or inability, to do anything more than insinuate the gradual breakdown of Michael's labor: the old man goes to the dell in order to build his sheepfold,
but when he gets there he does nothing, or so it is believed.[30] The poet,
unable to confess outright the shepherd's failure, falls back on common
hearsay. Work is endless and, apparently, thankless; and after Michael's
death his wife lingers, then dies, the estate is sold to a stranger, and agriculture replaces sheep herding:

> The Cottage which was nam'd the Evening Star
> Is gone, the ploughshare has been through the ground
> On which it stood; great changes have been wrought
> In all the neighborhood. . . .
>
> (ll. 485–88)

Civilization and progress have intruded, as a newer way of life replaces an
older, pastoral one. Only unfinished memorials remain, but these provide a
purely aesthetic legacy, first to the poet himself, who announced in his
opening apologia (ll. 1–39) that his tale, based on the sheepfold, represents
his earliest love of real shepherds, his first thoughts of other people, and his
capacity to feel "for passions that were not my own, and think / At random
and imperfectly indeed / On man, the heart of man and human life" (ll. 31–
33). Such a legacy he now extends to his own heirs, "a few natural hearts,"
those "youthful Poets, who among these Hills / Will be my second Self
when I am gone" (ll. 36–39).

Converting a material ruin into an aesthetic symbol, making art out of rumor (indeed, out of the economic ruin of an old couple), testifying to his sensitivity to "the heart of man," Wordsworth demonstrates how the leisure of tranquil emotional recollection is the necessary cause of artistic labor. Less than a decade earlier (June 17, 1791) he had jokingly—but a little anxiously—confided to William Mathews about his time in London that he was "whirled about by the vortex of its *strenua inertia,* and sometimes thrown by the eddy into a corner of the stream, where I lay in an almost motionless indolence. Think not however that I had not many very pleasant times" (*EY*, p. 49). Four months later, en route to Orléans, he confessed again to Mathews: "I am doomed to be an idler thro[ughou]t my whole life" (*EY*, p. 62). After his anxieties about career, family, and habitat had been to a large extent resolved, Wordsworth could still imagine himself as an idler, in a complacent tone, but secure in the knowledge that he was accomplishing his work: "I read, walk, doze a little now and then in the afternoon, and live upon the whole what you may call a tolerably rational life, I mean as the world goes" (to Francis Wrangham, January or February 1804, *EY*, p. 436).

No poem in the second volume of *Lyrical Ballads* attests more strangely than "The Brothers" to Wordsworth's effort to distinguish motionless indolence or senseless flitting—two versions of unproductive sloth—from creative leisure. The poem's oddness derives from the seeming peripherality of Wordsworth's obsession with these themes to the main action. Like "Michael," "The Brothers" uses an unnecessary framing device as a pair of asbestos gloves to protect the poet against truths otherwise too hot to handle. "Intended to be the concluding poem of a series of pastorals" (Wordsworth's apology for the "abruptness with which the poem begins" [*Lyrical Ballads,* p. 142]), "The Brothers" consists of almost three hundred lines of pure dialogue between a village priest and Leonard, a sailor who returns to his native village only to discover that his brother has died, accidentally, years before. The priest tells him the story, his own story in part, and then Leonard leaves his native soil. But the poem is framed by a narrator's mise-en-scène, an indirect discourse and a narrative of events before and after Leonard's reentry to a graveyard where neither is he recognized nor does he reveal himself.

Mary Moorman has emphasized the poem's simple restraint, its turn from the derangement of "The Thorn" and "The Mad Mother," and the moonlight world of "The Idiot Boy" and "Peter Bell," to the light of common day.[31] But the poem is more than an example of Wordsworthian elegy, a study of what she calls "the heart of man and human life," especially since it begins with an apparently irrelevant diatribe by the priest against tourists, in whose number he mistakenly counts Leonard as a "moping son of Idleness" (l. 11).[32] In its quirky concern with work, idleness, and the blurred middle ground between them, its clearest connections are to "Michael" and "Tintern Abbey."

Tourism to the Lake District was a burgeoning industry at the end of the eighteenth century, and Wordsworth's resentment of that industry, which built to an even greater intensity after the construction of the railroad, had its origins in his own return to his native soil.[33] "The Brothers" shares with several of the "Poems on the Naming of Places" a concern with mistakes in apprehension, and like "A Narrow Girdle of Rough Stones and Crags," but with less reason, it begins as a contrast, between the "homely Priest of Ennerdale" and his wife, models of domestic industry (like Michael and Isabel), and the unknown, loitering Leonard, who inspires the opening harangue:

> "These Tourists, Heaven preserve us! needs must live
> A profitable life: some glance along,
> Rapid and gay, as if the earth were air,
> And they were butterflies to wheel about
> Long as their summer lasted; some, as wise,
> Upon the forehead of a jutting crag
> Sit perch'd, with book and pencil on their knee,
> And look and scribble, scribble on and look,
> Until a man might travel twelve stout miles,
> Or reap an acre of his neighbour's corn.
> But for that moping son of Idleness
> Why can he tarry *yonder?* . . ."
>
> (ll. 1–12)

If tourists are butterflies, the Lake District natives are frugal, prudent ants, making a living but hardly profiting, reaping their own but not their neighbors' corn, and lacking the leisure merely to "look and scribble." The unusual chiasmus in line 8 betrays Wordsworth's scorn for the summertime flittering of holiday sketchers or poetasters (it is impossible to know exactly what they are doing),[34] but it also prepares us for the narrator's pendant and contrary description of Leonard, who has spent twenty years as a sailor. "Half a Shepherd" even at sea, he regularly heard and saw his native country on the main:

> he, in those hours
> Of tiresome *indolence* would often hang
> Over the vessel's side, and gaze and gaze,
> And, while the broad green wave and sparkling foam
> Flash'd round him images and hues, that *wrought*
> In union with the *employment* of his heart,
> He, thus by feverish passion overcome,
> Even with the organs of his bodily eye,
> Below him, in the bosom of the deep,
> Saw mountains, saw the forms of sheep that graz'd
> On verdant hills, with dwellings among trees,
> And Shepherds clad in the same country grey
> Which he himself had worn.
>
> (ll. 50–62; emphasis added)

With its virtual echoes of the language of "Tintern Abbey" and "I Wandered Lonely as a Cloud," this passage offers a paradigm of the Wordsworthian moment of imaginative apprehension. It also frames that apprehension within the language of investment and labor.

One thing seems deliberately unclear: whether we are to take Leonard's recreation of his native landscape as a fortunate product of his "tiresome indolence" or a fruitful counter to it. Leonard left his home to replace the family's small lost fortune because his grandfather, a surrogate father for the boys, like Michael "buffeted with bond, / Interest and mortgages" (ll. 212–13), lost his estate, house, and flock. Leonard has acquired the habits of industry and vision from his native hills; he has returned "with some small wealth / Acquir'd by traffic in the Indian Isles" (ll. 63–64). Even as a child he was exemplary. Model Wordsworthian children (cf. "Tintern Abbey," ll. 68–71), Leonard and his brother "like roe-bucks . . . / went bounding o'er the hills: / . . . Then they could write, ay and speak too, as well / As many of their betters" (ll. 273–76). For his brother's sake, Leonard "resolv'd to try his fortune on the seas" (l. 302). Wordsworth makes clear the connections between economic and imaginative reparations.

The poem serves some unknowable but inferable need of its author. We may conjecture, not entirely reductively, that the various resemblances between the Wordsworth family and the two brothers are too obvious to write off as mere coincidence. Wordsworth seems to have appropriated disparate details from his own family's life, reinvesting them in this narrative, making unity out of diversity. The five Wordsworth children were orphaned young. One became a sailor and was doing well in 1799 when Wordsworth wrote the poem. Wordsworth returned to his native hills after a decade of wandering to reestablish a home. Leonard resembles the young William in his overt or semiautobiographical poems. The eighteen-month difference in age between Leonard and James is the same as that between William and Dorothy.

This delicate self-referentiality verges at times on self-quotation. Consider Wordsworth's depiction of the sublime condition

> In which the heavy and the weary weight
> Of all this unintelligible world
> Is lighten'd:—that serene and blessed mood,
> In which the affections gently lead us on,
> Until, the breath of this corporeal frame,
> And even the motion of our human blood
> Almost suspended, we are laid asleep
> In body, and become a living soul:
> While with an eye made quiet by the power
> Of harmony, and the deep power of joy,
> We see into the life of things.
>
> ("Tintern Abbey," ll. 40–50)

The last three lines of this famous passage predict Leonard's situation, quoted earlier, in his indolently creative moments aboard ship. The first part, however, is echoed grimly by the priest's description of James's somnabulistic death:

> he had lain down
> Upon the grass, and, waiting for his comrades
> He there had fallen asleep, that in his sleep
> He to the margin of the precipice
> Had walked, and from the summit had fallen headlong—
> And so no doubt he perish'd: at the time,
> We guess, that in his hands he must have had
> His Shepherd's staff; for midway in the cliff
> It had been caught, and there for many years
> It hung—and moulder'd there.
>
> (ll. 393–402)

Physical suspension above or mental suspension within a liminal state defines the condition of many Wordsworthian figures, most notably the Boy of Winander, who "hung / Listening," and the young Wordsworth in *The Prelude*, "suspended by the blast which blew amain, / Shouldering the naked crag, oh, at that time / While on the perilous ridge I hung alone" (1.345–47).[35] In "The Brothers" the suspension is doubled, or divided, between Leonard's hanging over the side of the boat, converting tiresome indolence into productive recreation, and James's somnambulistic tragedy which leaves his suspended staff as a temporary memorial. But all mirroring and repeating comes to this: there is no legitimate reparation for loss. Work will never replace the past or the dead.

The multiplicity of "The Brothers," with its semi-narrative, semi-dialectic form, its divided references to Wordsworth and his siblings, its echoes from or predictions of other poems, its apparently irrelevant opening sermon, exposes many of its author's deepest feelings about the nature of home, family, separation, and the possibilities of compensation for economic, personal, and imaginative loss. Such problems of compensation were occupying Wordsworth's attention, but to greater purpose, during the simultaneous composition of *The Prelude*, which unfolds a narrative of harmony, loss, and work. At the heart of such imaginative work, indolence and play occupy a commanding position.

In the remainder of this chapter I explore Wordsworth's treatment of leisure as it informs the Intimations Ode and his most highly charged reminiscences in the early books of *The Prelude*, those from which he constructs his poetic vocation. In a poem that fervently claims that the base of the "mystery of man" is to be found in "simple childhood" (11.329–32) it is no surprise to observe an extensive survey of the activities, the pleasures and fears, of the poet's early years. More significant, the language, tropes, and rhetoric of books 1 and 2 continue throughout the whole;

childhood and its accompanying play provide the figurative, as well as the psychological, means for describing the poet's adult life. Play and work do not occupy the opposite ends of a socially determined scale, especially in the case of children and poets. It is, in part, for this reason, that the seventh stanza of the Intimations Ode ("Behold the Child among his new-born blisses"), which Helen Vendler has labeled a behaviorist's view of the child, resolutely avoids using the simple word *play* for its description of the child at play, always preferring some variation of *work* to elevate or dignify the activity.[36] Wordsworth maintains the mock-heroic tone that elsewhere defines his affectionate feeling for the play of childhood, but he is also asking us to take *literally* the idea that "the work of his own hand" amid which the child "lies" is the beginning of an adult labor that derives from a material amassing. What exactly is the child doing here?

> See, at his feet, some little plan or chart,
> Some fragment from his dream of human life,
> Shap'd by himself with newly-learned art;
>   A wedding or a festival,
>   A mourning or a funeral;
>   And this hath now his heart,
>   And unto this he frames his song:
>   Then will he fit his tongue
> To dialogues of business, love, or strife;
>   But it will not be long
>   Ere this be thrown aside,
>   And with new joy and pride
> The little Actor cons another part,
> Filling from time to time his "humorous stage"
> With all the Persons, down to palsied Age,
> That Life brings with her in her Equipage;
>   As if his whole vocation
>   Were endless imitation.
>
>   (ll. 90–107)

Wordsworth curiously equates play and work, implicitly connecting them through the deliberate intentionality of each. He also slides smoothly from—what are they?—drawings, building blocks, pieces of paper, or toys ("plan," "chart," "fragment") to their less material origin ("his dream of human life"). And from here he moves to an even less material arena of child's play as the youngster gives his heart to imitating the social rituals of adult life (Is he playing house? If so, is he doing it alone?), and then to imitating the dialectic of human conversation ("dialogues of business, love, or strife"). The child, who ages from the original "four year's Darling" of the 1804 poem to a six-year-old one in all editions after 1815, has his first experiences of work and play simultaneously. He is also talking in dialogues, probably to no one but himself, just as his social imitations (playing at a wedding) are rituals in which he takes all the parts. Childhood's calling is the fun of serious creation; the adult poet makes of his own imitations (of others' voices, of self-impersonations or recreations) a life's work. The concluding "as if" demands that we see the child's view as limited and deluded (Life's vocation, we say from the vantage of Blakean experience, had better be a whole lot more than this). But it is also ironically and proleptically true: life's work is genuinely a recreation, in both senses of that resonant word.

Such play, on the part of child and adult, is both purposeful (i.e., deliberate, conscious, self-willed) and useless (unmotivated, inexplicable, random). To the extent that we credit the adult's memory of his childhood, we can find a correlation between the ode's ambivalences and Wordsworth's remark that as an adult he loves the sun because it *symbolizes* something for him ("a pledge / And surety of our earthly life"), but that as a child he loved it entirely because it gave him pleasure:

> I had seen him lay
> His beauty on the morning hills, had seen
> The western mountain touch his setting orb
> In many a thoughtless hour, when from excess
> Of happiness my blood appeared to flow
> With its own pleasure, and I breathed with joy.
>
> (*Prelude* 2.188–93)

This distinction between an unmediated pleasure and a mediated, symbolic understanding is tempting but deceptive, because already built into the child's perception—or at least the adult's reconstruction of it, which may be something entirely different—is the child's personification of the sun as a divinity of aesthetics whose manifestation is "beauty" and whose effect on the beholder is thoughtless joy. The child has already participated in a symbolic order because of his playful engagement with external reality.

Within *The Prelude* Wordsworth's tropings of indolence fall roughly into two categories: those that betray his anxiety, and those that reveal his sensuous understanding of the fertility that derives from apparent waste. Significantly, the first category includes many activities that are social, whereas the latter contains largely solitary experience. For Wordsworth there is danger rather than safety in numbers. The image of a fun-loving, party-going, adolescent reveler, of which we have glimpses in books 3 and 4 (Wordsworth dancing till dawn or running tipsy to chapel) certainly squares ill with the emblem of craggy sobriety Wordsworth made himself into in middle age, but it is at one with the lighthearted tone and style of that large mass of his poetry that criticism can conveniently overlook.

Wordsworth's disapproval of his early, harmless dissipations at college and during summer vacation has the ring of the puritanical sternness we find in virtually all seventeenth-century religious literature. Take, for example, Richard Baxter's condemnation of

[v]oluptuous youths that run after Wakes, and May-Games, and Dancings, and Revellings, and are carried away by the Love of sports and pleasure, from the Love of God, and the care of their Salvation, and the Love of Holiness, and the Love of their Callings; and into idleness, riotousness, and disobedience to their Superiors.[37]

Strictures against both play and idleness were common coin to religious doctrine, and they also had an economic and social basis in the ruling class's fear that too much leisure could turn into a distraction and then a dangerous temptation to the working class. Later on, Henry Fielding's sardonic, tongue-in-cheek appraisal must have seemed serious to the very class it was mocking:

To be born for no other Purpose than to consume the Fruits of the Earth is the Privilege (if it may be really called a Privilege) of very few. The greater Part of Mankind must sweat hard to produce them, or Society will no longer answer the Purposes for which it was ordained.[38]

To the "leisured classes" the leisure of others, in the form of play or of doing nothing, was a threat. As Charles Hall wrote in 1805: "[L]eisure in a poor man is thought quite a different thing from what it is to a rich man, and goes by quite a different name. In the poor it is called idleness, the cause of all mischief."[39] Wordsworth's "hard task" (*Prelude* 2.232) is not merely "to analyze a soul" but to justify the apparent leisure of a middle-class poet.

M. H. Abrams has shown how the "glad preamble" of book 1 duplicates in miniature the shape of *The Prelude* as a whole: eagerness, confidence, and will strengthen the poet for his large project, but they are then undermined by self-induced doubts, anxieties, and a despondency that finds its own correction only at the end of the book, when his mind revives and he discovers his true epic subject in a rehearsal of childhood memories.[40] In addition, in its insistence on the motifs of play—not just play in childhood—book 1 readies poet and reader alike for further investigations of leisure. The "months of ease and undisturbed delight" (l. 28) which he anticipates, the pastoral *otium* of a new Lake District residence (ll. 70–94), encourage dreams of epic achievement.[41] But self-born frustrations and fear paralyze the would-be great poet, who angrily adduces as an alternative to "zeal and just ambition" the thoughtless, vacant indolence of "mere" self-indulgence:

> Ah, better far than this to stray about
> Voluptuously through fields and rural walks
> And ask no record of the hours given up
> To vacant musing, unreproved neglect
> Of all things, and deliberate holiday.
> . . . .
> 　　　I recoil and droop, and seek repose
> In indolence from vain perplexity,

Unprofitably travelling towards the grave,
Like a false steward who hath much received
And renders nothing back.
                    Was it for this . . .
                    (ll. 252–56, 267–71)

This passage, which comes just before the launching into the reparative discovery of greatness in childhood experiences (Was it for this, he seems to ask, that nature marked me out in childhood for special attention?), raises the question of indolence itself (significantly, Wordsworth changed "indolence" to "listlessness" in the 1850 text). Everything in lines 252–56 can be seen, mutatis mutandis, as the positive condition of Wordsworthian pastoral in both lyric and narrative verse—although here he presents it to us as the opposite of productive leisure. Only the atypical, mouth-filling, Latinate "voluptuously" (the longest word, along with "unprofitably," in the passage) rings false, and betrays Wordsworth's incipient puritanism. Voluptuousness is a bad investment, although some straying has productive consequences.[42] In his frustration Wordsworth defines himself only through the economic model of the false steward of Matthew 25. We may take the measure of his creative recuperation toward the middle of the book not simply by seeing that his spirits and energies have been revived but by attending to the economic conversion that has enabled him to transform vacancy to substance, play to work:

                    Not uselessly employed,
I might pursue this theme through every change
Of exercise and play to which the year
Did summon us in its delightful round.
                    (ll. 501–4)

Childhood play produces adult labor; in reproducing recreative moments, the poet renders what he has received and begins to amass his profits. Even here he remains skeptical: the litotes ("not uselessly") and the conditional mood, those standard rhetorical signs of Wordsworth's uncertainty, allow him ample hedging.

Books 3 and 4 offer a pair of opposing pictures: at Cambridge in book 3 Wordsworth plays at being at work; during summer vacation in book 4 he works at play. As in book 7 (on London) and books 9–11 (in France), but with less ferocious consequences, everything in book 3 tends toward mock-heroism, owing to the inflated, self-conscious struttings of a college man on his first forays into adult independence. As a first-year student, "a man of business and expense" (3.24), going about his own affairs, Wordsworth is also pretty much a truant, playing hooky in the fields, where his mind "seemed busier in itself than heretofore" (l. 104). Both a "freeman" (l. 89) and a slave to the "weekday works of youth" (l. 244), he cleaves to solitude at times, but "if a throng was near / That way I leaned by nature, for my heart / Was social and loved idleness and joy" (ll. 234–36). Although he never uses the dread word *sloth,* by the middle of the book we sense that the student has fallen into a spiritual paralysis that results from too much noisy, unprofitable socializing: "Hushed meanwhile / Was the under-soul, locked up in such a calm, / That not a leaf of the great nature stirred" (ll. 539–41). Such paralysis also protects: nothing happens to injure the buried soul. School becomes an exercise in vacuity, "a deep vacation," but not an "utter waste" (ll. 542–43) because it allows him to defer "mortal business" and "the conflicts of substantial life" (ll. 553, 559) until he matures naturally.

The productive unreality of the pseudo-scholar's life is presented as an allegorical pageant—as if Wordsworth matched his figurative devices to the odd phenomena that occasioned them—with Labour, Hope, "Idleness, halting with his weary clog" (l. 632), Shame, Fear, Pleasure, and finally the almost Popean "Feuds, factions, flatteries, Enmity and Guile" (l. 636) on parade. The permanent frieze of personifications is appropriate to an adolescent to whom nothing real is happening. The "submissive idleness" of a nine months' "labouring time" (ll. 669–71) rolls "pleasingly away" as if in a dream. When he continues his recollections of university life in book 6, he passes over his remaining years by saying only that he was caught within "the bonds / Of indolent and vague society"; that he read on his own and neglected his courses owing to his "over-love / Of freedom . . . / And indolence" (ll. 20–21, 44–46); that he enjoyed geometry even when its abtractedness was "no more than as a plaything, or a toy / Embodied to the sense" (ll. 184–85). Cambridge was apparently negligible and helpful in equal measure. "An idler among academic bowers" (8.649), the young would-be student reaped his rewards only later.

Vacation itself is more productive. (After the dismissal of university life at the start of book 6 come the lengthy, climactic, and apocalyptic revelations of Wordsworth's 1790 trip to France, which is initially treated as "an open slight / Of college cares." [ll. 342–43].) Even at the start of book 4, the face of every neighbor is "a volume" (l. 59), reminding us of what the student was reading, or *not* reading, at St. John's. Book 4, situated between the mockery of book 3 and the serious educational speculations of book 5 (on "Books"), is a corrective to the former and a testing ground for the latter. Whereas Wordsworth reduces his memories of university life to bare narration, mock-heroism, and personified abstractions, he now amplifies those of his summer at home with the specificity of heroic simile and paradigmatic human encounter. Even the formal organization of book 4 dramatizes the intricate relation between play and work: Wordsworth describes his juvenile attempts at poetic composition with a good-humored awareness of his adolescent self-absorption (ll. 84–180); at the center of the book comes the depiction of contemplation as a moment of heroic indolence (ll. 247–68); at the end comes the meeting with the discharged soldier.

Wordsworth presents his early efforts at "the toil of verse" (l. 102) with self-deprecating good humor. Talking to himself, composing *viva voce* on the public roads, he is luckily interrupted by his barking dog whenever a passerby approaches, and is spared the embarrassment of being thought a wandering Bedlamite. These efforts also result in some fruit, however unripe, which Wordsworth limns as "some fair enchanting image in my mind / [that] Rose up, full-formed like Venus from the sea" (ll. 104–5). The sexual basis of an adolescent male's daydreaming matches Keats's later, more famous remark concerning the imagination as Adam's dream: "He awoke and found it truth" (*Letters,* 1:185); it also stands as preparation for the sublime passage in book 6 when, as compensation for the traveler's disappointment in hearing that he has unknowingly crossed the Alps, Wordsworth makes his ardent address to the imagination as the "unfathered vapour that enwraps, / At once, some lonely traveller" (*Prelude* [1850] 6.595–96). If the latter passage represents the turbulent, troubled dimensions of Wordsworth's self-conceivings and the ego's Oedipal efforts to originate itself, the former is all easy self-assurance, poetic creation occurring *after* great toil but almost independent of it. What in Wordsworth is thoughtless and unwilled, seemingly self-begotten like (in this case) a motherless goddess, represents his first vocational "swellings of the spirits" (l. 153), his "new employments of the mind" (l. 269).

In spite of the happiness that attends a release from university work, in spite also of the early satisfactions of poetic toil, Wordsworth announces "an inner falling off" (l. 270) as a result of the vain "gawds / And feast and dance and public revelry / And sports and games" (ll. 273–75) which he can neither fully resist nor enjoy. Since the thematic and emotional rhythm of *The Prelude* depends on its formal organization more than its compositional or representational ones,[43] it is significant that this admission follows one of the few extended similes in the entire poem, one that isolates the moment of indolence as both metaphor and subject:

> As one who hangs down-bending from the side
> Of a slow-moving boat upon the breast
> Of a still water, solacing himself
> With such discoveries as his eye can make
> Beneath him in the bottom of the deeps,
> Sees many beauteous sights—weeds, fishes, flowers,
> Grots, pebbles, roots of trees—and fancies more,
> Yet often is perplexed, and cannot part
> The shadow from the substance, rocks and sky,
> Mountains and clouds, from that which is indeed
> The region, and the things which there abide
> In their true dwelling; now is crossed by gleam
> Of his own image, by a sunbeam now,
> And motions that are sent he knows not whence,
> Impediments that make his task more sweet;

> Such pleasant office have we long pursued
> Incumbent o'er the surface of past time—
> With like success. . . .
>
>   (ll. 247–64)

The fact as well as the language of exertion ("impediments," "task," "office," "pursued," "success") emerges only after that of pastoral lolling about. The excessive length of the opening *dependent* clause—which concerns *hanging*—makes the independent clause seem anticlimactic, to say the least. (The entire clause should remind us of the identical motifs in "The Brothers," which I discussed earlier.) The parallelism within grammar and metaphor is awkwardly skewed: "As one who hangs" and then "Such pleasant office have we long pursued." Not only does the single man of the metaphor's vehicle multiply to an educational or textual plural (as if to say, "You and I, dear reader"), but the very grammatical inversion does damage to the nature of the comparison.

Like Thoreau, Wordsworth might say that time is the stream he has gone fishing in, except that he is not fishing but gazing. "Incumbent" is part of that Wordsworthian arsenal that also includes "sustain," "hang," and "suspend"—all those (mostly Latinate) words of vertiginous balance that create maximum tension out of ease, and vice versa. It suggests physical weight and thematic seriousness, but also the gentle, mindless dreaming that begins when "we are laid asleep / In body and become a living soul." Lying on top of the water, the viewer is suspended by it while weighted down with other cares. In such a mood self-consciousness intrudes unavoidably and negatively, since seeing himself in the still water prohibits the viewer from seeing both the genuine aquatic life at the bottom and the reflection of the life of land and air above. His own image gets in the way of his work: a sunbeam can blind as well as illuminate, and a self-sighting can become as much a deterrent to seeing as it often is, from another perspective, a desired end. But in spite of everything, the light of self, like all the "impediments" that etymologically and perceptually weigh Wordsworth down, is a sweetening agent.

Wordsworth seems to need his indolence two ways. Almost simultaneously with the composition of book 4, he was resigning himself to sterner devotions: "Me this uncharter'd freedom tires; / I feel the weight of chance desires" ("Ode to Duty" [1804–5]). Unless we doubt the accuracy of his memory of events and feelings that occurred fifteen years earlier, we must grant that Wordsworth's later stoicism had its origin in moments like this one, when the poet in the act of composition describes his present labor with a metaphor appropriate to the mood of his adolescent self, who both enjoys and is troubled by such moments of easy looking. We can get a clearer view of Wordsworth's inherent puritanism by comparing a passage such as the one just cited with similar moments in Rousseau, especially in the fifth walk of *Les Rêveries du promeneur solitaire,* where an escape to an island solitude includes work that is both mock-heroic and self-absorbed. Or one might take a letter from a slightly younger Rousseau to the Marquis de Mirabeau (January 31, 1767):

> The fatigue even of thinking becomes more painful to me every day. I love to dream, but freely, letting my mind wander about without enslaving myself to any subject. . . . This idle and contemplative life, which you do not approve, and I make no excuses for, becomes to me more delicious daily. To wander alone endlessly and ceaselessly among the trees and rocks around my house, to muse or to be irresponsible as I please, and as you say, to go wool-gathering. . . . That, sir, is for me the greatest pleasure, to which I can imagine nothing superior in this life, or even in the next.[44]

Anti-Romantic critics from Irving Babbitt to the neo-Marxists have always been troubled by the escape from labor, responsibility, or reality that Romanticism in some of its moods recommends. Babbitt's early chastisement of both Rousseau and (in the excerpt that follows) Schiller foretells Terry Eagleton's later historicizing of the ideology of aestheticism:

> [B]y encouraging the notion that it is possible to escape from neo-classical didacticism only by eliminating masculine purpose from art, he opens the way for the worst perversions of the aesthete, above all for the divorce of art from ethical reality. In art, according to Schiller, both imagination and feeling should be free and spontaneous, and the result of all this freedom, as he sees it, will be perfectly "ideal."[45]

As the extended passage from *The Prelude* just quoted suggests, Wordsworth wants to make ease and work, *otium* and *negotium,* both equivalent and sequential. Too much ease is troubling; too little is nonproductive. It is to the credit of Wordsworth the autobiographer that nowhere does he succumb to the complacencies that might trouble even a less judgmental critic than Babbitt. In fact, as the paradigmatic conclusion to book 4 demonstrates, Wordsworth can relate indolence to morality and still be less than satisfied with his own place in the scheme of the world.

The episode of the discharged soldier has been thoroughly and variously analyzed, and it is not my purpose to give it a new reading.[46] What interests me here is the embedding of the episode within a framework of indolent self-absorption. As if in preparation for the encounter, Wordsworth gives us a recollection of an all-night revelry (ll. 316–45) at the end of which the young man, walking home at sunrise, sees an image worthy of a handbook on the picturesque:

> The sea was laughing at a distance; all
> The solid mountains were as bright as clouds,
> Grain-tinctured, drenched in empyrean light;
> And in the meadows and the lower grounds
> Was all the sweetness of a common dawn—
> Dews, vapours, and the melody of birds,
> And labourers going forth into the fields.

> Ah, need I say, dear friend, that to the brim
> My heart was full? I made no vows, but vows
> Were then made for me: bond unknown to me
> Was given, that I should be—else sinning greatly—
> A dedicated spirit. On I walked
> In blessedness, which even yet remains.
>
> (ll. 333–45)

The dedication to poetry comes automatically and unsought, indeed unknown at the time, and after the apparent wastefulness of dancing the night away. A Marxist critic might very well notice the appropriation of labor that Wordsworth includes as a part of the picturesque moment: he goes home to rest while others go forth to till the soil. Wordsworth never makes the revelry a sufficient or even a necessary condition for the blessing that follows it; but the ongoing rhythm of *The Prelude,* in which something fruitful results from something apparently wasteful, should encourage us to understand his blessing as both a product of and a counter to the youthful merriment that temporally preceded it.

Likewise, in the concluding episode Wordsworth wanders aimlessly at night, "with an exhausted mind worn out by toil" (l. 381), unconsciously "drinking in" the restorative properties of the surrounding stillness. His state verges on unconsciousness; at the very least he recalls his passive willlessness:

> Around me, all was peace and solitude;
> I looked not round, nor did the solitude
> Speak to my eye, but it was heard and felt.
> O happy state! what beauteous pictures now
> Rose in harmonious imagery; they rose
> As from some distant region of my soul
> And came along like dreams—yet such as left
> Obscurely mingled with their passing forms
> A consciousness of animal delight,
> A self-possession felt in every pause
> And every gentle movement of my frame.
>
> (ll. 389–99)

These lines are marked by insistent verbal repetition ("around . . . round," "solitude . . . solitude," "rose . . . rose"); by doublings ("peace and solitude," "heard and felt," "rose and came," "beauteous pictures . . . harmonious imagery"); by rhetorical antitheses ("all was . . . but it was"; "like dreams . . . yet such as left"; "in every pause . . . and every gentle movement"). Paradox and tautology work together as the stylistic hallmarks of those moments of tense calm throughout Wordsworth's poetry when he wishes both to amplify and to correct his definitions. Describing a moment in which something happens, he makes it seem as though nothing is happening.

At this point he spies the spectral figure of the discharged soldier, whom he engages in conversation, and whom he leads to a peasant's cottage for food and shelter. As in the apocalyptic crossing of the Alps in book 6, the young Wordsworth finds he must retrace his steps back from the village ahead to the cottage of the laborer behind. The act of returning to a prior spot is, of course, a version of the eddying spirals in which Wordsworth performs his acts of memory throughout his poem. I take it also as a figure for the kind of aesthetic experience that leads to epiphanic revelations (of the kind he has when he learns that he has crossed the Alps) and, as here, to moral action. A resonant phrase from "Tintern Abbey" rings with special meaning for the end of book 4. Wordsworth there claimed "beauteous forms," even when absent, as the basis for "that best portion of a good man's life; / His little, nameless, unremembered acts / Of kindness and of love." Beauty, contemplation, everything we might include within the rubric of "aesthetics," inspires ethical conduct; indeed, it is a prerequisite for it. Here the act is both named and remembered (it is the soldier who, like so many other human figures in *The Prelude,* remains anonymous), and it even earns for the young Wordsworth, who has patronizingly told the weakened man to stay off the public lanes late at night, an admonitory rebuke: with "ghastly mildness in his look," the solder replies, "'My trust is in the God of Heaven, / And in the eye of him that passes me'" (ll. 493–95).

Wordsworth prepared his readers for the meeting by stressing beauteous imagery that rose within him but did not *speak to his eye.* He ends by granting the soldier a voice and a mildly magnetic eye that holds his interlocutor, much as the Ancient Mariner's glittering eye traps the Wedding Guest. The passage is framed, in other words, by a concentration on speaking and seeing, or on *not* seeing and *not* looking (since the soldier trusts that God and other people will look out for him). Sauntering along in a semioblivious way, the young Wordsworth is in an aesthetic state of mind, one marked by the insistent arising from within of harmonious but invisible imagery. Thence follows the human encounter and dialogue, all of it significantly reported as indirect discourse. The organization suggests that the earlier state has prepared the youth—spiritually, logically, and psychologically—for the subsequent encounter and his moral response to it. It ends with a gesture that completes the former aesthetic one: the soldier speaks surprisingly and epigrammatically, and he speaks with, to, and about the eye.[47] The soldier trusts that someone will look at and then look after him. And he is, of course, correct: the young Wordsworth had encountered the soldier first by spying on him ("I could mark him well, / Myself unseen") before revealing himself. The whole episode confirms the centrality of viewing—not mere seeing but actual spectatorship—to Wordsworth's ethical conduct. From looking comes action, from mild sauntering human help.

Writing is labor. Reading is labor and it is also nutrition. So we learn in book 5, nominally on the subject of books, in which Wordsworth expends much energy considering whether the work of modern education (all work and no play, he might cry) is best suited to the needs of children like himself and Coleridge, who are better left to wander through the "open ground / Of fancy" (ll. 236–37) than to be bound, penned up at school

> like a stallèd ox shut out
> From touch of growing grass, that may not taste
> A flower till it have yielded up its sweets
> A prelibation to the mower's scythe.
>
> (ll. 242–45)

The extended simile (ll. 230–45) deliberately figures educational schemes in terms of agricultural, specifically pastoral, ones. Culture and agriculture unite in Wordsworth's implicit retrieval of their etymological cousinhood. The well-bred (well-fed) child has wandered "through heights and hollows and bye-spots of tales / Rich with indigenous produce, open ground / Of fancy, happy pastures ranged at will" (ll. 235–37). The georgic echoes—especially in "happy pastures," Wordsworth's appropriation of classical *arva laeta*—attest to his anxiety about what he later refers to as "these too industrious times" (l. 293), which imprison an infant prodigy in an educational straitjacket that develops his intellect at the expense of feelings and freedom:

> Meanwhile old Grandame Earth is grieved to find
> The playthings which her love designed for him
> Unthought of—in their woodland beds the flowers
> Weep, and the river sides are all forlorn.
>
> (ll. 346–49)

Play and pastoral are intimately related. Wordsworth has renewed the language of pastoral elegy, combining a floral procession with a Ruskinian pathetic fallacy. The growth and development of the "modern" child coincide with the murder of the "natural" or pastoral one, who should be playing with the unmentioned toys that Earth has laid in his path.

The goal of such education, as Wordsworth announces it several lines later, is, like those nameless and unremembered acts of kindness and of love he celebrates throughout his poetry, deliberately anonymous: the child who reads romances and fairy tales instead of science, history, and economics, "at least doth reap / One precious gain—that he forgets himself" (ll. 368–69). It seems as though one kind of symbolic death or another is the only possibility for growth into adult life: the infant prodigy is lamented, like a corpse in a pastoral elegy, whereas the natural child achieves for his toil the gain of self-loss. Nowhere else do we see Wordsworth's natural inclination to celebrate leisure and play so strongly connected to his elegiac temperament. The prodigious modern child is dead in one way, and the idealized natural child is equally but separately cut off, in his case from self-consciousness. The sober side of Wordsworth's disposition requires self-consciousness as a necessary part of adult life; the Epicurean side reserves playfulness for the child (or the child who survives as father of the man), but such playfulness has its own price.

The price is paid by the Boy of Winander. The formal organization of book 5 virtually begs us to see the boy as the epitome of the idealized Wordsworthian child, the boy raised alone and in nature, the boy who stands opposed to the infant prodigy whom Wordsworth has just satirized. When we get to the famous passage, excerpted and first printed in the second edition of *Lyrical Ballads,* later receiving pride of place among "Poems of the Imagination," we must shudder. No sequence depicts more forcefully the combined drama and discursiveness of Wordsworth's style, especially when applied to matters of growth, play and work, and death. Context is all. When read alone the miniature history tells the naked tale of this (semi)autobiographical child, the eponymous familiar of Winander's cliffs and islands, who blows his "mimic hootings to the silent owls / That they might answer him" (ll. 398–99), has an epiphanic experience, and dies. The richness of the boy's activity, his engagement in a pastoral contest in which provocation and response are virtually inseparable, assures him a place among Wordsworth's favored, though anonymous, sons. All is echo; there is no origin. But there is ending—first the multiple reception of sound and then of visible scene into the boy's heart, and within the visible scene the reception of heavenly image into the lake:

> a gentle shock of mild surprize
> Has carried far into his heart the voice
> Of mountain torrents; or the visible scene
> Would enter unawares into his mind
> With all its solemn imagery, its rocks,
> Its woods, and that uncertain heaven, received
> Into the bosom of the steady lake.
>
> (ll. 407–13)

And then the boy's death, impassively reported: "This Boy was taken from his mates, and died / In childhood, ere he was full ten years old." (ll. 414–15).

The effect of this passage within the context of book 5 is to make us wonder what kind of punishment Wordsworth is exacting from the boy or from himself. (Since we know that the original passage was autobiographical, Wordsworth seems at some level to be killing part of his earlier animal self.) The boy clearly epitomizes the virtues and habits Wordsworth holds up against the victims of modern pedagogy. Why, then, does he die? The text affords no answer, and none will satisfy, of course. But the fact that the boy is himself a model mimic, like the child in the seventh stanza of the Intimations Ode, makes it seem that Wordsworth associates his life of play with his early absorption by and into a ghostly natural realm. The church-yard in which he lies is overseen by a statue of the Virgin who forgets the graves; she prefers to listen, says the attending narrator, "only to the gladsome sounds / That, from the rural school ascending, play / Beneath her and about her" (ll. 429–31). Even the young "race of real children" (l. 436) is possessed of a ghostly fatality: *sounds,* not children, play around the statue. Undone by metonymy, the children are equally undone by simile. "Mad at their sports like withered leaves in winds" (l. 440), they bespeak Wordsworth's simultaneous attachment to and fear of playfulness even when it belongs to the young, who by rights should have nothing else. Knowing as he does that the shades of the prison-house will eventually trap the youths into the condition of adulthood, Wordsworth might logically be expected to praise unequivocally the temporary "sportiveness" (an epithet he applies to Lucy, another of his child–victims) of frolicking children. Instead, by proleptically associating that sportiveness with future desiccation in the trope of the autumnal leaves, he punishes it, sotto voce as it were, even while attesting to the educational value of childhood pleasures.

One smaller episode in book 5 deserves inclusion in a commentary on Wordworth's complex treatment of work and play. It is a minor but exemplary moment. Returning from school for summer vacation, the poet says he took delight in "that golden store of books" (l. 503) that he left behind. Those books, and the act of reading them, are figured as a surprisingly paradoxical combination:

> Full often through the course
> Of those glad respites in the summertime
> When armed with rod and line we went abroad
> For a whole day together, I have lain
> Down by thy side, O Derwent, murmuring stream,
> On the hot stones and in the glaring sun,
> And there have read, devouring as I read,
> Defrauding the day's glory—desperate—
> Till with a sudden bound of smart reproach
> Such as an idler deals with in his shame,
> I to my sport betook myself again.
>
> (ll. 505–15)

Books are here the enemy of the theoretically gainful employment of fishing. Reading becomes a subversive activity, distracting the child from his true work of angling. But that work is nothing more than *sport,* so the "smart reproach" and "shame" the child feels are, we must think, either ironic or misdirected. At the very least they are unexpected. Wordsworth has occluded rather than clarified the distinction between work and play. Reading takes place beneath the glaring sun, when we might think the boy would retreat from the *daemon meridianus* to some pastoral covert. He both ignores time and triumphs over it until, at last, he is sated and then guilt-ridden. Even the triple alliteration—"devouring . . . defrauding . . . desperate"—enacts a minidrama of englutting and cheating that amounts to sin. (The abundance of the dental "d" sound pervades the lines, beginning with "glad" and reaching a bitter anticlimax in "idler deals.")

Neither activity—fishing or reading—can qualify as pure work or leisure, *negotium* or genuine pastoral *otium*. The two are twinned opposites, resembling but combatting each other in equal measure. Such fruitful, deliberate confusion of work and play attests to Wordsworth's reformulation of the idea of the modern poetic vocation as a peculiar construct that derives equally from the freedom of childhood and the self-conscious, even self-created, obligations of the adult in society. *The Prelude* might be as accurately subtitled "The Growth of the Poet's Occupation" as of his "Mind."

Whatever educational function reading serves, it also confirms the youthful autobiographical subject in his commitment to poetry. Significantly, this commitment is to language as useless ornament. At the age of thirteen, he tells us, "My ears began to open to the charm / Of words in tuneful order, found them sweet / For *their own sakes*—a passion and a power" (ll. 577–79); such love opens the way for "something loftier, more adorned, / Than is the common aspect, daily garb / Of human life" (ll. 599–601). The glory in words for themselves, and the sense of aspiration to a higher and, equally, more ornamental dress for daily life, has prepared the adolescent for his future vocation. The "works / Of mighty poets" (ll. 618–19) that contain the mysterious visionary power celebrated in the climactic passage of book 5 (ll. 608–29) embody in words both darkness and light. The intricate turnings of verse make a home for elements that do not, perhaps, rightly belong there:

> There darkness makes abode, and all the host
> Of shadowy things do work their changes there
> As in a mansion like their proper home.
> Even forms and substances are circumfused
> By that transparent veil with light divine,
> And through the turnings intricate of verse
> Present themselves as objects recognized
> In flashes, and with a glory scarce their own.
>
> (ll. 622–29)

The search for home, destination, and occupation with which *The Prelude* began is redefined here by a claim for the indwelling capacity of poetry itself. Words make a working home for "shadowy things" and confer on them a glory by which alone they can be noticed. Work has seldom seemed so closely allied to interior decoration. Let us reconsider Wordsworth's memory of his adolescent attraction to the adornments of his "favourite verses":

> For images, and sentiments, and words,
> And every thing with which we had to do
> In that delicious world of poesy,
> Kept holiday, a never-ending show,
> With music, incense, festival, and flowers!
>
> (ll. 603–7)

Whatever else Wordsworth says about poetry and his sense of his own vocation within *The Prelude* or the Preface to *Lyrical Ballads* and elsewhere, it is clear that he was never released from his belief in the intimate connection between the *work* of art—as both occupation and adornment—and its genesis in the ardent, delicious, self-gratifying play of youth.[48] This play is transformed in adulthood into that tranquillity from which emotion is recollected, what Wordsworth refers to late in *The Prelude* as "that happy stillness of the mind" that enables genius to inherit and then to use nature's energy (12.11–14). Whether laboring or resting, the adult poet engages his energies in leisurely activity. The child in the Intimations Ode acts as though his whole vocation "were" endless imitation. As it turns out, the reverse is also true. The conditional mood of the verb ("were") is hardly necessary. Adult "work" derives from childhood "holiday." It also imitates it. Whether ambling about his local hills or merely standing inert, Wordsworth demonstrated to his sister (and first reader) the productivity of such leisure activity. Composing out-of-doors was for him the pleasurable idle prelude to that indoor effort at writing, which, as both he and Dorothy attest, was a source of strong physical debility to him. That labor or *negotium* had this leisurely beginning: "He walks out every morning, generally alone, and brings us in a large treat almost every time he goes," wrote Dorothy in a letter. "The weather with all its pleasant mildness, has been very wet in general, he takes out the umbrella and I daresay, stands stock-still under it during a rainy half-hour, in the middle of road or field."[49]

3

Coleridge and Dejection

His defective sight . . . prevented him from enjoying the common sports; and he once pleasantly remarked to me, "how wonderfully well he had contrived to be idle without them." Lord Chesterfield, however, has justly observed in one of his letters, when earnestly cautioning a friend against the pernicious effects of idleness, that active sports are not to be reckoned idleness in young people; and that the listless torpor of doing nothing, alone deserves that name. Of this dismal inertness of disposition, Johnson had all his life too great a share.
—Boswell, *Life of Johnson* (1725, *aetat.* 16)

It can be no coincidence that the two greatest critical intellects in English letters shared a temperament that was at once idle and paralyzing and also, paradoxically, inspiriting. Plagued by demons they could never fully exorcise, both Johnson and Coleridge thought of themselves as indolent, unholy, and unproductive. On the incompletion of "Christabel" Coleridge said, "I have only my own indolence to blame" (*CP*, p. 214), yet by affixing this self-reproach to the poem's preface, he reminds us sotto voce that something, at least, has been achieved. Few writers left bodies of work more substantial than those of these two chronic idlers; but Johnson, thinking himself a monster of lethargy, proclaims flatly, "Idleness can never secure tranquillity" (*Rambler*, no. 134), and in one of his last letters makes the surprising statement that idleness is a disease of the will: "[T]hat

58

voluntary debility" [as he terms indolence] . . . if it is not counteracted by resolution will render the strongest faculties lifeless."[1] Still, Coleridge's evaluation of his own sloth applies to Johnson's as well: *"indolence capable of energies"* (*CL,* 1:259–60).[2]

Especially for Coleridge, the man who in youth "became a proverb to the University for Idleness" (*CL,* 1:67), who referred later to his "constitutional indolence" (*BL,* 1:199; see also 1:45 and the accompanying note, and *CL,* 1:170), indolence—Chesterfield's "listless torpor of doing nothing"— goes hand in hand with metaphysics. The inability to *act* derives from the fact of too much thinking, as he admits in his famous self-analysis to William Godwin of January 22, 1802:

> Partly from ill-health & partly from an unhealthy & reverie-like vividness of *Thoughts,* & (pardon the pedantry of the phrase) a diminished Impressability from *Things,* my ideas, wishes, & feelings are to a diseased degree disconnected from *motion* & *action.* In plain & natural English, I am a dreaming & therefore an indolent man—. I am a Starling self-incaged, & always in the Moult, & my whole Note is, Tomorrow, & tomorrow, & tomorrow. (*CL,* 2:782)

And yet, recognizing like Keats the salubrious effects of receptivity, Coleridge is also able in other moods to sense somewhat wistfully the productive potential of mere passiveness. Two years after his letter to Godwin he writes in his notebook:

> The dignity of passiveness to worthy Activity when men shall be as proud within themselves of having remained an hour in a state of deep tranquil Emotion, whether in reading or in hearing or in looking, as they now are in having figured away one hour / O how few can transmute activity of mind into emotion / yet there are who active as the stirring Tempest and playful as a May blossom in a Breeze of May, can yet for hours together remain with hearts broad awake, and the Understanding asleep in all but its retentiveness and receptivity / yea, and the Latter evinces as great Genius as the Former. (*Notebooks,* 1, no. 1834)

Active playfulness, the youthful energy shared by Coleridge and Wordsworth in their more hopeful moods, occupies one side on the scale of these poets' emotional, intellectual, and speculative values. In such energy Coleridge earned a living through journalism, beyond that which came through the Wedgwood bequest, and he composed the first work on fells walking; generally, at least early in his life, he demonstrated a physical vigor composed in equal parts of daring and foolhardiness.[3] The other side is inhabited by the "deep tranquil" receptivity of mind and body in their static but creative capacities. As with all Romantic contraries, this pair generates its own demonic parody: activeness may too easily become frenzy; and patient, dignified passiveness "self-incaged" torpor.[4] In Coleridge, more than any of the other Romantic poets, we witness a psychomachia between these opposing forces. His poetry especially rehearses these struggles and, more important, dramatizes them rhetorically and figuratively in startling configurations. It is with Coleridge's figures for indolence, with special reference to "Dejection: An Ode" (of which a copy is printed as Appendix B), that this chapter concerns itself. I shall deliberately ignore one central biographical fact—Coleridge's opium addiction—not just because it has been much discussed but also because Coleridge's habits of mind and temperament antedate his drug problems. In addition, since my primary focus, in this chapter especially, is rhetorical and stylistic, I hope to prove a connection between Coleridge's scenes of indolence and one of his crucial poetic habits.

Coleridge's poetry surrounds, even derives from, an abyss, a psychic depression that he defines through certain reflexive rhetorical habits. Absence is everywhere at the heart of his poetry even when it is not overtly elegiac.[5] Self-incaged is self-engaged. As students are always quick to observe, however, the premise of the Dejection Ode is a poetic falsehood. What Coleridge terms his "shaping spirit of Imagination," far from being suspended or withdrawn, has been released to inspire and to build the poem that nominally laments its loss.[6] But to assert contrarily that dejection is "merely" a conceit is to debase both Coleridge and the general condition whose contours he attempts to delimit. More even than Keats, who refuses to address indolence or melancholy in his odes about them, Coleridge accommodates himself to a condition that is one of experiential as well as metaphysical nothingness. The mystery of representation is equivalent to the mystery of signification because dejection defies troping, or is known negatively, or is presented discursively rather than metaphorically. At the same time, it occupies a formally central and an experientially originary position in the ode. It is the *blank* out of which creation and representation derive, but it can allow no representation of its own self. Does it stimulate the secondary imagination (that which, according to Coleridge's famous formula, "dissolves, diffuses, dissipates, in order to recreate . . . struggles to idealize and to unify")? Certainly, to the extent that Coleridge has made poetry out of it. Does it derive from the primary imagination (the "prime Agent of all human Perception" [*BL*, 1:304])? Apparently it is the basis of all those perceptions he presents to us in the events of the poem. But according to Coleridge's stated discursive strategy throughout the ode, dejection also inhibits, paralyzes, and strangles. Paradoxically the same function kills and gives life.[7]

Before turning to "Dejection" and other poems, and to a discussion of Coleridge's schemes and tropes for spectatorship, I want to look briefly at a path not taken. Mary ("Perdita") Robinson, the celebrated actress–poet who died at the age of forty-two in 1800, and whom Coleridge called "a woman of undoubted Genius" (*CL*, 1:562; see also 575–76, where he comments on her ear and approves of her metrical experiments), wrote poems in the entirely archaic mode of eighteenth-century apostrophe and personification. Regardless of his admiration for Robinson's ear, Coleridge would have had to regard her odes "To Melancholy," "To Meditation," and "To Apathy" as periphrastic exercises in an outworn fashion.

For him the latter constitutes a *via negativa*. We can better take the measure of Coleridge's achievement by placing it beside Robinson's more stilted verses. Whereas Coleridge attempts to define a condition (in "Dejection" and the other conversation poems), he never once addresses it. Robinson invokes fully feminine goddesses: "Welcome, thou petrifying power! / Come fix on me thy vacant eye" ("To Apathy"); "Sorceress of the cave profound!" ("Ode to Melancholy"); "Sweet child of Reason! maid serene" ("Ode to Meditation").[8] Of her poems, "To Apathy" makes the most telling contrast with Coleridge's "Dejection" (and Keats's Indolence Ode). Like Coleridge, Robinson defines through accumulation—of personifications and apostrophes—a condition that turns out to be a richly confused hodgepodge of effects. Unlike Coleridge's comparable poem, however, her invocation to apathy is also a quasi-Keatsian quest, first welcoming the power, then requesting to be overwhelmed by it, then listing the various states of mind in which the power exercises its beneficent effects, and at last acknowledging that the power is both impermanent and potentially killing.

In her personifications Robinson adduces details that would naturally have appealed to the Coleridge of "Dejection": her goddess, a "dull maid" and a "numbing power," has a "vacant eye"; the speaker's pilgrimage takes her on a quest "through forest drear and unfrequented grove," until she tastes "one dream of solitary rest, / One dark unvaried dream." Like Coleridge, Robinson is unsure whether apathy can be sought or whether it inhabits the speaker's breast. (A stronger analogy here is with the state of the speaker in Keats's "Ode on Melancholy," who is both quester and victim, the recipient of a melancholy fit that "falls" from heaven and the hero who penetrates to the "sovran shrine.") Although Coleridge, significantly, never addresses his titular figure, he evidently associates it with both the pain and the achievement of his "abstruse research," and he works *through* (in both senses of that preposition) his dejection/indolence to administer his selfless blessing to Sara Hutchinson in the last stanza. Robinson, too, turns away—psychologically if not rhetorically (apostrophe is too strong an urge)—from her allegorical goddess in the poem's surprising last lines. Attempting to escape from the "tyrant power" of love into the dark, drear forest of forgetfulness, she finds an unexpected release:

> For I, by Apathy possess'd,
> Shall taste one dream of solitary rest,
> One dark unvaried dream—till fate
> Shall from this busy wildering state
> My spell-encircled soul set free—
> Ending thy short-lived power, congealing Apathy.

This suggests that a life of apathy is a mere dream, an earnest of the world after death, and that the speaker will be recalled to the things of this world and liberated from the enchantments of nonfeeling. At the same time, however, there seems to be an unexpected relief in this escape, especially if we sense the ambiguity of "busy wildering state." Does this refer to ordinary life within this world or to the strange state of the speaker's soul in her dark forest? More surprising is the final epithet for that power which has heretofore been sought as an unmitigated good; apathy freezes, congeals, and presumably deadens even as it seems to promise a release from the uncertainties of emotional and intellectual turbulence. "Short-lived" but also "congealing": apathy's last two epithets hold in check its ambiguous potential for salvation and damnation.

That Robinson offered Coleridge a perilous temptation is evident in his inconsequential "Ode to Tranquillity," first published with two additional stanzas in the *Morning Post,* December 4, 1801, four months before the Dejection Ode was written. The entire poem is cast in a weakly apostrophic manner, moving from the initial "Tranquillity! thou better name / Than all the family of Fame!" to the first lines of the last stanza: "The feeling heart, the searching soul, / To thee I dedicate the whole!" One of the few Romantic poems to praise earliness rather than belatedness (tranquillity comes not to one "who late and lingering seeks [her] shrine"), the ode posits the family relationships between its title goddess and her compeers—satiety, sloth, fatigue, hope, and remembrance—but does so without either discursive analysis or memorable figuration. Like Keats's melancholy, Coleridge's tranquillity cannot be found; rather, it finds its own subject, so he must already have won it if he knows that it will give him respite. In its declamatory, unexplorative, undramatic, and most of all painfully abstract manner, the poem is everything that Coleridge's more complex conversation poems are not:

> But me thy gentle hand will lead
> At morning through the accustomed mead;
> And in the sultry summer's heat
> Will build me up a mossy seat;
> And when the gust of Autumn crowds,
> And breaks the busy moonlight clouds,
> Thou best the thought canst raise, the heart attune,
> Light as the busy clouds, calm as the gliding moon.
>
> (ll. 17–24)

As in Robinson's poems, every element is rhetorically balanced, (one couplet by another, one hemistich by another, and so on), and virtually every noun has its qualifying adjective.

Coleridge's attraction to the substance, if not ultimately to the method, of Robinson's poetry allows us to appreciate the originality of "Dejection." Although hardly averse to personified abstractions in other poems, including the other conversation poems, Coleridge mostly does without them here. (As we shall see, his horrifying late poems seem to move ahead to the uncharted existential and rhetorical territory of bleak despair and self-canceling paradoxes by moving backwards to the language of rapt apostrophe.) His principal addressee is his "Lady," not his titular figure. The condition of "Joy" in stanza 5 is depicted but not fully personified; in the following stanzas "Fancy" and the poet's own "viper thoughts" assume a quasi-allegorical status. And, at the end, he invokes "Sleep" as a salutary force.

Nonetheless, these figurations seem almost incidental within the substance of the entire poem. Coleridge comes upon his true subject from afar. Even before he describes his accidie at the start of the second stanza, he surprises us at the end of the first. After eighteen lines of anticipatory description ("This night, so tranquil now, will not go hence / Unroused by winds, that ply a busier trade"), he remarks the difference between the expected storm and the wretched tranquillity of his own lifeless, internalized limbo, a tranquillity as empty as his natural surroundings. All hopefulness, he seeks arousal, animation, and life. The alexandrine of line 20 (matched by lines 46, 93, and 125 in similarly terminal positions, and 113, which significantly offers us men who "groan with pain," and 117) mimetically suggests dullness in its length, its alliteration, and its rhythmic balance. It also informs us that the speaker is suffering not from what we might conventionally label dejection but from something less intense and pointed, even less definable. An acute pain would be preferable by contrast, if only because more capable of being felt. An early notebook entry predicts Coleridge's present condition: "Real Pain can alone cure us of imaginary ills! We feel a thousand miseries till we are lucky enough to feel Misery" (*Notebooks,* 1, no. 28).[9]

Coleridge's grief is depicted most forcefully by what it does not have and by what it is not. Negation is the characteristic gesture of lines 21–25 ("without," "*un*impassioned," "no . . . no," "heart*less*"). Dejection is construed as a series of oppositions to known quantities but has no "real" identity of its own. He might as well have begun the second stanza with "A grief without a *name.*" One sees the precursor of Wallace Stevens's acknowledgment that imagination is required "even to choose the adjective / For this blank cold, this sadness without cause" ("The Plain Sense of Things"). In retrospect, even the litotes of lines 3–4 ("this night . . . will not go hence / Unroused") carries the freight of a negative rhetoric. The unusual (for Coleridge) stringing together of adjectives amounts to an attempt to accumulate a portrait from words that individually have no positive valence and that, more important, are virtually synonymous with one another. "Drear" is a case in point. Its obsolete meanings ("cruel," "bloody," "murderous") may have echoed faintly in 1802, but its predominant sense here is its modern one of drowsy dullness.[10] "Stifled" clearly suggests an earlier state of greater intensity: at one time, this past participle implies, the grief was *more* alive than it is now in its semiextinguished form. Significantly, Coleridge lit on the right word relatively late; he changed the original (1802) "stifling" only in the final 1817 version in *Sybilline Leaves.*[11] No longer does the grief (presumably) "stifle" him; rather, it has been itself lessened by a chronic psychic erosion.

Harold Bloom has proposed a twofold structure for this poem: stanzas

1, 7, and 8 develop Coleridge's response to the coming storm, which materializes at line 94, while the middle stanzas offer his reaction to the stimulus of Wordsworth's autobiography in the first four stanzas of the Intimations Ode, which were his original goal.[12] Critics have always found this poem more unruly, less manageable, than Coleridge's other conversation poems or those poems by Romantic contemporaries that fit under the rubric established by M. H. Abrams, the "greater Romantic lyric."[13] Whether fortuitously or by conscious craftsmanship, the ode, reduced from its original sprawling form in the "Letter to Sara Hutchinson," does have a shape and two governing tropes: the titular dejection and the poet's policy of trying to contain it. By beginning and ending with the external storm, Coleridge brackets himself (his own situation, as I mentioned earlier, is not ascertainable until line 19) and his diagnosis of his neurotic obsessions within the external meteorological data with which the poem opens and closes. At the heart of this poem is the poet's heart, surrounded first by the external world and finally by his prayer for Sara Hutchinson. For a man so self-obsessed he has a curious way of burying himself within his poem, stifling, so to speak, his own voice in the dark void of that grief which occupies his thoughts and the central section of his meditation. Another way of putting this is to say that in matters small as well as large, Coleridge is the master of chiasmus, the rhetorical device he employs more extensively and variously than any of his contemporaries. It is this device, I propose, that Coleridge finds most suitable as the vehicle of—virtually the image *for*—dejection as well as its opposites. A rhetorical scheme becomes, for Coleridge, a trope.[14] Chiasmus exists for containment, for good as well as ill. Indolence as dejection and indolence as the condition for aesthetic wonder elicit comparable rhetorical treatments.[15]

A brief survey of Coleridge's poetry (and of his prose) opens up the multiple uses of this trope, which became, one might say, the habit of his soul and the cross that he bore. In both "The Ancient Mariner" and "Christabel" it figures at least in part as a homage in the form of grace notes to the style of ballads and romances that Coleridge (like Wordsworth in *The White Doe of Rylstone*) wished to imitate: for example, "Down dropt the breeze, the sails dropt down," or "the sky and the sea, and the sea and the sky" ("The Rime of the Ancient Mariner," ll. 107, 250); "But Christabel the lamp will trim. / She trimmed the lamp, and made it bright"; "dreaming, fearfully, / Fearfully dreaming" ("Christabel" 1:185–86, 293–94). In his metrical exercise "Hexameters" we find a purely ornamental pairing: "place it on desk or on table; / Place it on table or desk." In a letter to Southey of August 11, 1801 (*CL,* 2:751) he transcribes two lines "in an old German Latin Book which pleased me": "Si tibi deficiant Medici, Medici tibi fiant / Haec tria, Mens hilaris, Requies, Moderata Diaeta." Surely the style as well as the substance of the dictum (which recommends joviality, rest, and a moderate diet as the best physicians) appealed to his senses.

At other points the chiasmus serves more complex and more varied functions. Writing of his own habits, Coleridge remarks in a letter (*CL*, 1:279): "I feel strongly, and I think strongly; but I seldom feel without thinking, or think without feeling." Here the chiasmus exists within a parallel construction that allows the heft of the sentence to be balanced in both an ongoing, linear fashion and a self-contained or enfolded one. More important are the privileged moments in the conversation poems (I shall discuss Coleridge's late, bleaker poems further on) that speak in favor of hoped-for, idealized circumstances. We have the prayer for Hartley's education by God, who teaches "[h]imself in all, and all things in himself" ("Frost at Midnight," l. 62); the wish that the poet's song "should make all Nature lovelier, / And itself be loved like Nature!" ("The Nightingale," ll. 33–34); the aphorism in a poem to Wordsworth ("Ad Vilum Axiologum"), "Love is the Spirit of Life, and Music the Life of the Spirit," which also places the chiasmus within a rhetorically parallel construction; the response to Wordsworth's depictions of great souls: "Time is not with them, / Save as it worketh for them, they in it" ("To William Wordsworth, ll. 53–54), a semichiasmus ("it . . . them / they . . . it) slightly repressed by its very context. As a conclusion I might cite the poem generally acknowledged as Coleridge's earliest important one, "The Eolian Harp," in which the much idealized and here personified "one Life within us and abroad" is depicted synesthetically as "[a] light in sound, a sound-like power in light" (l. 28). We might hypothesize that for Coleridge chiasmus best represents the unities that he seeks as a formal condition for poetry and as a psychological condition that the poetry duplicates.[16]

In "Dejection," and its original version in the "Letter," we can discover several crucial instances of this trope, and they will allow us first of all to say something about Coleridge's depictions of indolence and then to make some generalizations about the body of his poetry. We can begin with an early meteorological detail:

> For lo! the New-moon winter-bright!
> And overspread with phantom light,
> (With swimming phantom light o'erspread
> But rimmed and circled by a silver thread) . . .
>
> (ll. 9–12)

The chiasmus here ("overspread . . . light / light . . . o'erspread") was hard won.[17] The first version of the "Letter" in April 1802 (the Cornell MS) has

> And all suffus'd with phantom Light
> (With swimming phantom Light o'erspread,
> But rimm'd and circl'd with a silver Thread) . . .

As late as July 19, 1802, in his letter to William Sotheby which quotes part of the poem, Coleridge still has not reached his final adjustment:

> And overspread with phantom Light;
> (With swimming phantom Light o'erspread,
> But rimm'd and circled *with* a silver Thread)
>
> (emphasis added)

Having made the significant substitution of "overspread" for "suffus'd" to ensure a full chiasmus, Coleridge came to realize only a little later the stylistic repetitiveness of his third "with," and therefore replaced it with a "by."

His gestures toward containment are not always successful, or not simplistically so: the parentheses of lines 11–12 interrupt or syncopate the chiastic phrase that falls both without and within their boundaries. In addition, as at other crucial moments in the poem, a grammatical aporia opens up to reveal what I take to be a moment of psychic or poetic tension. Something seems to be missing from this section:

> For lo! the New-moon winter-bright!
> And overspread with phantom light,
> (With swimming phantom light o'erspread
> But rimmed and circled by a silver thread)
> I see the old Moon in her lap, foretelling
> The coming-on of rain and squally blast.
>
> (ll. 9–14)

As if to balance three major gestures of containment (the parenthetical couplet, the rhetorical chiasmus, the very image of the old moon in the lap of the new) there is a violent open-endedness here that is more than a typographical slip. "I see," the subject and predicate of a sentence, stands sentinel between what must be taken as two equal but grammatically separate objects, one that precedes and the other that follows it. "The New-moon . . . I see the old Moon," reads this sentence, but this turns out to be shorthand for another repressed chiasmus: "The New-moon I see / I see the old Moon."[18]

Coleridge's forging of the ode from the *disiecta membra* of the "Letter" involved the elimination of much material, including several characteristic chiastic phrases, which though dropped reveal significant associations he must have made unconsciously with the trope. At line 120 of the "Letter" he addresses Sara: "Thee, Best-beloved! who lovest me the Best!" At lines 145–47 he moves from rhetorical symmetry to semi-chiasmus:

> Peace in thy Heart and Quiet in thy dwelling,
> Health in thy Limbs, and in thy Eye the Light
> Of Love, and Hope, and honourable Feeling . . .

Coleridge dispatches his family of abstractions variously, starting with a pair of balanced hemistiches, proceeding to the chiasmus in the middle (abstraction in body / in body abstraction), and then opening through the enjambment to the richer cornucopia of the last line. The fact that any of the abstractions might legitimately replace any of the others (e.g., "Quiet in thy Heart and Health in thy Dwelling . . . and in thy Eye the Light of Peace") may have contributed to Coleridge's decision to omit the lines from the ode, but chiasmus had also become too habitual to be casually tossed aside. Last of all, in stanza 17 of the "Letter" (ll. 248–49) comes the apostrophic: "But Thou, DEAR Sara! (Dear indeed thou art) / My Comforter! A Heart within my Heart!"

Coleridge's fondness for parentheses is attested to by a telling aperçu in his letter to Thomas Poole of January 28, 1810 (*CL,* 3:282), where he remarks that in addition to representing the *"drama* of Reason" and the development of a ramifying mind, they also serve the rhetorical function of simultaneously advancing and containing an argument. The line just quoted both withholds and breaks apart as the chiasmus (thou dear / dear thou) joins the main thought and the sotto voce aside of the parenthetical afterthought. As Sara is characterized as the heart within his heart, Coleridge has also lit upon chiasmus as the trope best suited for gestures of enfolding, mimicking, or mirroring. Having referred earlier to the "habitual ills" of his unhappy domestic situation, "when two unequal minds / Meet in one House, and two discordant Wills" (ll. 242–44), a phrase we may read as a collapsed chiasmus with one middle term omitted (*a b a* rather than *a b b a*),[19] he has himself been reduced to the accidie for which he adduces only intellectual causes in the final redaction of the ode: "Past cure and past Complaint! A fate austere, / Too fixed and hopeless to partake of Fear" (ll. 246–47). If Coleridge's dream of human perfection is equivalent to a Shelleyan epipsyche, a soul within his soul to alleviate his psychological deadness, chiasmus is the trope that permits equal rhetorical parts to meet in one linguistic house.

Chiasmus as the rhetorical gesture of enclosure everywhere counters the unnameable, indefinable dread at the heart of Coleridge's poetry. In an anticipation of Emersonian circles and the obsession of a contemporary poet such as A. R. Ammons with determination and entropy, Coleridge proposes the two "conflicting principles of FREE LIFE, and of the confining FORM" as the "primary forces from which the conditions of all possible directions are derivative" (*BL,* 1:197).[20] But if the form of "Dejection" read large involves the containment of the poet's self-analysis, it also possesses its own momentary breakdowns, gestures that in the language of Coleridge's distinction signal freedom. The grammatical doubling of "the New-moon . . . I see . . . the old Moon" is one example. Another comes, perhaps naturally, after Coleridge's desperate and negative attempt to define his indolent grief: line 24 simply breaks off as if to signal its failure to provide closure of definition or even the grammatical continuity that might allow "A grief" (l. 21) to stand as the subject *or* the object of the sentence. But it is neither. Instead, the exasperated speaker interrupts himself and begins again: "O Lady! in this wan and heartless mood, / To other thoughts by yonder throstle woo'd / . . . Have I been gazing" (ll. 25–28). The mood, that which was originally *in* Coleridge, is now construed as something that encloses him. This reversal of inner and outer corresponds to his failure to fix or define his state. It is also connected with the opposing problem of identifying the origin of the "Joy" that is its nominal opposite: in stanza 5 Coleridge construes it as a natural beneficence ("Joy that ne'er was given, / Save to the pure, and in their purest hour [ll. 64–65]), which must logically come from *somewhere,* like Keats's melancholy "fit" falling like grace from heaven. Nonetheless, he takes pains through the middle stanzas to stress the purely internal origin of such blessedness: "from the soul itself must issue forth . . . from the soul itself must there be sent" the light and the voice of joy (st. 4). One may be reminded of Blake's epigram: "To be in a passion you good may do, / But no good if a passion is in you." (This couplet might be construed as a *double* chiasmus: "you . . . good / good . . . you" mingled with "passion . . . good / good . . . passion"!) Having abandoned his quest to define his "grief," Coleridge begins the poem again, using the first four lines of stanza 2, now separated by the anacoluthon of the dash, as an apposition to the "wan and heartless mood" he is *in*.

If this grief "finds no *natural* outlet, no relief" (l. 23), it must still be bottled within the speaker, who can neither exorcise it nor find any external (i.e., natural) language for it. This mutual self-containment (he contains it, it him) has a manifest outlet in the poet's ongoing effort to discover the "word" for it. He recapitulates through his imagery in the rest of the stanza his grammatical and rhetorical gestures of simultaneous containment and discursiveness. On the one hand, he claims the "blankness," the unfeelingness, of his own merely aesthetic response to the outward scene. On the other, he has constructed a little picture of natural "relief" in the "clouds . . . / That give away their motion to the stars" (ll. 31–32), and the new moon that is "fixed" and centrally located "[i]n its own cloudless, starless lake of blue" (l. 36). We have a metonymic drama of self-abandonment in the clouds and a metaphor of movement-in-stasis in the crescent moon. These personifications of evanescence and stability are in fact the *natural* (in the several senses of that word) and artistic outlet the poet has been claiming he lacks.[21]

Aesthetic responsiveness or spectatorship derives from nonfeeling. Keatsian indolence, here in its peculiarly negative, Coleridgean manifestation, is once more the sine qua non for aesthetic appreciation. We may apply to Coleridge his label for Wordsworth: the *spectator ab extra,* who at least in this poem admits his own position as an observer on a periphery looking in at things whose beauty he can no longer "feel." It is significant that the entire second stanza has a prose gloss in "On the Principles of Genial Criticism," which appeared in *Felix Farley's Bristol Journal* for September 10, 1814, along with two sections of the poem. Distinguishing the "beautiful" from the "agreeable," Coleridge says that the sensation of pleasure precedes and determines the judgment that an object is agreeable, whereas with the beautiful, the contemplation of an object's beauty "precedes the *feeling* of complacency, in order of nature at least: nay, in great depression of spirits may even exist without sensibly producing it" (quoted in Stephen Maxfield Parrish, p. 51). Coleridgean dejection, as it develops throughout the poem, looks like a combination of deep pain and severe nonfeeling. Crushed by a "smothering weight" (l. 41), deprived (or so we infer) of the "Joy" that is given only to the "pure" in stanza 5, and bowed down by afflictions, and infected by his habit of "abstruse research" (st. 6), the poet is also curiously apathetic about his condition: "I may not hope" (l. 45); "Nor care I that they rob me of my mirth" (l. 83); until, at last, he disappears from the poem in the palinode of stanza 8, which turns entirely toward the "Lady" ("'Tis midnight, but small thoughts have I of sleep" [l. 126]), an exorcism or natural outlet for the fears and anxieties that earlier poisoned—but also inspired—his consciousness.

Coleridge knows neither the nature of his condition nor his own proper response to it. What I have labeled the grammatical aporia at the start of the second stanza is matched by another, equally vexed passage further on. According to Parrish (p. 47), the poet quoted lines 87–93 to friends ("For not to think of what I needs must feel . . .") more than any other section of the poem. But these are also rhetorically the most difficult lines of the poem: Coleridge's sense of their truthfulness to his condition must have been matched by his own difficulty in clarifying his definition. In a sensitive analysis of the ode, Marshall Suther concludes that Coleridge's "whole presentation of the psychological history of this most important development in his life is confused, contradictory, and factually inaccurate," and asserts that the entire sixth stanza is "like a parenthesis in the poem" because it omits the major symbols of light and wind which inform the rest of the work.[22] What for Suther is anomalous in the poem seems to me its most characteristic part. In parsing Coleridge's self-analysis, Suther is perplexed by the logical contradiction between two ways of hearing the lines. The poet wishes "either to deaden pain or to compensate for the absence of feeling." Either his defense mechanism has itself become an infection, or (given the evidence from the "Letter") he now lacks all occasion for genuine feeling because of the failure of his marriage.[23] In fact, I think, the poem's uncertainty is at the heart of its originality, combining two standard senses of melancholy as the indolence (lack of pain) that is also a Carlylean center of indifference (dejection as a condition definable only through negation) or as that crucial humor associated by Burton and other earlier anatomists—whether physicians or philosophers—with philosophical speculation.[24]

The moment of speculation that occupies these lines comes with its own aporias. There is the strongly felt absence of (I presume) verbs of being and acting in line 88. One must paraphrase thus: "But to be still and patient [is] all I can [do]." There is the anacoluthon at the end of line 90 which places the preceding four lines into a timeless world governed only by infinitives ("not to think," "to be still," "to steal"). There is the barely suppressed, wistful echo of "happily" in "haply," intimating the pathos of the poet's efforts at self-redemption, and the illusion of criminality ("to steal") undercutting those efforts immediately. There is, at last, the equation of theft with the poet's human "nature," regardless of whether we take his "sole resource" as the cause of his criminal pain or as its result. His only plan is to rid or empty himself of his "nature," a gesture that has turned back on him to heighten the very disease it had attempted to eliminate.

Coleridge is on the horns of a dilemma; his metaphysical speculations offer both salvation and damnation, as an 1818 letter reminds us: "Poetry is out of the question. The attempt would only hurry me into that sphere of acute feelings, from which abstruse research, the mother of self-oblivion, presents an asylum" (*CL,* 4:893).[25] Rather than stemming from tranquillity (the Wordsworthian formula for poetry), Coleridge's poetry leads *into* strong, or strongly negative, feelings, for which the only antidote is provided by metaphysical research and self-forgetfulness. But, to conflate the remark in the letter with the language of the poem, since we also know that abstruse research results in a painful rather than an *in-dolent* oblivion, we see that Coleridge has no way out of his dilemma. The will is poisoned by feelings, and it in turn poisons all efforts at abolishing itself. It is to the negativity of the will that indolence and unself-consciousness offer a salve, just as (to argue from the other side) dejection, as the intensely negative manifestation of indolence, threatens to destroy both "Joy" and its effluent "shaping spirit of Imagination."[26]

A middle course between those "viper thoughts" that strangle, obliterate, and deaden the soul, and the "Joy" from which the poet feels himself cut off, whether as a result of birth, damnation, or habit, emerges in the form of what we might label spectatorship, or the aesthetics of watching.[27] "Dejection" is a poem of looking, witnessing, and attending, as well as of thinking and analyzing. So ardent is Coleridge's self-concentration that the central *fact* within the poem, the beginning of the storm for which the first·stanza was a hopeful anticipation ("And oh! that even now the gust were swelling"), is deliberately evaded or buried somewhere between lines 20 and 97. Although it initially appears that Coleridge's move from self-analysis to the external storm is an effort of the conscious will ("Hence, viper thoughts / . . . I turn from you" [ll. 94–96]), the subsequent lines reveal that he has been snapped from his dark dreams by the sound of the lute in the window, the aeolian harp which has served, since his earlier poem about it, as the metonymic symbol for the responsive human mind. Not through an act of willing but through one of responding does the mind animate itself.[28] And, in fact, with Coleridge we bear witness to a *doubled* passivity: his mind responds to the lute which responds to the wind. The self has been emptied of both consciousness and identity in its indolence, and it regains its healthy—that is, imaginative—status only through its notice of an external version of itself—the lute—that is acted upon.

Such notice, however, is not a conscious gesture. Neither thinking, in the form of abstruse research and articulate self-examination, nor looking, in the form of the gazing that occupies the second stanza, provides solace or aid. Both paths lead to misery, the latter because it reminds the poet of his alienation from the world of external beauty from which he thinks himself cut off. To put it otherwise, what can be seen (the green light lingering in the west) does not help. What *cannot* be seen or heard *does*. The crucial moment in the ode is the poet's realization that he has in fact been hearing the wind for some unstated time, although he has not been listening to or for it. The senses, like thought itself, can be suspended, and when one returns to them, the new experience is excitingly self-animating. This then permits the release generated within the blessing of the poem's last stanza.

There are other Coleridgean paradigms for this kind of unconsciously specular activity. The primary one, of course, belongs to the moment in "The Ancient Mariner" when gazing at the watersnakes encourages the Mariner to bless them "unaware." Only with the relaxation or, to use the Wordsworthian word, the suspension of the will do understanding, sensitivity, and moral duty come alive.[29] More important from the standpoint of "indolence" are the absences at the heart of "This Lime-Tree Bower My Prison," and "Frost at Midnight," poems that revolve around what is not immediately discernible but is available only *after* the suspension of will and vision. A detour through these poems will enable us to return to the conclusion of "Dejection."

The former is in some ways Coleridge's most original poem within the conversation or "greater Romantic lyric" genre. Although it is clearly the inspiration for "Tintern Abbey," Wordsworth never fully took up Coleridge's obsession with absence in his rendition of a similar dilemma. That is, Coleridge, unlike Wordsworth, consciously creates a landscape from which he is separated, vicariously participating in an experience that he can only imagine, but can never have at firsthand. (In this regard it is of considerable significance that the original manuscript version of the poem, in a letter to Southey of July 17, 1797, does not contain the full description of what was to become lines 1–28.) The poem is premised on the indolence that results from physical immobility—the poet is trapped at home after his wife accidentally spills boiling milk on him—and that triggers the imaginative reconstruction of the experience of his peripatetic friends as a means of compensating for, and indeed surpassing, the original loss.

No poem more stunningly announces the paradox that I earlier posed as "self-incaged is self-engaged." From the start the physical setting is both a pastoral "bower" and an entrapping "prison," as though Coleridge were rehearsing the positive and negative alternatives of leisurely solitude and psychic or moral isolation. The opening tone is as offhand as that of "Dejection" ("Well, they are gone, and here must I remain") and even more exaggeratedly self-pitying: "I have lost / Beauties and feelings, such as would have been / Most sweet to my remembrance even when age / Had dimm'd mine eyes to blindness!" What follows (ll. 5–37) is a voyeuristic travelogue in which Coleridge reviews, in a continuous present tense, the supposed path his friends are taking, a path initially proposed to them by him. Wandering in gladness, first down to a dell and then up to a hillside clearing that grants a view of sea and land, Charles Lamb and the others clearly inhabit a *paysage moralisé* that corresponds to the absent Coleridge's state of mind. As a metonymic projection of his own condition, the symbolic landscape charts a movement from abjection to ecstasy, beginning in the "roaring dell,"

> Where its slim trunk the ash from rock to rock
> Flings arching like a bridge;—that branchless ash,
> Unsunn'd and damp, whose few poor yellow leaves
> Ne'er tremble in the gale, yet tremble still,
> Fann'd by the water-fall!
>
> (ll. 12–16)

As in his definition of dejection, Coleridge relies on negation ("branchless," "unsunn'd," "ne'er") and other gestures of diminution (the echo of the "yellow leaves or none or few" of Shakespeare's seventy-third sonnet must be intentional) to paint the scene. Not only is he absent from the landscape; he also consciously constructs a scene *of* absence.

From this image, through the subsequent one of an eerie waterfall, to the emergence of the group upon an exposed height under the presumed protection of "the wide wide Heaven" whence they view the majestic surround, Coleridge has taken a miniaturized voyage of Dantean proportions. First by imagining the landscape, then by identifying with and directly addressing himself to Charles Lamb, the most appreciative and "glad" of the group, Coleridge has all unwittingly proceeded along a course of self-enlightenment, entirely through an act of self-forgetfulness. Just as the landscape represents his condition, so also does Lamb, who many a year "in the great City pent," like Coleridge in *his* bower–prison, could only "[win his] way / With sad yet patient soul, through evil and pain / And strange calamity!" (ll. 30–32).

What is for my argument the most telling gesture in the poem is *not* the subsequent ecstatic address to the sun, flowers, clouds, and ocean which attains the status of a beneficent legacy to Charles Lamb ("So my friend / Struck with deep joy may stand, as I have stood, / Silent with swimming sense" [ll. 37–39]). It is, rather, the observation that follows this rapt and transcendent visionary moment. After vicariously gazing with Lamb on the landscape till "all doth seem / Less gross than bodily" (ll. 40–41), Coleridge returns to his own lot with a renewed enthusiasm:

> A delight
> Comes sudden on my heart, and I am glad
> As I myself were there! Nor in this bower,
> This little lime-tree bower, have I not mark'd
> Much that has sooth'd me. Pale beneath the blaze
> Hung the transparent foliage; and I watch'd
> Some broad and sunny leaf, and lov'd to see
> The shadow of the leaf and stem above

Dappling its sunshine! And that walnut-tree
Was richly ting'd, and a deep radiance lay
Full on the ancient ivy, which usurps
Those fronting elms, and now, with blackest mass
Makes their dark branches gleam a lighter hue.

(ll. 43–55)

By and large, critics have not commented on the tenses of the poem's verbs at this point.[30] Coleridge is no longer describing what he sees or imagines, but rather what he *has* seen during (we assume) the previous monologue. His "marking" of the beauties of his bower has been entirely unconscious, but he can now report it as if he *had been* conscious of it all along, even though he has not been. The section is both a climax and an afterthought, as if to say: "By the way, I forgot to mention that the transparent foliage hung beneath the blaze while I was prattling on about Charles and the others." Vision has occurred retroactively or, we might say, retrospectively. The spectator's status has been enlarged by virtue of the suspension of at least one part of his will; by focusing on the others, by conjuring an absent landscape, Coleridge returns to himself and *his* surroundings in a way that can hardly be called self-involved.

As he moves seamlessly from the past to the present tense (at line 53), Coleridge homes in, as evening darkens round, on himself and the lesson taught by his previous observation:

Henceforth I shall know
That Nature ne'er deserts the wise and pure;
No plot so narrow, be but Nature there,
No waste so vacant, but may well employ
Each faculty of sense, and keep the heart
Awake to Love and Beauty!

(ll. 59–64)

This doctrine of compensation, of having been "bereft of promis'd good" *in order to* "contemplate / With lively joy the joys we cannot share" (ll. 65–67) demonstrates the Coleridgean tactic for making sense of deprivation and, even more, for moving beyond deprivation, abandonment, and absence through an imaginative reconstruction that partakes equally of conscious, willed notice and unconscious, unwilled spectatorship. His poem converts the negative potential of indolence into the positive fact of active prayer in its final moment of imaginative enclosure: Coleridge sees the "last rook" heading home, infers that Lamb is also witnessing the same bird, and thereby establishes the rook as the bond, whether metaphor or abridgment, between the two of them. The human connection is constructed out of the flimsiest possible vehicle. This vanishing bird—is it absent or is it present?—links the two separated friends. Out of such absences can Coleridge in his hopeful moods alleviate his self-pity or repopulate vacancy. And these are moods in which physical immobility and the temporary suspension of the will compel the compensating imagination to begin its own work.[31]

"Frost at Midnight" embodies more elegantly than any other of Coleridge's poems his obsession with absence and, as a compensating gesture, reflective mirroring. It, too, is a poem of indolence and spectatorship, in which the Coleridgean "idling Spirit" (l. 20) finds its "companionable form" in a series of images, each of which comes as the climax to one of the poem's four verse paragraphs. The poem begins with a stunning epigrammatic pronouncement: "The Frost performs its secret ministry, / Unhelped by any wind." Coleridge returns to his opening inspiration only at the end, providing readers such as Abrams with evidence for the "circularity" of Romantic lyric. The whole poem is enclosed by the image of the frost, which depicts an independent, self-willed, and (most important) invisible action seemingly unconnected to the goings-on indoors, where the poet sits with his slumbering infant. The frost does something; the poet sits idly, contemplating the sooty film—or "stranger"—on the grate of the fireplace and begins to establish a sequence of resemblances that counter the independent, active performance of the frost.

All is quiet or asleep. The poet has been abandoned, as he was in "This Lime-Tree Bower My Prison," by everyone except his sleeping infant, and finds provocation in abandonment for "abstruser musings" (which he never reveals to us). Father and child provide one mirror, poet and "stranger" a second, stronger one. But since the "puny flaps and freaks" of the film replicate the mood and mind of the "idling Spirit," the film reduces the poet to the status of a child himself, and the paragraph ends with a doubled identification:

> Methinks, its motion in this hush of nature
> Gives it dim sympathies with me who live,
> Making it a companionable form,
> Whose puny flaps and freaks the idling Spirit
> By its own moods interprets, every where
> Echo or mirror seeking of itself,
> And makes a toy of Thought.
>
> (ll. 17–23)

The densely hypotactic syntax suggests the impossibility of discovering an origination for the poet's mental activity: *it* seeks a self-image, but has been provoked to do so, perhaps, *by* the motion of the film. The mind seeks its own resemblance but, having found it, is reduced to a child's play by the diminished thing that the film actually is. The two components, film and mind, are self-enclosed so tightly that one cannot determine what causes what. The film's "motion" *makes* it a form and also (as I read the lines) *makes* the poet's thought a toy. These lines have the spirit, if not the letter, of a chiasmus, the two verbs of "making" surrounding the activity of the Spirit ("interprets" and "seeking"); but since the Spirit has itself actively sought its own mirror, matters of priority and cause are deliberately obscured. The will has been thwarted, either from within or from without. The closing image must be an unsuccessful one: the poet has become a child, his own active spirit finding an image of itself only in a will-o'-the-wisp.

And so the poem attempts a second gesture, this time through an act of memory, to discover a fitting double for the poet's mind. If the first paragraph thwarts his effort by rendering it mock-heroic, the second mirrors and reverses, as well as literalizes, the first by returning Coleridge to childhood, when, at school, he gazed hopefully on the film, expecting to see a companion from home:

> still my heart leaped up,
> For still I hoped to see the *stranger's* face,
> Townsman, or aunt, or sister more beloved,
> My play-mate when we both were clothed alike!
>
> (ll. 40–43)

Like the one in the first stanza, this moment of expectation comes during an indolent reverie compounded of meditation and mock-study: scanning his "swimming book" (recall Coleridge and Charles Lamb in "This Lime-Tree Bower" standing "silent with swimming sense"), the young Coleridge plays at thought, and is, we assume, disappointed in the nonarrival of the sibling–mirror he awaits.[32]

Whereas the first half of the poem presents thwarted efforts at self-repetition, attempted acts of discovering one's mirror half while idly summoning up ghosts from either the mind or home, the second half gives us more assured reciprocities, precisely because they no longer involve the poet himself. Hope for repetition devolves solely upon young Hartley, as it does upon Sara Hutchinson in "Dejection": he shall be the beneficiary of the chiastic act of a pedagogic God who "doth teach / Himself in all, and all things in himself" (ll. 61–62). And, though not strictly chiastic, the last lines of the paragraph depict a comparable enclosing in the reciprocal relationship between God and child, teacher and pupil: "Great universal Teacher! he shall mould / Thy spirit, and by giving make it ask" (ll. 63–64). The comforting enwrapping of chiasmus is here matched by the comfort of tautology: God will inspire the child to ask for what He has in fact already given. The circularity of the pedagogic relation forms another image of unity from which the adult poet has clearly been cut off, except in his roles as prayer giver and observer.

It is for this reason that the moving benediction of the last stanza, which places Hartley in a world of natural variety and loveliness, is the only one from which the first-person poet has entirely disappeared.[33] The aesthetic act, a projected observing of an idealized landscape, removes Coleridge completely from his poem, except as its creator. It is he who constitutes the absence at the end of the poem, where child and nature submit to the general sweetness of seasonal change.[34] But although the poet is nominally absent from his prayer, he returns us to his opening meteorological detail, not only completing the circle that Abrams posits as the hallmark of the Romantic nature lyric, but, also, more important, ending on a note of reciprocal activity:

> Therefore all seasons shall be sweet to thee,
> Whether the summer clothe the general earth
> With greenness, or the redbreast sit and sing
> Betwixt the tufts of snow on the bare branch
> Of mossy apple-tree, while the nigh thatch
> Smokes in the sun-thaw; whether the eave-drops fall
> Heard only in the trances of the blast,
> Or if the secret ministry of frost
> Shall hang them up in silent icicles,
> Quietly shining to the quiet Moon.

(ll. 65–74)

As in other key moments in Coleridge's poetry, a grammatical or rhetorical problem jars the apparent tranquillity of this benediction. He seemingly attempts an act of pure rhetorical balance in his two dependent clauses ("Whether . . . or / whether . . . Or"), but he tips the scales first of all by offering three parts winter to one part summer, and next of all by making even *more* conditional the ultimate detail: the "if" of line 72 has no mate anywhere in the paragraph, and the stated futurity of "shall hang" is off-key with the present tense of "eave-drops fall"—unless, that is, one thinks of the temporality of the last stanza as itself an implied chiasmus: the futurity of the general "shall be sweet to thee" repeated by that of the penultimate line. One other chiastic gesture now seems obvious: the bracketing of the interior intransitive verbs ("sit and sing," "smokes," "falls") by the two outer, active ones ("clothe" and "shall hang").

All of these stylistic details vivify Coleridge's insistence on enclosure and repetition as happy conditions from which he is himself, alas, cut off.[35] Harmony will come to Hartley alone, and finally through the image of a paradoxical self-sufficiency that is also a dependency. The downward-growing icicles, created by the falling eave-drops, are hung *up*; they pay homage *to* a regent moon, *in* whose cold light their own is reflected.[36] At the heart of this cool, elegant world of silent reciprocities and clear, icy visibility lies one last gesture that draws us outside the nearly perfected, enclosed figure. It is the same gesture with which the poem began. If the frost, that secret performer, is also a minister, we must wonder in what or whose service it is operating. As always Coleridge mars his attempt to create perfect figures of harmonious stillness with an aporia—this time figuratively as well as grammatically or rhetorically—that leads us outward or beyond to a mysteriously unknowable first cause. *Sweetness* will come to Hartley, but the quiet of the last lines, observed by the indolent aesthetic spectator, comes at a price: the ignorance of causality. Even at its most beautifully still moment, Coleridge's poetry yearns for a knowledge of "secret," because absent, origins.

Returning from the strategies of "This Lime-Tree Bower My Prison" and "Frost at Midnight" to the seventh stanza of "Dejection," we can better understand the harmony in Coleridge's only apparently sudden or willed tossing off of his coiled, viperish "thoughts." Dejection is not the only thing that disappears from the poem at this point; Coleridge himself does as well. The wind becomes a "Mad Lutanist" playing on the lyre, and on the poet himself with motifs from gothic, tragic, or pathetic texts, those tales it *tells* about (l. 110). As such, the wind replaces not only the actors, poets, and musicians whose work it mimes but also the central poet, who has become an audience for that work. There are only six first-person deictic references in the last two stanzas (ll. 94, 96, 103, 126, 127, and 138), of which only the first two are strong enough to command a verb of willing; the rest render the poet either a respondent or a mere describer. He exits the poem slowly, exorcising himself along with "reality's dark dream." What remains, as at the end of "Frost at Midnight," is all futurity: an entire stanza is governed by the optative mood ("Full seldom *may*," and so on). The poet's "vigil" (l. 127) has kept him attentive to meteorology and autobiography. By now the habit of self-analysis has worn itself out, and dejection has played itself out. Although the poet will never possess the joy he took such pains to define in the middle stanzas, the last stanza vouchsafes the only possible substitute for him, a blessing proffered on behalf of another. The poet's negative indolence, manifestation of his dejection, has transformed itself through a series of acts of seeing and listening into its positive twin, the imaginative sympathy or outpouring of self in which both will and self are emptied.

In a famous aphorism Nietzsche encapsulated much Romantic thought: "It is only as an *aesthetic phenomenon* that existence and the world are eternally *justified*."[37] Whereas for Nietzsche aesthetics is inextricably bound up with a masculinist will to power, for Coleridge the act of observing has a laudably self-denying, rather than self-affirming, basis. This is due in part, of course, to the self-incriminating charges of weakness and effeminacy that attend mere looking in poems such as "The Eolian Harp," where the "indolent," "idle," "flitting" brain is troped specifically as feminine.[38] (Wordsworth, as I have noted, has distinctly different doubts about his own "voluptuous" or "indolent" side, but they are not connected to the matter of gender.) In line 14 of "The Nightingale" he condemns as an "idle thought" Milton's label of the bird as "melancholy." One notices how even in his quasi-Wordsworthian associationism Coleridge goes where Wordsworth never would: "flitting" does not appear in Wordsworth's vocabulary, nor do "pretty" and "peep'd," Coleridge's words from the opening lines of "Reflections on Having Left a Place of Retirement." Looking, for Coleridge, is often tainted with voyeurism, as it is here and in "Fears in Solitude," or with a proto-Marxist sense of economic wish fulfillment, as in the egregious figure of the wealthy Bristol citizen whose "thirst of idle gold" accompanies his envious "gaz[ing]" upon the happily retired Coleridges. Mere being is "a luxury" (l. 42) and must therefore be justified in action. The moral cowardice of isolation supersedes its attractions, so Coleridge replaces those slothful loves and dainty sympathies that threaten to un-man him with his active setting forth to "fight the bloodless fight / Of Science, Freedom, and the Truth in Christ" ("Reflections," ll. 61–62).[39]

Coleridge never again attained the gracious charity he achieved at the end of "Dejection." Throughout this poem, thinking rather than looking and hearing (or *being*) has been the cause of dejection, and that thinking, occupying the middle of the poem, has vanished from its seventh and eight stanzas, replaced by the wholly positive exclamations and queries ("Thou mighty Poet . . . / What tell'st thou now about?" [ll. 109–10]) that characterize aesthetic engagement. Even in their pain, or especially so, the tales the storm is presumed to be telling move us from Aristotelian fear ("trampled men, with smarting wounds" [l. 112]) and pity ("[a] tale of less affright" [l. 118]) to their cathartic draining in the break between the seventh and eighth stanzas. Abstruse research and joy, located at the poem's heart, are absent from its periphery, except as a trace. Both have been temporarily ignored or buried, collapsed through their own weight, and succeeded by artful inquiries. The language of friendship has replaced the language of marriage. Sara has replaced Coleridge.

The active and passive poles of the Coleridgean poetic are clearest in "Dejection." Although he famously equates will with self (*BL*, 1:116), Coleridge suggests a more fanciful, elaborate, and ultimately appropriate image of the mind's workings later in the same chapter in an often quoted simile:

> [A] small water-insect on the surface of rivulets, which throws a cinque-spotted shadow fringed with prismatic colours on the sunny bottom of the brook . . . the little animal *wins* its way up against the stream, by alternate pulses of active and passive motion, now resisting the current, and now yielding to it in order to gather strength and a momentary *fulcrum* for a further propulsion. This is no unapt emblem of the mind's self-experience in the act of thinking. (*BL*, 1:124)[40]

The self-diminishing that we saw in "The Eolian Harp" and "Frost at Midnight" here achieves an entirely nonpejorative form. *"Like a long-legged fly upon the stream / His mind moves upon silence"*: Yeats's famous image for Caesar, Helen, and Michelangelo owes something to Coleridge's earlier figuration. Both poets construe thought as small but hardly nugatory. The Coleridgean watcher, like the mind and like the insect, surrenders himself to the current. According to "The Nightingale" he does so to "share in Nature's immortality" and to increase its loveliness. In that poem, where "we have been loitering long and pleasantly" (l. 89), nature requites his filling it with *un*melancholy associations. In "Dejection" Coleridge propels himself out of the poem; thinking retreats into observation and aesthetic questioning, and then transcends itself. The mind does not *win* the joy it once sought; instead it remains momentarily gratified and energized by the hope it entertains for the absent, sleeping beloved.

Few victories are either so tentative or so hard won. Coleridge never achieved such hopeful, even though temporary, solace in his later poems. The dark and even more despondent works of his later years may be said to pick up where the second stanza of "Dejection" had left off. Indolence no longer possesses the potential for even momentary pleasure or aesthetic gratification. In their efforts to depict a state of existential blankness, they surpass the earlier poem in their negative rhetoric. He blames, perhaps too easily, abstruse thought as the root of his problems, referring to himself as one "who, soul and body, through one guiltless fault / Waste daily with the poison of sad thought" ("To Two Sisters"), exonerating and inculpating himself at the same time. "Happy thought" would be, presumably, not poisonous, but it is also presumably not possible. Bleakness and self-pity are once again carried through semichiasmuses, as in "The Pains of Sleep," where Coleridge laments the unquenchability of "the powerless will / Still baffled and yet burning still," and transforms his interest in the active–passive dimensions of thought and creativity into a lament about love, its absence, and its possible encouragement: "To be beloved is all I need, / And whom I love, I love indeed."

Aside from the terrifying ending of *The Dunciad,* there is no real precedent for the language of blankness, nothingness, and self-canceling paradoxes that Coleridge developed in these later poems. "Human Life" (1815) begins with conditionals that never reach a final independent clause:

> If dead, we cease to be; if total gloom
>   Swallow up life's brief flash for aye, we fare
> As summer-gusts, of sudden birth and doom,
>   Whose sound and motion not alone declare,
> But are their whole of being! If the breath
>   Be Life itself, and not its task and tent,
> If even a soul like Milton's can know death;
>   O Man! thou vessel purposeless, unmeant,
> Yet drone-hive strange of phantom purposes!

That last apostrophe never takes a verb (it might read: "Man, thou *then would be* a vessel . . ."), and thereby undoes the entire conditional sequence with which it began ("If the breath / . . . If even a soul"). And so the poem goes, an apostrophic list composed of negation ("purposeless, unmeant," and, later on, "Blank accident! nothing's anomaly!," "rootless," "substanceless," "costless shadows"), redundancy ("Image of Image, Ghost of Ghostly Elf"), and, at the last, a helpless acknowledgment: "Thy being's being is contradiction." The contradiction is most forcefully borne out by the poem's subtitle, "On the Denial of Immortality," a toneless tag that might, mutatis mutandis, speak on behalf of man's immortal soul, but that in this case wraps itself up within the frustrated hostilities of a poem that seems to affirm and to deny everything and nothing at all. Coleridge wishes to disprove the apparent disproof of immortality but can muster only halfclauses, incomplete utterances, and self-canceling paradoxes in his blighted effort.

The Coleridgean will can go only so far in the direction of affirmation. All is conditional. "It may indeed be phantasy, when I / Essay to draw from all created things / Deep, heartfelt, inward joy / . . . So let it be" ("To Nature" [1820]). "Phantasy" alone gives hope. In what is arguably his most original poem, Coleridge even refuses to specify an antecedent for an unnamed power that occupies a negative space in which it terrorizes: "The sole true Something—This! In Limbo's Den / It frightens Ghosts, as here Ghosts frighten men" ("Limbo" [1817]). Limbo itself, *not* a place though called one, may be the Coleridgean ideal of nonfiguration and nonfeeling, his last effort to depict an outward boundary for the condition he described in "Dejection: An Ode."

"Limbo" proceeds as a sequence of denials, of negations that lead to still further negations. In this nonplace, two nonfigures *seem* to contend but are undone by the very sequence of dashes that prevent them from even assuming full allegorical figuration. The aporias in "Dejection" are as nothing compared to those in this poem (originally, according to *CL,* 6:758, a fragment spoken by the mad playwright Nathaniel Lee in Bedlam) that starts, stops, and resumes its lurching pace:

> Lank Space, and scytheless Time with branny hands
> Barren and soundless as the measuring sands,
> Not mark'd by flit of Shades,—unmeaning they
> As moonlight on the dial of the day!
> But that is lovely—looks like Human Time,—
> An Old Man with a steady look sublime,
> That stops his earthly task to watch the skies;
> But he is blind—a Statue hath such eyes;—
> Yet having moonward turn'd his face by chance,
> Gazes the orb with moon-like countenance,
> With scant white hairs, with foretop bald and high,
> He gazes still,—his eyeless face all eye;—
> As 'twere an organ full of silent sight,
> His whole face seemeth to rejoice in light!
> Lip touching lip, all moveless, bust and limb—
> He seems to gaze at that which seems to gaze on him!
>   No such sweet sights doth Limbo den immure,
> Wall'd round, and made a spirit-jail secure. . . .

(ll. 15–32)

Space and time appear, only to be replaced by moonlight. Moonlight metaphorically becomes "lovely" Human Time, the Old Man who seems to watch. His activity, too, is undone, and he becomes a mere statue, or a moonlike figure himself, the Emersonian eyeball a grotesque synecdoche for the whole man. Such gruesome parody of unmeaning, motiveless, and feckless human activity (the man can *see* nothing, and only appears to be be

looking) balances those moments of lovely harmonies in Coleridge's poetry (most notably the end of "Frost at Midnight") in which spectatorship
opens up divine reciprocity. Identity is both asserted and undermined by
the horrible punning of Eye–I. If Coleridge can be said to have absented
himself at the end of "Dejection" and "Frost at Midnight," here he denies
and confirms *all* human existence, his own as well as that of his nominal
human subject. Looking is now mooted by blindness, and Coleridge's
parodic image of reciprocal looking (l. 30), a construction of mingled
chiasmus and parallelism, leads nowhere—twice—first because the man is
blind and second because the poem proceeds to remind us that even such
blindness is too lovely for the prison-house of a limbo that admits of no
escaping.[41]

"Ne Plus Ultra" (1824), preceded in manuscript by the first draft of
"Limbo" and evidently a continuation of it, develops around a series of
apostrophic paradoxes ("Sole Positive of Night! / Antipathist of Light!").
Likewise, "Limbo" itself ends with what might be regarded not only as the
beginning of such self-canceling paradoxes but also as the confirmation of
Coleridge's ongoing experiments with the condition of dejection that he
limned in the second stanza of his earlier ode:

> No such sweet sights doth Limbo den immure,
> Wall'd round, and made a spirit-jail secure,
> By the mere horror of blank Naught-at-all,
> Whose circumambience doth these ghosts enthral.
> A lurid thought is growthless, dull Privation,
> Yet that is but a Purgatory curse;
> Hell knows a fear far worse,
> A fear—a future state;—'tis positive Negation!
>
> (ll. 31–38)

Referentiality gives way here to the unspecified horror implicit in vagueness. Are "these ghosts" equivalent or opposed to the "sweet sights" of line
31? If opposite, then what exactly are they? How do we situate limbo,
psychologically as well as theologically, with respect to both purgatory and
hell? Obviously it is different from the latter, but with regard to the former
(the origin of the negative "growthless, dull Privation" at the center of the
Dejection Ode) we cannot be as clear. If hell is worse than limbo/
purgatory, it is also, paradoxically, better in its certainties: positive negation, utter cursed hopelessness, is preferable to the dull privation of a grief
without a pang.

Coleridge's poetic habits of negation were associated, as I observed at
the start of this chapter, with the several phenomena of metaphysical contemplation. One might never guess, but is not surprised to learn, that the
moving late sonnet titled "Work Without Hope" was originally intended
as a complaint by Jacob spoken to Rachel, the traditional representative of
the *vita contemplativa*. Anxious and fearful that he will never attain his goal,
Jacob assumes from Laban's daughter the feminized condition of self-

absorption. Coleridge gives us one final mirror, now embedded within the joint enclosures of parentheses *and* chiasmus:

> "My faith (say I: I and my Faith are one)
> Hung, as a Mirror there! and face to face
> (For nothing else there was, between or near)
> One sister Mirror hid the dreary Wall. . . ."
>
> (*CL*, 5:414–16)

In its final printed version, the poem does without its biblical apparatus and eliminates as well its mirroring. All that remains is the pathos of alienated, dejected individualism: while "all Nature seems at work," Coleridge touchingly returns to the language of "Frost at Midnight," this time without a son or a stranger to comfort him: "I the while, the sole unbusy thing, / Nor honey make, nor pair, nor build, nor sing" (ll. 5–6). He knows where amaranths blow, where nectar flows:

> Bloom, O ye amaranths! bloom for whom ye may,
> For me ye bloom not! Glide, rich streams, away!
> With lips unbrightened, wreathless brow, I stroll.
>
> (ll. 9–11)

Like Eliot's Prufrock, Coleridge knows or sees the sources of a blessing denied him. Jacob's labor has been shunted aside, for the simple reason that it resulted in his winning his bride, and for the simpler reason that *no* work or business better suits the poet's despair. Such despair is mitigated only at the end of his life, by the poem printed as Coleridge's epitaph and dated November 9, 1833. Its middle lines read:

> O, lift one thought in prayer for S. T. C.;
> That he who many a year with toil of breath
> Found death in life, may here find life in death!

Coleridge's poetic last words contain his last chiasmus. The enclosure of the grave grants peace, in a form transcending both prison and bower, and providing at the last a type of indolence accompanied by neither pain nor punishment but only by comfort.

4

Keats's Figures of Indolence

With Keats it makes sense to start at the end. In the center of what readers have always taken as his symbolic valediction poses, or reposes, a worker-goddess, his ultimate and most sublime embodiment of indolence:

> Who hath not seen thee oft amid thy store?
>> Sometimes whoever seeks abroad may find
> Thee sitting careless on a granary floor,
>> Thy hair soft-lifted by the winnowing wind;
> Or on a half-reap'd furrow sound asleep,
>> Drows'd with the fume of poppies, while thy hook
>> Spares the next swath and all its twined flowers;
> And sometimes like a gleaner thou dost keep
>> Steady thy laden head across a brook;
> Or by a cyder-press, with patient look,
>> Thou watchest the last oozings hours by hours.
>
> ("To Autumn," ll. 12–22)

Keats presents his titular figure in four standard visual guises that resemble candid snapshots hurriedly pasted into an album. Rhetorically he has given us two pairs of *almost* parallel clauses: X or Y (ll. 14–18), and X or Y (ll. 19–22). But though the two sections seem grammatically and thematically equivalent, Keats has tipped the scales in favor of a lackadaisical figure: in only one of her four appearances is Autumn *doing* anything (and, it is significant that here she is merely *like* a gleaner, and then not even in the act of gleaning but bringing home her grain), while in one she is watching,

83

and in the two others she verges on or actually inhabits a state of sleep. In addition, by line 19 Autumn is no longer the object of our vision; rather, she becomes the grammatical subject of the new clauses that present her as a more active semiparticipant in the processes that she oversees. This complex image is part statue (whether reclining or staying upright and steady) and part drugged farm girl. She can afford to appear a beneficent rather than a grim reaper because ultimately even that which does not fall beneath her scythe will succumb to time. Poised temporally between moments of labor—harvesting, gleaning, apple pressing—the autumnal deity is a transparent object of aesthetic contemplation (anyone with half an impulse to do so can find her), and is herself a patient onlooker at those processes over which she presides.[1] She is the obverse of the goddess Melancholy, who is approachable only by the epicurean hero who reaches her shrine, tastes her might, and is sacrificed among her cloudy trophies.

A Virgilian parallel suggests itself: the Sybil's warning to Aeneas in book 6 that "facilis descensus Averno . . . sed revocare gradum, hoc opus, hic labor est." To the laborious quest involved in the "Ode on Melancholy," Keats has added the easeful triumphs of "Autumn" in which neither struggle nor effort is required for the sighting of the goddess. That melancholy and indolence were conditions related by physiology, psychology, philosophy, and mythology from the Middle Ages through—at least—the Enlightenment encourages us to think of these odes, along with the "Ode on Indolence," as a small family connected by more than simply generic bonds. It is with this family that this chapter concerns itself. As with Coleridge, I find a curious *absence* at the heart of Keats's figurative grapplings with indolence: alone among the six odes, "On Indolence" neither personifies nor addresses its titular subject. The reasons I propose for such a stunning omission are, strictly speaking, aesthetic and formal rather than political or social.[2]

Autumn herself remains an aesthetic object in the middle of a georgic poem: work is temporarily suspended in favor of rest, indolence, looking (the goddess is both object and subject of observation), and contemplation. We have here the components of the aesthetic moment. The standard time of pastoral *otium,* noon, has been replaced by a late afternoon siesta, as the day and the season wind down to and in the delicate abandonments figured in the poem's last stanza.[3]

The personification of Autumn is exemplary for many reasons. She is the only human figure in the poem, aside from the quasi-human friends of sun and season in the opening lines, which Reuben Brower long ago sensed as ambiguously gendered co-conspirators.[4] She is positioned spatially at the center of the poem and in the midst of her own work, but is also removed from the cottage of the first stanza and the garden croft of the third. She occupies a status at once central and peripheral, appropriate to her gendered embodiment of labor-in-repose. As Helen Vendler has shown, Keats was able to solve many artistic problems in his composition of "To Autumn" through his negotiation among kinds or levels of language.[5] He simultaneously lit upon the most satisfying way of figuring the trope that I take as the master obsession of his career. Indolence occupies the central place in Keats's aesthetics as well as in his poetic achievement.

Of all the Romantic poets Keats—along with Coleridge, but for different reasons—was stylistically the most conservative. He was certainly the most responsive to Spenserian allegory and to techniques of personification.[6] I find it helpful to consider his oeuvre as a series of ongoing experiments in depicting indolence because the idea or possibilities of leisure occupy such a prominent place in his letters and poetry, and because physiology rather than politics was at the heart of his conceptions of self and world.[7] The rhythms of labor and repose concerned him for significant personal reasons (most obviously his inevitable worries about physical decline in the face of his vocational ambition, and his sensitivity to his social status). His poetry thematizes these rhythms, sometimes tensely, sometimes harmoniously. What for Wordsworth was "majestic indolence" became for Keats "delicious diligent indolence" (*Letters,* 1:231), something at once purposeful and lazy, necessary and contingent, sanctioned and self-indulgent.[8]

Keats's personifications are related to his general indebtedness to Spenser, to the neo-Spenserians of the eighteenth century, and to the Milton of "L'Allegro" and "Il Penseroso," whom Geoffrey Hartman adduces as the literary origin of one strain of Romanticism: "If mythology old-style showed the mind at the mercy of humors or stars or heavy abstractions, these personifications of easy virtue, which constitute a mythology new-style, reflect a freer attitude of the mind toward the fictions it entertains." In placing this strain within the dominant literary history of the past three hundred years, Hartman himself resorts to an allegorizing gesture: "[T]he writers of the Enlightenment want fiction and reason to kiss." Hartman rescues the seeming archaism of Keats's allegorical figures by categorizing them as part of the ongoing literary and philosophical effort to accommodate romance—an eternal component of the human mind—to history, and by defining poetry as the "purification" as well as the expression of such an accommodation: "[E]very poem will be an act of resistance, of negative creation—a flight from one enchantment to another."[9] It is specifically to Milton's carefree mingling of *kinds* of mythological gestures—classical divinities, personified abstractions, and spirits of place—that Keats owes his greatest allegiance.

Before returning to Keats's figures for indolence, I would like to examine some of his precursors, starting with Milton. In her study of the Renaissance typology of melancholy, Brigit Gellert Lyons looks closely at the structure and rhetoric of Milton's paired poems. Whereas the transitions in "L' Allegro" are abrupt ("then" is the most common word, as the individual scenes are strung paratactically together), those of "Il Penseroso" are more gradual, "an expression of the awareness of time." While "L'Allegro" tends to omit first-person deictic pronouns and adjectives as a self-distracting means of warding off melancholy, the pendant poem is governed by the greater self-awareness of the melancholic figure. Melancholy, ultimately, refers to feeling rather than to thought or behavior; it retains its traditional link with imagination and contemplation.[10]

Perhaps even more attractive and useful to Keats than the organization of Milton's poems is the way they offer invitations to, or variations on, pastoral experience, with their defining moments of contemplative and aesthetic leisure. As such, "L'Allegro" is also an invitation to liberation:

> And in thy right hand lead with thee,
> The Mountain Nymph, sweet Liberty;
> And if I give thee honor due,
> Mirth, admit me of thy crew
> To live with her, and live with thee,
> In unreproved pleasures free.
>
> (ll. 35–40)[11]

Such easy pleasure not only echoes Marlovian eroticism but also anticipates the artistic observances of late eighteenth-century landscape painting in which labor may be witnessed but never engaged in by members of the class for whom the paintings are intended. Although he depicts such a picture with workers—plowman, milkmaid, mower, and shepherd—Milton then turns his eye to "new pleasures" (ll. 69–70) of the landscape. It is never clear exactly how the first-person subject is stationed vis-à-vis these people and these natural items. Distanced enjoyment rather than participation is the object. Milton devotes his poetic energy to the creation of the leisure to witness: "These delights, if thou canst give, / Mirth, with thee I mean to live" (ll. 151–52). Delights, of course, to go to the theater, to hear music, to be lapped "in soft Lydian airs": to remain, in other words, the privileged aesthete.

"L'Allegro" figures a state of mind purely by association with its traditional attributes. Aside from the initial conventional genealogy, Mirth herself is hardly presented at all. Melancholy, here dismissed, is entirely dark, while Euphrosyne is "fair and free," a goddess who is pictured solely by her train, by that which accompanies her. The poem is a study in metonymies and attributes. In addition, the speaker–courtier, the would-be mirthfully indolent person, does nothing himself. Far from being a characterization of a titular goddess, or a depiction of a specific temperament, the poem looks only glancingly at its nominal subject, indirectly accumulating references, associations, and attributes. Mirth—herself or itself—is either the sum of its attributes or a lacuna at the heart of the poem, barely visible. Something in the condition inhibits depiction.

"Il Penseroso" makes greater demands on its readers. Melancholy, the sober nun, brings in her train "retired leisure" and "the cherub contemplation," and the speaker actually participates in the melancholy mood: "I woo to hear thy Even-Song; / And missing thee, I walk unseen / On the dry smooth-shaven Green" (ll. 64–66). The insistent first-person demands and participation ("I hear the far-off Curfew sound"; "me Goddess bring / To arched walks of twilight groves"; "Hide me from Day's garish eye"; "But let my due feet never fail / To walk the studious Cloisters pale"; "Dissolve me into extasies, / And bring all Heav'n before mine eyes"; and so on) make the passivity or leisure of this poem a much richer, and paradoxically a much more active, condition than the parallel state in "L'Allegro." Whereas the social happiness of the carefree state allows one the freedom to witness, the solitary sobriety of the thoughtful state generates an active freedom.

Although Melancholy is only slightly more personified than her opposite, Euphrosyne, we can sense in Milton's arrangement a struggle with poetic figuration that will influence Keats's subsequent depictions of abstractions—or his avoidance of depicting them. The relationship among figure, abstract quality, speaker, and reader is so much less clear than the easy diction of the poems would suggest that we are forced to consider them as nothing less than radical experiments in allegorical gestures. A remark by Steven Knapp on some Wordsworthian figures (in "Yew-Trees" and "Resolution and Independence") is relevant here, especially in regard to Milton's legacy to the Romantics: "Personifications on vacation from allegory, these casual worshippers neither frighten one away from their sacred enclosure nor invite one to join them. They neither challenge nor assuage our sense of our own agency, but simply shrug it off."[12] Knapp's larger point is that such Wordsworthian figures (and, I shall argue, Keatsian ones as well as the Miltonic pair from which they derive) occupy a strange middle ground that neither includes nor excludes the reader. It is as though the poet has borrowed space in, or from, someone else's poem or life. It is for this reason that the figure (or figures) of Autumn in Keats's ode seems both reassuring and careless, occasionally active but mostly passive, central to the poem's structure but peripheral in its depicted landscape.

A second, obvious precursor for Keats's deliberations on indolence was James Thomson's "Castle of Indolence." Its Spenserian stanzas, its neo-Spenserian archaisms, its organization based on "L'Allegro" and "Il Penseroso," as well as its subject matter might naturally appeal to Keats; but if it was exemplary, it was so in a clearly negative way. This is the path not taken, in spite of Keats's claim to his brother and sister-in-law on March 19, 1819: "This morning I am in a sort of temper indolent and supremely careless: I long after a stanza or two of Thompson's [*sic*] Castle of indolence" (*Letters*, 2:78–79). Thomson gives us two views of indolence, the first (canto 1) of its charms and delights, the second (canto 2) of its alluring deceits and dangers. Both halves lead, mutatis mutandis, to Tennyson's "Lotos Eaters" via Keats's odes.

Thomson presents a parodic *locus amoenus* in which the wizard Indolence hides his castle (st. 6–7), a "delicious nest . . . mid bowering trees." He entices passing pilgrims to his land of Cockaigne, where there exists neither ploughing or sowing nor "hard-hearted Interest." This communal social experience, composed of "candour," "indulgent ease," and "good-natured lounging" turns into a parody of Epicurean ataraxia in stanzas 16 and 17:

> "What, what is virtue but repose of mind?
> A pure ethereal calm that knows no storm,
> Above the reach of wild ambition's wind,
> Above those passions that this world deform,
> And torture man, a proud malignant worm!
> But here, instead, soft gales of passion play,
> And gently stir the heart, thereby to form
> A quicker sense of joy; as breezes stray
> Across the enlivened skies, and make them still more gay.
>
> "The best of men have ever loved repose:
> They hate to mingle in the filthy fray;
> Where the soul sours, and gradual rancour grows,
> Imbittered more from peevish day to day.
> Even those whom fame has lent her fairest ray,
> The most renowned of worthy wights of yore,
> From a base world at last have stolen away:
> So Scipio, to the soft Cumaean shore
> Retiring, tasted joy he never knew before."[13]

The wizard's victims melt under his power (st. 23), and simultaneously retreat to their solitary pleasures (st. 29). The land of indolence combines sensuous freedom and the vague orientalism of "The Eve of St. Agnes," its only rule being "that each should work his own desire, / And eat, drink, study, sleep, as it may fall" (st. 35). As a land of art it contains tapestries inwoven with old tales of Arcadian delights, pastoral scenes, landscapes by Claude and Poussin, and music of "soul-dissolving airs" that relaxes and un-mans. Morpheus sends sweet dreams, all the more delicious for the storms that occasionally rage out-of-doors, making *us* (the speaker includes himself) more grateful for our protective enclosure. One great amusement of the inhabitants is to look in a magic crystal ball that shows the "idly-busy" doings of men on earth, all in search of vain pleasures, and running hither and yon in wasteful vanity. Indolence, in other words, while ignoring the vanity of its own conditions, affords one a perspective from which to observe the vanity of others. Self-deceit is the lot of the satirist who prides himself on understanding the deceits of others, whether authors, scholars, urbanites, soldiers, or politicians. Although some of the inhabitants are virtual Shakespearean melancholics (sts. 57–61), dirty, ill-kempt, and photophobic, many are given to social and artistic pleasures. The worlds of "L'Allegro" and "Il Penseroso" have merged.

Regardless of their temperament, all the inhabitants face one end. Beneath the castle lurks a dungeon, into which everyone is thrown when diseased, loathsome, or "unpleasing grown," where "[f]ierce fiends and hags of hell their only nurses were" (st. 73). Here the ruling deity is

Lethargy, a snoring monster who teaches his prey how to find "the softest way to death." His court consists of Hydropsy, Hypochondria ("Mother of Spleen"), Apoplexy, and Intemperance. The appearance of this hellish allegorical crew, an earnest of what follows, ends canto 1.

In canto 2 the Knight of Art and Industry, the son of Selvaggio (a "rough unpolished man, robust and bold") and Dame Poverty, comes to overthrow the castle. Brought up in ways that are stern, rural, stoic, careless, and Siegfried-like, the knight has also been nurtured in every art and science. He journeys to England where "by degrees his master-work arose" (st. 19), but the land has been blighted by the soul-enfeebling calls of Indolence, who dulls public virtue and spreads rank, luxurious vices. An embittered, desperate people beg the knight to save them and their land from Indolence's grip. With his old Druid bard Philmelus the knight vows to rescue as many of the castle's inhabitants as he can, on the theory that vice and virtue are always mixed. With heroic, energizing song, the bard rouses a clarion call to the castle's denizens, urging them away from ease to ardent, active grace. Whereas greatness—cities, art, history, and government—derives from ambition, the service of indolence leads only to death. Toil releases one from vanity; work increases pleasure (of appetite, for example) through healthful exercise. The advice mixes Burton's famous motto—"Be not solitary, be not idle"—with an early advertisement for the moral and physical advantages of cardiovascular exercise. The final call appeals to the will:

> "Resolve! resolve! and to be men aspire!
> Exert that noblest privilege, alone
> Here to mankind indulged; control desire;
> Let godlike reason from her sovereign throne
> Speak the commanding word *I will!* and it is done."
>
> (st. 62)

Based on evolutionary theories of man's progress toward perfection, the advice is heeded by the best of the castle's inhabitants, who are transported, presumably to lives of active toil and an awakened consciousness of virtue. Whereas some escape phoenixlike, however, most mutter curses and refuse the knight's wisdom. With an anti-magic power he unveils the falseness of their landscape and of their lives: streams and groves turn into blackened marshes. To the repentant inhabitants of the subterranean prison, the knight advises the release that can come only through patient suffering: hope for salvation through mental purification. With this the pleasure house/prison is instantly transformed into a hospital, a joint symbol of human misery and hopefulness. Some sinners are saved, but those who had merely feigned meek repentance are doomed to a life in a wild desert, "bare, comfortless, and vast," a wasteland with neither pleasure, comfort, nor hope for salvation. In a true Circean end, Gaunt Beggary and Scorn become the prevailing deities of a blighted landscape in which men have been changed to beasts.

Both Keats and Wordsworth were especially attracted to Thomson's poem,[14] but it is easy to see why—the matter of literary quality aside—they may have been uncomfortable with it as a potential model. "The Castle of Indolence" attempts to be both psychological and moral or didactic, and these two aims are not mutually compatible. The religious salvation offered by the Knight of Industry should, from the standpoint of Christian theology, be available to any sinner leading a life of self-indulgent excessive indolence, but Thomson makes it into a once-in-a-lifetime opportunity to receive grace. The final transformation of men into swine is permanent, irrevocable, and damning. Interestingly, the late Victorian editor, J. Logie Robertson, deems the first half of the poem ("which sets forth the pleasures of indolence") "an apology for an indolent life; the second is a warning to discourage the indulgence of indolence. There is poetry in the first canto; the second is mostly didactic" (pp. 306–7). But this claim is untrue: the whole first canto is filled with warnings about the fraudulence and the incipient dangers of indolence, however attractive it may be. Likewise, the second is filled with "poetry," although to a critic weaned on Tennyson and Swinburne (the inheritors of Keatsian excess), poetry had come to mean the placid portrayal of sunny climes and mellow landscapes. Poetry equals the picturesque, whereas didacticism involves all that is grim, horrifying, and appalling.[15]

Keats elaborates (as does Shelley) on the pleasures of the first canto of Thomson's poem and removes the potentially negative implications that a Christian apologist–allegorist appends in the second. At the same time, he employs indolence as part of a poetic–psychological–physiological program that enables the individual to embody a new, progressive, more complicated sense of activity and will, one that contains within itself its very opposites. The bard who inhabits the Castle of Indolence certainly sounds like a much later figure:

> A bard here dwelt, more fat than bard beseems,
> Who, void of envy, guile, and lust of gain,
> On virtue still, and nature's pleasing themes,
> *Poured forth his unpremeditated strain,*
> The world forsaking with a calm disdain:
> Here laughed he careless in his easy seat;
> Here quaffed, encircled with the joyous train;
> Oft moralizing sage; his ditty sweet
> He loathed much to write, ne cared to repeat.
>
> (canto 1, st. 68; emphasis added)

An embodiment of Epicurean *apatheia*, the poet looks forward to those "forsaking," "careless," and most of all "unpremeditated" harbingers of Romantic music, Keats's nightingale and Shelley's skylark, who evade both human mortality and the inherent ardent deadliness of writing by their constant reliance on sweet, because unrepeatable and unparaphrasable, ditties.

From Richard Steele's "good-natured indolence" down through Dr. Johnson's labeling of indolence as "that voluntary debility," the eighteenth century saw such a varied series of experiments in coping with, and troping, the phenomenon that it deserves for this, as for other reasons, the label "pre-Romantic." In addition to Thomson, both Gray and Shenstone wrote about the subject in their poems and letters.[16] The latter's 1750 "Ode to Indolence" may represent the last use of the title word in its literal meaning (freedom from pain) before the Romantics made of both word and its associations a richer force field:

> Lo! on the rural mossy bed
> My limbs with careless ease reclin'd;
> Ah, gentle sloth! indulgent spread
> The same soft bandage o'er my mind.
>
> For why should lingering thought invade,
> Yet every worldly prospect cloy?
> Lend me, soft sloth, thy friendly aid,
> And give me peace, debarr'd of joy.[17]

The rhetoric and the conception of indolence here anticipate Wordsworth and Keats, but we can also see why the author of *Lyrical Ballads,* with his distaste for poetic inversions and personified abstractions, and Keats, who recommends "wakeful anguish" in the "Ode on Melancholy," should find Shenstone's invocation insufficient and facile.[18] More important is the aversion, shared by Coleridge, Keats, and Wordsworth, to the automatic gendering of indolence, whether as male (in Thomson) or as female (in Shenstone). Coleridge's poems especially, as I suggested in chapter 3, refuse to define, allegorize, or even to name the state without character; indolence represents the condition that most demands catachresis as its salient trope. Shenstone, by contrast, courts his pastoral "puissant queen" so that she may:

> Dissolve in sleep each anxious care;
>> Each unavailing sigh remove;
> And only let me wake to share
>> The sweets of friendship and of love.

Far from representing the other side of action, social life, or even consciousness, Shenstone's figure is merely a goddess of unstressful ease, an anodyne to pain that can be shunted aside once "the sweets of friendship and of love" make themselves readily available. To none of the Romantics does such psychology or such figuration make convincing sense.

In Milton and Thomson, especially, Keats saw two possible ways of figuring indolence: he wished to avoid the relative impersonality of the former, in whose works the speaker occupies at most an ambiguous position, and the labored didacticism of the latter, whose poem has, if anything does, that "palpable design upon us" that Keats claimed always to abhor.[19]

Turning to the "Ode on Indolence" (written in May 1819, but having—as Vendler asserts—its "experiential" beginning in details from two letters of two months and even one year earlier), one may be surprised to note that Keats, in the poem the writing of which he claimed was the thing he "most enjoyed this year" (*Letters,* 2:116), does not bother, or perhaps dare, to depict his titular character. Generally regarded as the weakest of the odes, the "Ode on Indolence" is unique in never personifying, describing, or even invoking the quality at its heart. (Although she is personified, Melancholy is never invoked, and for related reasons.) Indolence seems, at this point in Keats's career, to be the trope that defies or inhibits naming. Why is this so? In addition, we may wonder why, given the basis for the ode in his journal letter of March, it took Keats two months to revise, update, and otherwise make use of his earlier feelings at a time when such ruminative delays were uncommon for him. Either (I surmise) the feelings concerning indolence and its potential threats as well as attractions are so strong as to be memorable, repeatable, and recordable well after the initial experience, or else they are so troublesome that Keats is unable to exorcise them immediately, and instead absorbs and digests them.

A reluctance or fear to envision informs many characteristic moments in Romantic poetry, from Wordsworth's refusal to rely on visual motifs in "Tintern Abbey" ("I cannot *paint* what then I was"), through Coleridge's inability to describe the black melancholy that tortures him in "Dejection: An Ode," to Keats's own blindness at the heart of the Nightingale Ode ("I cannot *see* what flowers are at my feet," and so on). As Wordsworth, the least visual of the Romantics, fears the tyrannies of the bodily eye, so even Keats, in many ways the *most* visual, is equally aware of the danger of sensuous vision and figuration. There may be a relationship between this fear and his frequent (early) reliance on the language of abstraction, as John Hamilton Reynolds unconsciously observed in an unsigned favorable review of October 11, 1818, in *The Examiner:* "Poetry is a thing of generalities. . . . The mind of Keats, like the minds of our older poets, goes round the universe in its speculations and its dreams. It does not set itself a task."[20] Not setting a task might encourage a poet to write indolently or *about* indolence. Keats transformed this early weakness into a later strength, if we credit the "process" school of Harvard Keatsians.[21]

The depiction of indolence under the name of Autumn was Keats's final way of avoiding a direct confrontation with his master trope; but four months earlier, in the May ode, he managed to depict everything *except* his title character:

> One morn before me were three figures seen,
>   With bowed necks, and joined hands, side-faced;
> And one behind the other stepp'd serene,
>   In placid sandals, and in white robes graced:
> They pass'd, like figures on a marble urn,
>   When shifted round to see the other side;

> They came again; as when the urn once more
> Is shifted round, the first seen shades return;
> And they were strange to me, as may betide
> With vases, to one deep in Phidian lore.
>
> (ll. 1–10)

In his own indolence the speaker hardly even sees the three tempting abstractions who interrupt him; rather, they are seen *by* him, and they immediately retreat into a further distance, relegated by a simile (they are not real figures on a marble urn, but are treated as such for the remainder of the poem) to an even vaguer status. The speaker's surprise, his being caught in medias res, resembles the comparable shock at the beginning of "On First Looking into Chapman's Homer": in both cases a self-confident, worldly sophisticate ("Much have I travell'd in the realms of gold"; "one deep in Phidian lore") is undone, startled by an unforeseeable event. And Keats's momentary ignorance, his inability to recognize the three figures until stanza 3, is like the much shorter suspension that occurs at the end of the first stanza in the "Ode to Psyche," when, wandering "thoughtlessly" (one might say "indolently") through the forest, he catches a glimpse of a pair of mythological lovers, of whom he recognizes Cupid immediately, but Psyche only after a hesitation.

The cause of such temporary blindness is the indolence that is dramatized only by its effects, but never described or depicted, throughout the ode. The "figures" (later labeled "shades," "shadows," "ghosts," and "phantoms," as if Keats's inability to see them properly were reflected by an unwillingness even to name them consistently) are viewed as silent tempters, engaged in "a deep-disguised plot . . . / To steal away, and leave without a task / My idle days" (ll. 13–15). This last is a deeply puzzling phrase, since we might expect Keats to object to just the opposite, that is, to the figures' bringing *to* rather than removing *from* him an occupation that might spell the end to idleness.

The poem mentions indolence only twice; its crisis of representation is so powerful that it circles its main subject, in much the same way that the trio of tempters circles the speaker, making faint but strongly felt demands on his attention. In stanza 2 the poet depicts a psychological condition comparable to the suspension of will and vision that Wordsworth had rendered in "Tintern Abbey" ("we are laid asleep / In body, and become a living soul: / While with an eye made quiet by the power / Of harmony, and the deep power of joy"), the disarming of consciousness that in Wordsworth (but not, significantly, in Keats's ode) ensures a deeper wisdom ("We see into the life of things"). Keats, however, describes what amounts to a whimper at being being awakened from a nap:

> Ripe was the drowsy hour;
> The blissful cloud of summer–indolence
> Benumb'd my eyes; my pulse grew less and less;
> Pain had no sting, and pleasure's wreath no flower.

> Oh, why did ye not melt, and leave my sense
> Unhaunted quite of all but—nothingness?
>
> (ll. 15–20)

The combination of physiological detail and naturalistic or pastoral fecundity (the hour grows ripe as the man sinks into oblivion) is Keatsian common coin; his tepid "annoy" (l. 38) is no greater than that of a man bothered by pesky flies (which later, in "To Autumn," contribute to, rather than detract from, the natural harmony). The sure sign of Keats's difficulty in depicting his condition, or personifying both his distractions and his drowsiness, is the ambiguously gnomic power of the concluding question.[22] Keats resorts to puns, other rhetorical duplicities, and the language of paradox, especially at those moments when intellectual and emotional tension is rising (as in, for example, "Cold Pastoral!" as the climax of the fifth stanza of the "Ode on a Grecian Urn," an exclamation that embodies the strong, conflicting feelings the urn has engendered in the speaker, and also acts as a rhetorical pivot between the hostile, punning, and therefore self-protecting ironies of the first five lines of the stanza and the consolations of its second half). In this case, working with tropes of absence/presence and emptiness/fullness, the speaker demands with his double negatives ("Leave me *un*haunted with everything except *nothing,*" he is saying) a release from temptations of the will which is simultaneously a repletion of "nothingness," for which another word is, of course, indolence itself.

The tension in this last couplet is equivalent to the comparable paradoxes embodied in the famous, aphoristic "the feel of not to feel it" ("In Drear-Nighted December"), the longed-for ability to articulate a state of anesthesia or apathy. It is also dramatically and philosophically comparable to the peculiar ending to the poem formerly known as "What the Thrush Said":

> O fret not after knowledge—I have none,
> And yet the evening listens. He who saddens
> At thought of idleness cannot be idle,
> And he's awake who thinks himself asleep.

The idea that consciousness or will is the antinomy of idleness, that self-contemplating leisure opposes leisure itself, sits squarely at the heart of Keats's ambivalences about the productive potential, as well as the alluring deceits, of indolence. This unrhymed sonnet comes at the end of a letter to John Hamilton Reynolds of February 19, 1818, more than a year before the other, nominally epistolary beginning of the Indolence Ode, which I discuss shortly; both letters bear witness to the ways in which Keats, working through various configurations of indolence, conjures through association the sexual, creative, and even political benefits of passiveness. The richness of paradox in both letters and poems serves as an equivalent to Kant's notion of the aesthetic as "purposefulness without purpose." Keats's rhetoric supplements the deep truths toward which the philosopher gestures. The letters, especially the earlier one (*Letters*, 1:231–33), thus recommend themselves as models of the Keatsian method.

The 1818 letter begins as a deliberation on reading but quickly leaves behind any inspiring text:

> I have an idea that a Man might pass a very pleasant life in this manner—let him on any certain day read a certain Page of full Poesy or distilled Prose and let him wander with it, and muse upon it, and reflect from it, and bring home to it, and prophesy upon it, and dream upon it—untill it becomes stale—but when will it do so? Never—When Man has arrived at a certain ripeness in intellect any one grand and spiritual passage serves him as a starting post towards all "the two-and thirty Pallaces" How happy is such a "voyage of conception," what delicious diligent Indolence! A doze upon a Sofa does not hinder it, and a nap upon Clover engenders ethereal finger-pointings.

What he later refers to as the "mere passive existence" of "noble Books" works as if by osmosis to generate "conception," both the abstract "thought" which he elsewhere opposes to "sensations" (*Letters*, 1:185) and the self-conceiving, self-constructing means of creating a spiritual life. The delicate filigree continues with an elaborate conceit of a spider spinning her web, weaving a self that may have innumerable contacts with other selves or other lives as they spin their own individual webs and resume contact "at the Journeys end." Such soul-making has an organic basis and a political consequence: "[T]hus by every germ of Spirit sucking the Sap from mould ethereal every human might become great, and Humanity instead of being a wide heath of Furse and Briars with here and there a remote Oak or Pine, would become a grand democracy of Forest Trees."[23]

From reading to soul-making Keats moves on to a peculiar reconstruction of Acts 20:35:

> [W]e should rather be the flower than the Bee—for it is a false notion that more is gained by receiving than giving—no the receiver and the giver are equal in their benefits—The f[l]ower I doubt not receives a fair guerdon from the Bee—its leaves blush deeper in the next spring—and who shall say between Man and Woman which is the most delighted? Now it is more noble to sit like Jove tha[n] to fly like Mercury—let us not therefore go hurrying about and collecting honey-bee like, buzzing here and there impatiently from a knowledge of what is to be arrived at: but let us open our leaves like a flower and be passive and receptive—budding patiently under the eye of Apollo and taking hints from eve[r]y noble insect that favors us with a visit.

The rich confusions of reference, logic, and metaphor attest to the strenuous complexity of Keats's feelings about an indolence that he conceives as both delicious (sensuous, receptive) and diligent (strenuous, active). On the one hand, the passive flower receives the "guerdon" of the bee (although Keats must have realized that the bee *takes* the pollen from flower to flower and also returns it to the hive); we assume the flower is the female to the fertilizing male. On the other hand, a staid, masculine Jupiter (cf. the later depiction of Lycius in "Lamia" as "a young Jove with calm uneager face") embodies the virtues of patience against the active flitting of Mercury (who, significantly, performs an equivalent fostering, fertilizing deed in the first part of "Lamia").[24]

Mercury is an apt representation of the Keatsian intellect as it develops throughout the rapidly changing landscape of the letters. Weaving and unweaving, working through associations at times seemingly random and at others logical, Keats actively pursues a definition of idleness that will excuse his own laziness, as he jocularly confesses at the end of the letter, when he also virtually undoes much of what he constructed earlier. Reading is the first thing to go: "I was led into these thoughts, my dear Reynolds, by the beauty of the morning operating on a sense of Idleness—I have not read any Books—the Morning said I was right—I had no Idea but of the Morning and the Thrush said I was right." (There follows the sonnet.) To write about, to contemplate, reading, and then to confess that the voyage of conception has been provoked by no book, suggests a deep skepticism about the possibilities for such "ripeness in intellect," just as the apparent confusion about the conventional wisdom of giving and receiving, and the accompanying ambiguity (botanical, sexual, and mythological) about activity and passivity result in a paradoxical stalemate. But this jibes with the self-canceling paradoxes at the end of the sonnet, and with the more modest self-appraisal that Keats offers by way of leave-taking at the end of the letter:

> Now I am sensible all this is a mere sophistication, however it may neighbour to any truths, to excuse my own indolence—so I will not deceive myself that Man should be equal with jove—but think himself very well off as a sort of scullion-Mercury or even a humble Bee—It is no matter whether I am right or wrong either one way or another, if there is sufficient to lift a little time from your Shoulders.

Keats's valediction confirms the soothing and elevating potential of such metaphor making and intellectual journey taking as he has indulged in. It also occupies a place within his ongoing program of defining poetry and his relation to it. Poetry, we may recall from "Sleep and Poetry," should "soothe the cares and lift the thoughts of man," even while it is also depicted in a sculpted, heroic pose: "'Tis might half slumb'ring on its own right arm."

According to the scenario of the "Ode on Indolence," poetry occupies a position along with love and ambition among the three tempting urn figures. In stanza 4, where indolence is referred to for the second (and last) time in the poem, poetry is the antithesis of ease, slumber, and pastoral half-consciousness:

> For Poesy!—no,—she has not a joy,—
>   At least for me,—so sweet as drowsy noons,
>   And evenings steep'd in honied indolence;
>   O, for an age so shelter'd from annoy,

That I may never know how change the moons,
Or hear the voice of busy common-sense!
(ll. 35–40)

As stimulus. enemy, and antidote to forgetfulness, poetry takes one away from the pastoral bower into the workaday world that Keats's Lycius has almost left forsworn until he is recalled to it by the "thrill of trumpets" at the beginning of the second part of "Lamia." Poetry is, in short, labor, effort, a product of the will, and a response to the demands of the marketplace and to vocational ambition.

Marjorie Levinson and other New Historicists read Keats's attractions to and fears of this marketplace—and, as corollary, to indolence—as responses to his self-consciousness as an outsider essaying an entry into the comfortable but higher reaches of the bourgeoisie. "Keats hadn't the luxury for a 'wise passiveness,'" says Levinson, exiling Keats from the havens of both the earlier and the later Romantics. "[T]he graciously conformable bowers and dells enjoyed by Wordsworth and Coleridge were no more available to Keats than were the glory and grandeur of Greece and Rome, Byron's and Shelley's enabling resorts" (Levinson, pp. 8, 7). Levinson's generalization rings untrue for Wordsworth and Coleridge, who were hardly immune in their youth to worries about money, career, and self-advancement. In addition, Keats dreamed about Italy, in ways typical of Englishmen since the Renaissance, even before his illness made going there a practical necessity (see his letter to Reynolds of April 10, 1818: "Who would live in the region of Mists, Game Laws idemnity Bills etc when there is such a place as Italy? It is said this England from its Clime produces a Spleen, able to engender the finest Sentiment" [*Letters,* 1:269]). The land of dolce far niente is the opposite of a foggy and politically repressive England which is *also* the Mother of Melancholia, and of melancholics who embody the sentimental, creative, and introspective forces traditionally associated with spleen.

Marxist critics such as Levinson derive from class alone the origin of Keats's most characteristic ideas and anxieties. To them ideology is all, especially with regard to Keats's conflicting notions about leisure as wise passiveness or self-narcosis, and about fame and disinterestedness as correlatives to a toiling middle-class ambition: "on the one hand, the middle-class commitment to a program of social mobility (Keats's 'chameleon poet': an ethic of becoming, or, less Romantically, a work ethic), and on the other, its longing for the authority connected with the general passivity, stable identity, and 'quiet being' which was an influential fantasy of the leisure class" (Levinson, p. 24). Such a generalization plays false, as I have suggested, with the facts of the social and economic situations of Coleridge and Wordsworth, even after they inherited their benefactions from the Wedgwoods and Raisley Calvert, respectively. More important, it does a disservice to the complex motives of Keats, whose anxieties concerning passiveness and leisure, whether figured as pastoral lounging or as the trope of a nonpersonified indolence, have a physiological as well as a political root.

Stuart Sperry, and more recently Hermione de Almeida and Donald Goellnicht, have examined the medical and scientific basis for many of Keats's ideas and his characteristic vocabulary (words such as "essence," "distill," "etherize") whose contemporary chemical meanings have been largely replaced, for us, by more general philosophical connotations.[25] Far from representing merely the attractions of a higher social status (which Levinson construes as a proto-Veblenesque leisure class) to which the young cockney poet aspires, indolence works itself into a program of self-help compounded of equal doses of science and aesthetics. The category of "the aesthetic," whose origin Terry Eagleton has traced to the bourgeois Enlightenment and whose effects he rightly identifies as body-centered, coincides in Keats, more than in any of the other Romantics, with an organic notion of mind and body, consciousness and physiology, leisure and work, passivity and will (Eagleton, esp. pp. 1–12). Another way of viewing what a cultural critic might label conspicuous consumption is embodied in a remark by Henry James (himself, of course, susceptible of being labeled an aesthetic drone): "It is in the *waste*—the waste of time, of passion, of curiosity, of contact, that the true initiation resides."[26] The seeming wastes of leisure and of indolence have genuinely productive results.

In the second letter from which the "Ode on Indolence" derives (to George and Georgiana Keats, March 1819, *Letters,* 2:77–80), Keats distinguishes "easy" from "uneasy" indolence, that waste which initiates from that which deadens. He characterizes the former: "An indolent day—fill'd with speculations even of an unpleasant colour—is bearable and even pleasant alone—when one's thoughts cannot find out anyth[i]ng better in the world; and experience has told us that locomotion is no change." This is not exactly what we might initially imagine. For one thing, the state involves "speculations" (thoughts as well as sensations) that may be other than entirely pleasing; for another, the indolence does not eliminate locomotion (of the Wordsworthian, "wander[ing] lonely" variety). Such ease contains, we conjecture, its own brand of activity. And yet,

> to have nothing to do, and to be surrounded with unpleasant human identi-
> ties; who press upon one just enough to prevent one getting into a lazy
> position; and not enough to interest or rouse one; is a capital punishment of a
> capital crime: for is not giving up, through goodnature, one's time to people
> who have no light and shade a capital crime?

Uneasy indolence turns out to be no indolence at all: the people who press upon one inhibit laziness, just as the trio of abstractions in the ode rouse the dreamer from his honied state. Ironically, if we pursue the logical correlation between letter and poem, Keats might have generated the energy to "think" or "speculate" had he been left to his own indolent devices without the interference of those figures who remind him after all of the demands of ambition, worldiness, and common sense.

Such obsessions with laziness fill Keats's letters virtually from start to finish. At best he views the state as the organic incubation period necessary for giving birth to solid work, as in his remark to his brother and sister-in-law right before printing "On Sitting Down to Read *King Lear* Once Again": "[A] little change has taken place in my intellect lately—I cannot bear to be uninterested or unemployed, I, who for so long a time, have been addicted to passiveness—Nothing is finer for the purposes of great productions, than a very gradual ripening of the intellectual powers" (*Letters,* 1:214). At the end of his great creative period (September 22, 1819), however, he writes to Charles Brown, lamenting his chronic failure to redeem himself through work: "I have never yet exerted myself. I am getting into an idle minded, vicious way of life, almost content to live upon others. In no period of my life have I acted with any self will, but in throwing up the apothecary-profession. That I do not repent of. . . . I have not known yet what it is to be diligent" (*Letters,* 2:176).[27] This polarity reveals more than a simple tension between hopeful and anxious moods of confidence and self-doubt. We may regard the continuation of his March journal letter to his brother and sister-in-law (*Letters,* 2:78–79) as further evidence of the complexity of his feelings.

Donald Goellnicht (pp. 204–5) has suggested that Keats alludes to, without naming, yet a third kind of indolence in his March 19 entry. He surmises that Keats was given a dose of opium (which the letter does not mention), in addition to a leech (which it does), by Charles Brown as treatment for an eye inflammation caused by his being hit in the face with a cricket ball. The opium would have produced a weakened pulse and muscular contractions, creating an indolent state that is neither completely beneficial nor entirely torpid, lifeless, and oppressive. Keats's ode, by this standard, has an entirely somatic origin (and as such recommends itself to our attention as an example of Eagleton's "aesthetic" category):

> This morning I am in a sort of temper indolent and supremely careless: I long after a stanza or two of Thompson's [*sic*] Castle of indolence—My passions are all alseep [*sic*] from my having slumbered till nearly eleven and weakened the animal fibre all over me to a delightful sensation about three degrees on this side of faintness—if I had teeth of pearl and the breath of lillies I should call it langour [*sic*]—but as I am I must call it Laziness—In this state of effeminacy the fibres of the brain are relaxed in common with the rest of the body, and to such a happy degree that pleasure has no show of enticement and pain no unbearable frown. Neither Poetry, nor Ambition, nor Love have any alertness of countenance as they pass by me: they seem rather like three figures on a greek vase.

The state of feminized languor (whose pearly teeth may foretell those of Lamia later in the year) leads to a contemplation of the circumstances that mass around one like clouds, "gathering and bursting" (Keats is thinking of the imminent death of the father of his friend William Haslam), and of

COLORADO COLLEGE LIBRARY
COLORADO SPRINGS
COLORADO

the possibilities afforded by these tragic circumstances for (aesthetic) contemplation: "[W]e have leisure to reason on the misfortunes of our friends; our own touch us too nearly for words." Like Wordsworth's peddler who "could *afford* to suffer / With those whom he saw suffer" (*The Excursion*, 1:370–71), Keats implicitly connects leisure with the possibility of Aristotelian catharsis. Aesthetic responses require relaxation and distance; personal suffering, that which "touches" us physically, deadens both reason and articulation.

Keats continues to deliberate "aesthetically," speculating on the few possibilities for "disinterestedness of Mind" among men. Self-interest normally intervenes, whereas "amusement" and "leisure" (synonyms, evidently, for indolence in its positive guise) are the necessary conditions for the truly disinterested hearts of Jesus and Socrates: "The noble animal Man for his amusement smokes his pipe—the Hawk balances about the Clouds—that is the only difference of their leisures." Only when the body overpowers the mind, in the state of effeminate indolence depicted earlier, can the mind develop the necessary conditions for aesthetic speculation and disinterested leisure. Self-interest (what he calls "instinctiveness"), an "unwandering eye from . . . purposes" or "animal eagerness," spells survival. That is the Keatsian unconscious will. But such instinctive efforts at preservation are balanced by equally powerful, more self-conscious moments of leisure, at once unwilled (because selfless) and deeply self-gratifying. That is the Keatsian aesthetic. The "speculative Mind" is that which derives "the Amusement of Life" from the sighting of stoat, field mouse, or man, catching glimmers of a shared identity at those moments when distance and separation are initially more evident than relationship.

Keats's movement from one idea, speculation, or circumstance to the next presents the dramatic evidence of how he works with, from, and *in* an initial state of indolence: using it at first as the antithesis to creation (the temptations of poetry), to masculine will, and to selfhood, he finally makes it the sine qua non for self-consciousness and for the leisure that engenders rather than destroys aesthetic responsiveness. Such leisure paradoxically develops from selflessness (disinterestedness of mind) that empathy with human and nonhuman creatures embodied in Keats's slightly misquoted rendering of Wordsworth's "We have all of us one human heart." By the end of this day's entry in the journal letter (p. 81), when Keats records his sonnet "Why Did I Laugh Tonight?" his mood has moved from one of languor, relaxation, and apathy, through the contemplation of leisure and disinterestedness, to a series of remarks in his more traditionally feisty, masculine vein: "Though a quarrel in the streets is a thing to be hated, the energies displayed in it are fine"; "Do you not think I strive—to know myself?"; "Nothing ever becomes real till it is experienced"; "I have . . . that in me which will well bear the buffets of the world." The (still unwritten) "Ode on Indolence" derives from and discusses a provocation that is shunned. "Why Did I Laugh Tonight?" describes an equal but opposite movement. In the ode the weary speaker continues to shoo away and bid farewell to his unwanted visitors; in the sonnet his initiating gesture (which is also a response to an unnamed, unnameable provocation) leads to a recognition that "[v]erse, fame and Beauty"—his equivalents for poetry, ambition, and love which tempted him earlier in the letter (and later in the ode)—"are intense indeed / But Death intenser—Death is Life's high mead."

Keats's deliberations in his letter as well as in his poems call into question the very nature of the will and its relation to other human faculties. It is tempting to regard Keats politically, as Levinson and Jerome McGann have done, especially in poems such as the *Hyperion*s and "Lamia." Certainly to that poem we might apply Nietzsche's observation on "willing": "'[F]reedom of the will' is essentially the affect of superiority in relation to him who must obey. . . . [H]e who wills sincerely believes that willing suffices for action."[28] But Keats's thoughts about, and depictions of, the will are ambivalent at best. In regard to friendship, he wrote to Benjamin Bailey (January 23, 1818) in terms that suggest the positive obverse of the "uneasy indolence" he describes in his 1819 letter to George and Georgiana: "[T]he sure way . . . is first to know a Man's faults, and then be passive, if after that he insensibly draws you towards him then you have no Power to break the link" (*Letters,* 1:210). However much Keats politicizes human relationships, he also figures them in physiological terms such as he uses in his letters. As he also announced in his 1818 "Epistle to John Hamilton Reynolds," things "cannot to the will / Be settled, but they tease us out of thought" and the provocations of "thought" and of "things" as various as nightingale and Grecian urn provide the starting point, and often the resolution, to many characteristic poems. Even in *Endymion* we can detect those conditions that Keats, as man and medical student, would have recognized as related to will, and to its failures. Exhibiting, according to Goellnicht, the classic symptoms of nervous fever, Endymion is a melancholic whose physical condition results from, as well as symbolizing, his diseased mind (pp. 173–88).

What Keats would have learned about melancholy is apposite to his sense of the will and its relation to indolence. As we see in writers as diverse as Montaigne, Burton, and Hume, the condition of melancholy produces copious and ridiculous "Phantasms, and fills the Imagination with a thousand uncouth Figures, monstrous Appearances and troublesome Illusions; so it is no less fertile in producing disquieting and restless Passions, while they affect the Heart with Anxiety, Sadness, Fear and Terror."[29] The virtually automatic suspicion of figuration and of imagination is evident not only in the English empirical tradition that stretches from Locke through much philosophical and medical thought of the eighteenth century but also in more immediate contemporaries of Keats's. For example, he would have heard his lecturers at Guy's Hospital discuss the mental form of hypochondriasis in melancholy, among the causes of which are "indolent inactive life" as well as "intense study."[30] As early as his letter of May 16, 1817, to John Taylor and James Hessey (*Letters,* 1:146; see also his habit of despair [*Letters,* 1:142 and 2:352]), Keats expresses his fear of being thought a congenital melancholic and his idea that poetry will be the superior force to destroy his innate morbid anxieties. Poetry, like love and ambition, is a counter to the naturally indolent mood that in its extreme, perverse manifestation evinces a dangerous melancholic state. And yet, Keats can imagine such a state—of indolent will-lessness—as the necesssary and beneficial precondition for mental as well as poetic health. Such a situation begins not only the ode on indolence but also the odes on melancholy and to Psyche, the nightingale, and Autumn.

Keats steers his path between construing passivity as the sign of listless illness and making it the initial sign of ripeness; or between will as a frenzy of morbid, active phantasms and will as a man's healthy determination to make himself and his work. Between ready watchfulness and uneager ripening the human condition will establish psychic and physical health. We can measure such a balance by comparing an early letter and a poem with a later one. Writing to John Hamilton Reynolds on November 22, 1817 (significantly, on the same day that he wrote his famous letter to Bailey that discusses the lack of "any determined character" in "Men of Genius," as well as the relationship between "the holiness of the Heart's affections and the truth of Imagination"), Keats comments effusively on Shakespeare's sonnets:

> I neer found so many beauties in the sonnets— they seem to be full of fine things said unintentionally—in the intensity of working out conceits—Is this to be borne? Hark ye!

> > When lofty trees I see barren of leaves
> > Which not [*sic*] from heat did canopy the heard,
> > And Summer's green all girded up in sheaves,
> > Borne on the bier with white and bristly beard.

> He has left nothing to say about nothing or any thing. (*Letters,* 1:188–89)

It is often tempting, and in this case I think legitimate, to make something of Keats's notorious misspellings. We can see, as well as hear, in "heard" his effort to produce a dialectic of literary production and reception.[31] He commands Reynolds to listen ("Hark ye!"), to read *aloud* that which appears on the page, much in the same way he deliberately synthesizes reading and listening in "On First Looking into Chapman's Homer" ("Yet did I never breathe its pure serene / Till I heard Chapman speak out loud and bold"). Writing seems to be unconscious and unwilled activity ("fine things said unintentionally"), but also an intense "working out" of and through conceits. By contrast, reading is an act of discovery and of active, strenuous listening which arouses and perhaps threatens the will ("Is this to be borne?" he asks with mock-indignation that may disguise a deeper seriousness).

This threat picks up the language of the sonnet ("Borne on the bier") but it also, in the course of the letter, comes before it, subjugating the literary provocation (reading sonnet no. 12) which temporally precedes the response to a subordinate position after it in Keats's reworking of the experience. Matters of priority and anteriority are more than just suggested here: they are at the heart of Keats's effort to dramatize the state of healthy passivity in which imaginative responsiveness, whether to a literary or to a nonliterary provocation, occurs.[32] To the double puns (borne–borne, hark–he[a]rd) Keats adds at last another of the self-canceling, gnomic paradoxes that represent the failure of his will either to respond or to create: since Shakespeare has "left nothing to say about nothing or any thing," the writer–reader's response is, as in the Chapman sonnet, one of silence (although the letter goes on for another high-spirited page), but a silence that betokens respect as well as envy, stimulation as well as subjugation, youthful energy as well as an identification with the ravages of time that are "borne on the bier."[33] Just as one cannot be idle who saddens "at thought of idleness," so a reader who realizes that nothing is left to say about nothing will find his own provocation to say much himself. Nothing will come of nothing, as Lear announces, and as Keats knows full well (his own sonnet on rereading *King Lear* would come two months later): he must speak—something—again.

Four months after the letter to Reynolds, Keats writes to Bailey from Teignmouth that "every mental pursuit takes its reality and worth from the ardour of the pursuer—being in itself a nothing," and proceeds to distinguish three species of ethereal things ("Things real . . . Things semireal . . . and Nothings"). "Passages of Shakespeare" are numbered among the legions of the real, while "Nothings . . . are made Great and dignified by an ardent pursuit" (*Letters*, 1:242–43). Keats then inserts his own Shakespearean sonnet, "Four Seasons Fill the Measure of the Year," a poem that appeared with significant variations in Leigh Hunt's *Literary Pocket Book of 1819*. What is most surprising is the fact that the poem, a reflection on the topos of seasonality and its human analogies, should essentially refute everything about ardor and pursuit that precedes it in the letter. It is thoroughly a poem of indolence, of waiting, of leisurely observation:

> Four seasons fill the measure of the year;
>   Four seasons are there in the mind of man.
> He hath his lusty spring, when fancy clear
>   Takes in all beauty with an easy span:
> He hath his summer, when luxuriously
>   He chews the honied cud of fair spring thoughts,
> Till, in his soul dissolv'd, they come to be
>   Part of himself. He hath his autumn ports
> And havens of repose, when his tired wings
>   Are folded up, and he content to look

On mists in idleness: to let fair things
  Pass by unheeded as a threshold brook.
He hath his winter too of pale misfeature,
Or else he would forget his mortal nature.

With its predictions of "To Autumn," and its resemblance to the "Ode to a Nightingale," this study of seasonality is in fact a study of repose.[34] Keats's depiction of the human life span precludes virtually *all* labor.

The sonnet proceeds through levels of passiveness, from the analogous grammatical constructions of the opening lines through the relative weakness of all the verbal constructions that follow. "Man" here does nothing. Even youth is a time of aesthetic leisure: "takes," the strongest verb, is used in the service of quiet observation. Summer merely continues the waiting game of ingesting, absorbing, and transforming aesthetic data for future use. The season of mists and mellow fruitfulness finds the man in ports and havens which he never really left. There can be no homecoming, no arrival, as there was never any departure. Life is passed entirely upon a border, or on a threshold between states that is never abandoned. The utter stasis of *all* conditions harmonizes the four seasons in a distinction without a difference. Even the misfeature of winter is presented not as "the weariness, the fever and the fret" of the Nightingale Ode, or as the withered post-harvest landscape of "La Belle Dame sans Merci," but as a condition that—owing largely to its unfigurative, rhetorical blandness—comes anticlimactically as the presumed proof, or remembering, of human mortality rather than as "Life's high mead." Everything in the poem is proleptic: in such a state of waiting there can be neither real growth nor real harvest nor death. Suspending the will and its activities has suspended even the brook, which does not so much move purposefully as exist in a liminal state that can be observed but hardly passed through.

Four months after this poem, in a letter from Scotland to his brother Tom, Keats remarks the flight of eagles: "They move about without the least motion of Wings when in an indolent fit" (*Letters,* 1:338). Like the hawk which he observed balancing about the clouds in his leisure (*Letters,* 2:79), the eagles look like an earlier version of Yeats's self-delighting, self-balancing aviator ("An Irish Airman Foresees His Death"), a combination of power and grace, all effortless ease and godlike *apatheia*. But "fit" gets in the way here: it does not square with the comfortable motionlessness of the eagles, and it hardly seems appropriate to the onset of an otherwise enviable condition. What it certainly should put us in mind of is the "melancholy fit" that falls "sudden from heaven like a weeping cloud" in the second stanza of the "Ode on Melancholy" and the more than incidental physiological and psychological connections between melancholy and indolence.[35]

The indolent but fitful grace of eagles is a temporary condition, to be cherished for its ephemerality like any of the images listed by Keats in the Melancholy Ode:

But when the melancholy fit shall fall
　　Sudden from heaven like a weeping cloud,
That fosters the droop-headed flowers all,
　　And hides the green hill in an April shroud;
Then glut thy sorrow on a morning rose,
　　Or on the rainbow of the salt sand-wave,
　　　Or on the wealth of globed peonies;
Of if thy mistress some rich anger shows,
　　Emprison her soft hand, and let her rave,
　　　And feed deep, deep upon her peerless eyes.

Keats had rejected what we might call "uneasy" (because conventional) melancholy in the first stanza of the ode, cautioning against suicide, forgetfulness, intoxication, or any comparable dulling of the senses. Here he begins his rendering of an "easy" (that is, positive) or, paradoxically, *arduous* melancholy, a condition that, like indolence, generates and fructifies. Both conditions demand the Keatsian "aesthetic" response: a determination to cancel for a moment the plea of the will in favor of active observing of a dramatic pageant, whether of abstract personifications on an urn or of natural details. In this way the "mo[u]rning rose" legitimately becomes the appropriate vehicle first to represent and then to convert the viewer's own unexpressed sorrows.[36] And just as Keats has distinguished negative, conventional melancholy from its positive, imaginative counterpart, so he also insists here that the patient to whom he is addressing his advice become his own physician, curing both himself and, in the final lines cited, the mistress whose hand he is holding (as if taking an actual as well as a metaphorical pulse). That the diagnosis obliquely alludes to Paeon, physician to the gods and namesake of the "globed peonies," gives additional strength to the poet's diagnostic admonitions.

　　Like indolence, melancholy comes *in* and *as* a fit; it is never pictured, and it can be known only through the pulse and not the intervening figures of poetry. It arrives to bring fostering grace, falling *like* a weeping cloud; as such the state resembles the speaker's condition in the fifth stanza of the Indolence Ode:

My soul had been a lawn besprinkled o'er
　　With flowers, and stirring shades, and baffled beams:
The morn was clouded, but no shower fell,
　　Though in her lids hung the sweet tears of May;
　　The open casement press'd a new-leaved vine,
　　Let in the budding warmth and throstle's lay;
O shadows! 'twas a time to bid farewell!
　　Upon your skirts had fallen no tears of mine.

Keats remains in the liminal state that he had depicted in his letter to his brother and sister-in-law. The poet's soul sits passive, awaiting the May showers that never come from the personified spring morning. He merely observes the open casement (see the comparable ones in the odes to Psyche and the nightingale), never violating or passing through it. The spectator refuses to mourn, or to perform his own gesture of emotional requital. Personal will has been silenced in favor of a more impersonal aesthetic responsiveness.

Since melancholy and indolence descend fitfully and defy troping, it is startling but appropriate to find in the last stanza of the "Ode on Melancholy" that the "fit" of melancholy, a clinical condition, has spectacularly turned into a goddess who, like Milton's metonymic figures in "L'Allegro" and "Il Penseroso," is peripheral as well as central:

> She dwells with Beauty—Beauty that must die;
> 　And Joy, whose hand is ever at his lips
> Bidding adieu; and aching Pleasure nigh,
> 　Turning to poison while the bee-mouth sips:
> Ay, in the very temple of Delight
> 　Veil'd Melancholy has her sovran shrine,
> 　　Though seen of none save him whose strenuous tongue
> 　Can burst Joy's grape against his palate fine;
> His soul shall taste the sadness of her might,
> 　And be among her cloudy trophies hung.

Melancholy is the poem's titular figure; she inhabits the center of the "temple of Delight"; she is divine. But she is depicted only by her train, that fraternity of abstractions (Beauty, Delight, Joy, Pleasure) who are also her servants and opposites. She is named but not invoked; she is veiled, but can be seen by the hero who comes Siegfried-like to break through (to) her. And his efforts are at once active and passive, arduous and, we might say, somewhat listless. The peculiar synesthesia of the last four lines allows the epicurean hero a glimpse of the goddess, but strangely in the passive voice. She is seen *by* him. Such a triumphant sighting seems almost accidental: it comes as a by-product of oral pleasures (bursting Joy's grape), and it then causes the hero's suicidal release among the other cloudy, invisible heroes who have gone before him to win, and be simultaneously captured by, the goddess.[37] To achieve Melancholy (i.e., to cure *it* and to win *her*) requires the patience of indolence and the simultaneous indulgence of heroic effort.

She is, like Autumn, a presiding genius of arrival, but where Autumn can be pictured as well as invoked, Melancholy can be described only through her attributes, but neither confronted nor addressed directly. Autumn undergoes a typically Keatsian series of changes, from "sitting careless" as an object susceptible to the wind, through falling asleep on the job, a victim of narcosis, and then being reanimated into a balancing act like that of Keats's hawks and eagles, before finally subsiding into a state of pure spectatorship. Keats here sandwiches activity (gleaning) between forms of inactivity: the structure of Autumn's poses is hardly arbitrary, though it may seem to be so. The aesthetic state—watching and seeing—is the end of both action and inaction. Autumn herself embodies what we may ambiguously call the *work* of art. She is a laborer who, in the completion of her tasks, has metamorphosed into an image of elegant stasis, leisure, and ornament. As for Indolence, the sister of both Melancholy and Autumn, she is quite literally nothing herself because the impossibility of describing her results from her etymological origin as a state of *non*-pain. She remains the deity of conception and inception, never to be known or seen or named. We may dub her, at last, the goddess of beginnings, of origination.

5

States of Possession: Shelley's Versions of Pastoral

To begin, two homages—only one of them deliberate—to Shelley and his pastoral. In *Mrs. Dalloway* (1925) Virginia Woolf's eponymous heroine is contemplating the moving fields of human life within her London landscape: "[S]omehow in the streets of London, on the ebb and flow of things, here, there, she survived, Peter survived, lived in each other, she being part, she was positive, of the trees at home." Thereafter, temporarily distracted from the present moment, Clarissa Dalloway thinks about the question of falling in love with women; her adolescent infatuation with Sally Seton fills her reverie. The bohemian Sally, with a beauty Clarissa herself lacks, possessed "a sort of abandonment . . . a quality much commoner in foreigners than in Englishwomen," the kind that inspires an erotic involvement at once deeply sexual and almost purely pre- or asexual, a love based on the sharing of time, experiences, and ideas. It is a love associated with the secrecy and evasiveness of adolescence, and with radical political gestures that must also be kept secret. The gift of a book by William Morris is made in brown paper to disguise the revolutionary contents from the eyes, we assume, of disapproving parents. The two girls are always, conspiratorially, together:

> There they sat, hour after hour, talking in her bedroom at the top of the house, talking about life, how they were to reform the world. They meant to found a society to abolish private property, and actually had a letter written, though not sent out. The ideas were Sally's, of course—but very soon she was just as excited—read Plato in bed before breakfast; read Morris; read Shelley by the hour.

108

In order to rationalize her strongly erotic involvement with Sally, Clarissa desexualizes and sanctifies it: "The strange thing, on looking back, was the purity, the integrity, of her feeling for Sally. It was not like one's feeling for a man. It was completely disinterested, and besides, it had a quality which could only exist between women, between women just grown up. It was protected, on her side." One might add: between women of the upper classes, accustomed to living, in vast and lovely country houses, lives like those of Yeats's contemporary and equally idealized Anglo–Irish aristocracy. But in spite of the youthful bravado, the playing at radicalism, the view of marriage as catastrophe, it is the pure eroticism of the relationship that most stays with the mature Clarissa. "The most exquisite moment of her whole life," she recalls, was the time when Sally, at a summer party, picked a flower, kissed her on the lips, and everyone else disappeared, at least until Peter Walsh interrupted (as she knew all along something would, to "embitter her moment of happiness") with the innocuous but murderous interjection: "Star-gazing?"[1]

The second homage involves Casey Robinson's 1939 screenplay for *Dark Victory,* based on the stage play by George Brewer, Jr., and Bertram Bloch. The spoiled Judith Traherne (Bette Davis), an aristocrat by American standards, learns of her fatal illness and abandons her thoughtless, frivolous life, or most of it. "I'm going to sell my house and my apartment—everything—my horses. . . . No, I'll keep Challenger—He's a champion," Judith says, with self-denial matched by common sense, to her best chum, Ann King (Geraldine Fitzgerald), the pseudosister who we assume will take Judith's place by marrying her widower after her death. Judith leaves the *jeunesse dorée* in order to pursue an unexpectedly noble life as the wife of her even nobler doctor–husband (the grimly earnest George Brent), who has given up his lucrative medical practice in favor of pure research in order to protect future humanity from the tumors from which he will not be able to save his own wife. Going off, Judith says, "to be useful people in the world" ("I'll be 'Mrs. Pasteur'"), they exchange the world of New York and Long Island—cocktail parties, horse races, café society—for that of Vermont—scientific research, a clapboard farmhouse, an occasional "dance on Saturday night." Ann wants to visit but has trouble renting her own house ("I'm not going to let tramps have it"), and Judith responds to these long-forsworn problems of the bourgeoisie by remarking to her servant, Martha, in a setting that looks like a late thirties version of a Ralph Lauren pseudo-English country kitchen: "Why do people complicate their lives so? All those horses—that house. . . . *Here we have nothing—and yet we have everything*" (emphasis added).

Shelley's greatest unintended legacy may have been his encouragement of aristocratic hauteur among bourgeois artists, whether those, like Woolf, from the high reaches of the late Victorian intelligentsia or those, like the makers of *Dark Victory,* who appropriated to the needs of a popular medium the Shelleyan trope of worldly escape for self-improvement and the salvation of humanity. Neither Clarissa Dalloway nor Judith Traherne could experience such generous, gracious nobility were it not for the class apparatus that allows her a life of relative ease from which the quest for beauty or for truth can spring most easily. The delicacy of the one, the earnestness of the other: both derive from the prerogatives of class. One must first possess the complications of society in order to banish them in favor of the simplicity of rural life. In a final scene cut from *Dark Victory,* Judith's horse Challenger wins his race, inspiring the Lawrentian groom (Humphrey Bogart) to remark: "She could have told them. . . . She knew. . . . It's in the breeding."[2]

By one way of figuring it, pastoral has always been the genre best suited to "naturalizing" an essentially conservative, not to say oppressive, worldview, one that allows kings and queens to masquerade as swains and milkmaids and thereby to cast off the artificial trappings of monarchy, worldliness, and class in favor of nature, pleasure, and simplicity. It is the genre of "breeding."[3] Pastoral has never been, of course, quite so simple, and its habits of incorporating criticism of both a political and a self-consciously literary sort have allowed it the amplitude to *seem* narrow and artificial while at the same time developing a resilient capacity to contain and reflect whatever its readers and critics wish to define as the chief qualities of literature itself. Pastoral, in other words, may be taken as the paradigm for all deliberate literary forms that give pride of place to matters of convention and artifice. Like indolence, a condition to which it traditionally grants privileged status, the pastoral in its multiple versions may encourage hostile or approving ideological responses to its "mere" aestheticism, its factitious treatments of shepherds and the lower orders, its nostalgia for a world either long vanished or never real. Although Renaissance pastoral was, at best, a form laced with georgic elements, it is true, as Alastair Fowler has noted, that in its purest form, pastoral "was concerned with otium, with art (singing, narrative), with emotions . . . and parenthetically with the herding of sheep or goats."[4]

Shelley's pastoral everywhere bespeaks his deeply ambiguous feelings about the relation of the self, especially what I label the "aristocratic" self, to the world, especially to *hoi polloi.* Shelley was, of course, no genuine aristocrat; his father received a political baronetcy in 1806 and, dying in 1844, well after his son, bequeathed the title to Percy Florence Shelley, the poet's son, over the objections of the poet's mother, who would have preferred the title to go to Shelley's brother John. Nevertheless, given his associations with Byron in Italy, as well as his education, his attitude toward money, domestic economy, and human relationships, and the strong sense of a gentleman's privilege that informs his poetry, it is legitimate to apply the label "aristocratic" (or at least "pseudo-aristocratic") to Shelley's self-portrayals in his pastoral poetry.[5] Shelley was a gentleman before he was a radical. This unarguable biographical fact has important effects, I would maintain, on his choice of subjects, his poetic self-presentation, and his style, all of which we may connect—however loosely— to "temperament." In addition, alone among the Romantics he incorporates the aestheticism of pastoralism, as well as its communal aspects, into his program for political change. Shelleyan "indolence" appears as a topos within his pastoral poetry, and Shelleyan passivity, as more than just a psychological condition, may be measured even by close looks at the voices of his verbs in a range of poetic utterances.[6] In the discussion that follows I examine some aspects of Shelley's pastoral in those capacious works where it signifies an end to struggle, labor, and history.

Keats's famous appraisal of his contemporary's essence encapsulates half the truth: "You might curb your magnanimity and be more of an artist, and load every rift of your subject with ore. The thought of such discipline must fall like cold chains upon you, who perhaps never sat with your wings furl'd for six Months together" (*Letters*, 2:323). So does the conclusion of Matthew Arnold's estimate: "a beautiful *and ineffectual* angel, beating in the void his luminous wings in vain."[7] Attempting to save his hero ("our former beautiful and lovable Shelley" [p. 213]) from the demystifying biography of Edward Dowden, Arnold senses that Shelley's importance as a cultural icon to subsequent generations rests on the implicit conflict between idealism and skepticism, luminousness and worldliness, radical-ism and a deeply entrenched sense of his own entitlement. Shelley the gentleman, "of high and tender seriousness, of heroic generosity, and of a delicacy in rendering services which was equal to his generosity" (p. 246), was capable of haughtily refusing £2,000 rather than consenting to entail property, in a letter quoted by Arnold: "I desire money because I think I know the use of it. It commands labour, it gives leisure; and to forward leisure to those who will employ it in the forwarding of truth is the noblest present an individual can make to the whole" (p. 247). Shelley was beset with financial problems throughout his adult life; this cavalier refusal im-plies a gentlemanly unwillingness to compromise as well as a rationaliza-tion of class privilege by an appeal to the *usefulness* of leisure in the fight against ignorance, falsehood, and oppression.

Shelley's pastoral moments are most prominent in the poetry he wrote in Italy, where he went in part because of the relatively inexpensive cost of living there. These are moments (in "Lines Written Among the Euganean Hills," *Prometheus Unbound,* "Epipsychidion," the lyrics to Jane Williams, and *Adonais*) that picture the highest good as a life of leisure, even indo-lence, apart from the *profanum vulgus* and with not much consideration of them. Shelley's summum bonum is to sit with his wings furled in an elegantly simple setting (Judith Traherne's "nothing . . . and yet every-thing"), beyond mere Horatian sufficiency and beyond mundane toil. In spite of their situation in caves, dells, islands, or otherwise secluded *loci amoeni,* Shelley's pastoral scenes have less to do with a "hard" Wordsworthian life in nature, or even with the nobler efforts of the Wordsworthian will, than with the softer, refined, even rococo indolence embodied in Voltaire's elegant couplet, "J'aime le luxe et même la mollesse, / Tous les plaisirs, les arts de toute espèce" ("Le mondain," from *Satires* [1736]).[8] To my knowledge, only Shelley has dared to suggest that "the

Enchanter in the first canto [of Thomson's *Castle of Indolence*] was a true philanthropist, and the Knight of Arts and Industry in the second an oligarchical impostor overthrowing truth by power."[9] In the Shelleyan hierarchy of value, indolence comes first, effort second.

Shelley's poetic paradises always come as conclusions, either as the climax of what has preceded their depiction or as an escape from it.[10] "Lines Written Among the Euganean Hills" is a case in point. Although Earl Wasserman claims that it represents the "Hymn to Intellectual Beauty" seen from the other side,[11] it shares with its hymnal forebear and with many of Shelley's most characteristic lyrics a structural principle that moves from abstraction to observation, or from generality to specificity. The inferrable first-person "self" in a Shelley lyric is often depicted at the end, either as respite and diversion from, or as logical extension of, the philosophical and symbolic speculations with which the poem begins. "Lines" may embody what Donald Davie calls Shelley's urbanity,[12] but it achieves this urbanity primarily by means of its ending. As a poem in the loco-descriptive tradition, it peculiarly lights upon its true subject after speculations of other sorts, careening from a random, wishful allegory to a visual and personal retreat to an island paradise. The first three quarters of the poem are seemingly without purpose, except to prepare us for the calm of the ending, where anxieties, complaints, fears, and darkness give way at last to pastoral calm.

The poem is a study of islands.[13] The first 285 lines constitute a series of reflections on an opening generalization: "Many a green isle needs must be / In the deep wide sea of Misery." The direction of the poem is haphazardly speculative, symbolic, and political. At line 285 the poet takes a turn, attempting to counter, or escape from, the world he has previously depicted. A look at the first section of his ending puts us in touch with Shelley's style:

> Noon descends around me now: 285
> 'Tis the noon of autumn's glow,
> When a soft and purple mist
> Like a vaporous amethyst,
> Or an air-dissolved star
> Mingling light and fragrance, far
> From the curved horizon's bound
> To the point of heaven's profound,
> Fills the overflowing sky;
> And the plains that silent lie
> Underneath, the leaves unsodden   295
> Where the infant frost has trodden
> With his morning-winged feet,
> Whose bright print is gleaming yet;
> And the red and golden vines,

Piercing with their trellised lines
The rough, dark-skirted wilderness;
The dun and bladed grass no less,
Pointing from this hoary tower
In the windless air; the flower
Glimmering at my feet; the line   305
Of the olive-sandalled Apennine
In the south dimly islanded;
And the Alps, whose snows are spread
High between the clouds and sun;
And of living things each one;
And my spirit which so long
Darkened this swift stream of song,—
Interpenetrated lie
By the glory of the sky:
Be it love, light, harmony,   315
Odour, or the soul of all
Which from heaven like dew doth fall,
Or the mind which feeds this verse
Peopling the lone universe.

(ll. 285–319)

This excerpt is officially a single sentence, although obviously one might reduce it to smaller units that remain grammatically complete. Still, its effect is of inundation: Shelley has constructed a catalogue of details, one of his strongest legacies from the pastoral tradition, in order to represent a natural harmony and his place within it.

Such harmony is characterized above all by a sense of laziness, especially in the *seeming* winding of Shelley's grammar. Indolence works, in other words, as both theme and grammatical principle throughout Shelley's poetry. All the natural objects in the landscape are objects of the verb "fills" (l. 293): "a soft and purple mist" (l. 287), which itself is like an amethyst or a star, *fills* the overflowing sky, the silent plains beneath, the red and golden vines, the dim and bladed grass, the flower at his feet, the line of the Apennines, the Alps, and at last "my own spirit." It turns out, however, that these phrases, separated by semicolons, are not, or not only, grammatical objects but subjects of the subsequent verb "lie" (l. 313). The passage dramatizes an effort at containment as well as enumeration: "the plains that silent lie . . . interpenetrated lie." And, as if to create a synthetic *tertium quid,* Shelley's list forces us to consider the elements of the natural world as a sequence of objects, then as a sequence of subjects, and finally as another sequence of objects, since, although the nouns are grammatical subjects of the intransitive "lie," they are at the same time the passive recipients of that penetration that emanates from "the glory of the sky" (l. 314). The parts of speech perform a magic act—filling first one grammatical role, then another—leaving us uncertain of grammatical causation but sure of an "interpenetrated" unity. Likewise, the main causal principle, "the glory of the sky," appears initially as "a soft and purple mist" and finally as a sequence of not entirely equivalent synonyms: love, light, harmony, odor, soul of all, poetic mind. The confusions of plenty begin with a bejeweled nebulous "mist" and culminate in single abstract nouns, crowned by "mind."

Shelley's catalogue does not follow the normative pattern of a loco-descriptive poem such as Pope's "Windsor Forest"; it makes no attempt to force the reader's imaginative eye across a real or depicted landscape, examining first one element or section and then another. Instead, it works to accumulate a series of details in an only apparently topsy-turvy manner, setting us loose amid typically Shelleyan images while simultaneously requiring us to understand a scene through syntactic parsing. All is amassed, and all is passive. The naturalized sexuality of the interpenetrated elements includes the human observer as merely one element, albeit the concluding and perhaps climactic one.

This section of twenty-five lines is the first part of the poem's conclusion. There follows a bridge (ll. 320–34), which allows the speaker to move from noon to evening, and to return to the leitmotif of imagined nautical passages to safe harbors. At last Shelley escapes entirely, finding peace, comfort, and community in the calmest haven of all:

> Other flowering isles must be   335
> In the sea of Life and Agony:
> Other spirits float and flee
> O'er that gulph: even now, perhaps,
> On some rock the wild wave wraps,
> With folded wings they waiting sit
> For my bark, to pilot it
> To some calm and blooming cove,
> Where for me, and those I love,
> May a windless bower be built,
> Far from passion, pain, and guilt,   345
> In a dell 'mid lawny hills,
> Which the wild sea-murmur fills,
> And soft sunshine, and the sound
> Of old forests echoing round,
> And the light and smell divine
> Of all flowers that breathe and shine:
> We may live so happy there,
> That the Spirits of the Air,
> Envying us, may even entice
> To our healing Paradise   355
> The polluting multitude;
> But their rage would be subdued
> By that clime divine and calm,

And the winds whose wings rain balm
On the uplifted soul, and leaves
Under which the bright sea heaves;
While each breathless interval
In their whisperings musical
The inspired soul supplies
With its own deep melodies,   365
And the love which heals all strife
Circling, like the breath of life,
All things in that sweet abode
With its own mild brotherhood:
They, not it, would change; and soon
Every sprite beneath the moon
Would repent its envy vain,
And the earth grow young again.

(ll. 335–73)

Another, even lengthier sentence, this section continues the depiction of a deserved indolence, here specifically allied to aristocratic privilege through the allusions to *The Tempest* and Dante's sonnet to Cavalcanti ("Guido, I would that Lappo, thou and I, / Led by some strong enchantment, might ascend / A magic ship"). The desired destination, a bower in a dell, will like the earlier landscape be filled, now with sea murmurs. Rage will "be subdued" by the climate, the wind, and the power of love. Shelley's verbs are insistently passive: important actions *are performed*. Effort and energy have been left behind or ignored altogether. Even (or especially) the construction of the island retreat is at once automatic and willed: "May a windless bower be built" (l. 344) without any evidence of labor or agency. Shelley has decreed his island equivalent of Kubla Khan's stately pleasure dome, and it arises, the result of a conditional or jussive verb and a muted velleity. Determination and reverie have become synonymous.

Shelley's pastoral seclusion promises redemption for the *profanum vulgus*, whom he simultaneously invites and keeps at arm's length. (They exist in some anticipated, generalized future moment.) The poem's catalogue of island havens, beginning with imagined and symbolic ones, and extending through Venice as a "nest" for Byron, the "tempest-cleaving Swan" who has fled from England to Italy, has concluded with a "peopled solitude" different from the urban emptiness of Padua. With quasi-dialectic force the poet manages to retain his vaunted superiority without sacrificing his radical, millenarian dreams of transforming society. The "blooming cove," originally the haunt of the poet's selected loved ones, incites the envy of those "Spirits of the Air" who willfully attempt its spoliation by inviting the "people" to the paradise: even as Shelley labels it "healing," he readies us for the conversion that follows in the passive voice. The "mild brotherhood" of love, circling and enabling, reaches back even to the vain and envious "sprites," whose sudden though predictable repentance foretells an unwinding or rejuvenating of history and human society.

What kind of poem is this? As I have mentioned, it is not really conventionally descriptive, nor does it easily fit into the genre of the Romantic nature lyric as defined by M. H. Abrams.[14] Its different sections, although tied together by the imaginary and actual islands that symbolize safety and repose, deal thematically with such various topics—actual sea journeys, existential isolation, lonely unmourned death, the political state of contemporary Italy, the role of poets in giving voice to the soul of liberty—that we might naturally wonder at the degree of association (or lack thereof) among the thirteen paragraphs. The charming divagation of Shelley's tetrameter couplets sets a mood repeated in several of the later lyrics to Jane Williams; it is a mood of indolent dolce far niente, one that Shelley's poetry composed in England seldom struck, and one that we may legitimately associate specifically with the last three profitable years of his life in Italy. Shelley's pastorals, whether entire poems or partial, magical moments like the ending of these "Lines," share an expatriate's deepest wish for discovering home, or, more specifically, the aristocratic expatriate's wish that "a windless bower be built" for him far from the madding crowd's ignoble strife. The new paradise will implicitly compensate for past sins as (we assume) the earth and its inhabitants retreat to a primal state. Childhood, Eden, all that is first and golden arrives as a wish fulfillment at poem's end.

These moments may appear connected—logically, symbolically, thematically—to the other sections of the longer poems in which they fit, but they often seem arbitrary as well. Shelley might very well have ended "Lines Written Among the Euganean Hills" before he reached his bower–cove; we have no reason to expect the poem to take a personal, escapist turn. And yet, at the end of "Epipsychidion" the retreat with Teresa Viviani (called Emilia in the poem) to an island paradise signals a climax to an adulterous episode and marks a movement away from the poem's philosophical investigations into the nature of erotic gratification.[15] The last third of the poem (ll. 407–604, including a thirteen-line envoi) constitutes Shelley's lengthiest depiction of a paradisal haven; it adds to its catalogue of pastoral topoi an aristocrat's dream of unearned comfort, luxuries sufficient to one's needs for tasteful elegance, and the apparatus necessary to maintain artistic energies amid civilized exile. Shelley's "favoured place" (l. 461) far exceeds Milton's happy rural seat, that decidedly English version of paradise, in its Mediterranean abundance.

Like the opening landscape of Keats's "Fall of Hyperion," Shelley's here is informed throughout by its author's awareness of belatedness. Unlike Keats's dreamer, Shelley does not arrive upon a scene recently abandoned by its inhabitants; instead, he refurbishes the landscape and its architecture to ensure a perfect mating of the antique and the contemporary. The isle, "beautiful as a wreck of Paradise" (l. 423), is both a remainder and a promise of future bliss, but it is not at all clear whether its current inhabitants, from an ancient race, represent the end of a line:

And, for the harbours are not safe and good,
This land would have remained a solitude
But for some pastoral people native there,
Who from the Elysian, clear, and golden air
Draw the last spirit of the age of gold,
Simple and spirited; innocent and bold.

(ll. 424–29)

Implicitly lurking within Shelley's topos of the golden age are suggestions of its imminent destruction. "Would have remained" and the adversative "but" of lines 425–26 might lead us to expect a subsequent clause depicting Shelley's own adventurous trip to the island. This is clearly bound to take place. Instead, we have something like a compromise between two possibilities: the pastoral people are rooted, native, and ancient, but are themselves something of an intrusion in the primal "solitude." At the same time Shelley and Emilia, equally "spirited" and "bold" but not "simple" or "innocent," will brave the waves to reach the blessed isle. Whether their arrival in these Elysian Fields will redeem them among the happy natives or destroy the preexisting quasi-"solitude" can only be guessed.

Shelley's depiction of the golden age clearly surpasses Ovid's or Milton's by including actual (rather than metaphorical) architecture. The "chief marvel of the wilderness" (l. 483), a "lone dwelling" (l. 484) constructed by some precivilized Ocean King, combines characteristics of the simple and the sophisticated: it is tall but not strong, central to the place but not threatening, a "pleasure-house / Made sacred" (ll. 491–92). It is the architectural equivalent of Horatian *simplex munditiis*. Above all, the constructed palace has become as it were naturalized, an element of and from the landscape rather than merely set within it:

It scarce seems now a wreck of human art,
But, as it were Titanic; in the heart
Of Earth having assumed its form, then grown
Out of the mountains, from the living stone,
Lifting itself in caverns light and high:
For all the antique and learned imagery
Has been erased, and in the place of it
The ivy and the wild-vine interknit
The volumes of their many twining stems.

(ll. 493–501)

The self-conscious elaboration of the natural metaphor attests vividly to Shelley's mingling of opposites in his wished-for island paradise, and to a style that can blithely say two things, if not at once, then sequentially: here is a building that is so old it seems no longer made but natural and inevitable. The architecture has a will of its own, and its growth is organic. In one way we have retreated to an earlier state of being or consciousness, as the writing on the walls has been replaced by the natural volumes of intertwined plantings. But in another we have been lifted to a subtler, higher plane of sophisticated or even witty consciousness, as the clearly meta-phoric, figural naturalizing of the building makes it more, rather than less, removed from a natural reality. That Shelley should resort, as he seldom does, to a Latinate punning ("volumes") suggests the serious as well as the playful tone captured in his depiction of an antique-turned-garden.[16]

The richness of the wrecked dwelling, it becomes clear, attests to its owner's tastefulness; its semidecay requires of him some redecorating and refurbishing, the putting into effect of innate good taste. Shelley's state-ment of possession makes a claim to the property as an enticement to Emilia to accompany him as they presumably will step in for the original Titanic builder–owner and the sister–spouse for whom he built the edifice:

> This isle and house are mine, and I have vowed
> Thee to be lady of the solitude.—
> And I have fitted up some chambers there
> Looking towards the golden Eastern air,
> And level with the living winds, which flow
> Like waves above the living waves below.—
> I have sent books and music there, and all
> Those instruments with which high spirits call
> The future from its cradle, and the past
> Out of its grave, and make the present last
> In thoughts and joys which sleep, but cannot die,
> Folded within their own eternity.
> Our simple life wants little, and true taste
> Hires not the pale drudge Luxury, to waste
> The scene it would adorn, and therefore still,
> Nature, with all her children, haunts the hill.
>
> (ll. 513–28)

"True taste," that which comes to an aristocrat by *nature* (i.e., birth and early nurture) rather than by later effort, needs no luxury to adorn a setting. Instead, good sense harnesses "Nature" and her brood (ring-dove, owls, bats, spotted deer) as perfect ornaments for the country estate. The primal and natural here become secondary or subservient to the artistic impulse that orders the house, its interior, its inhabitants, its furnishings, and even its exterior setting. Shelley sends to his new estate the apparatus for the aesthetic life: books for reading, music for listening, and unspecified "instruments" for psychic or magical researches. The "music" is presum-ably musical instruments, but Shelley's catalogue daintily replaces agency with result, as though the island music will be automatically or "naturally" produced without human effort. (Earlier he remarks that "all the place is peopled with sweet airs" [l. 445].)[17]

Shelley's invitation constitutes an aristocrat's seduction to sexual dal-liance, however much he renders it glamorous by lofty philosophizing. The depiction of the island, house, and household as an organic unity composed in equal parts of art and nature, simplicity and "true taste," golden age and sophisticated modernity, culminates in successively impassioned moments of sexual union, beginning metaphorically and proceeding to the lovers themselves. Thus:

> The blue Aegean girds this chosen home,
> With ever-changing sound and light and foam,
> Kissing the sifted sands, and caverns hoar;
> And all the winds wandering along the shore
> Undulate with the undulating tide.
>
> (ll. 430–34)

Or:

> And, day and night, aloof, from the high towers
> And terraces, the Earth and Ocean seem
> To sleep in one another's arms, and dream
> Of waves, flowers, clouds, woods, rocks, and all that we
> Read in their smiles, and call reality.
>
> (ll. 508–12)

Such examples, two among many, attest both to the sexual nature of Shelley's invitation and to his mania for detailed lists, amassed to impress upon Emilia the richness of his possessions and the inevitable, natural sexuality of the universe to which he wishes to take her.

Since all elements in the surroundings partake of real or metaphoric sexual union, the famous depiction of sexuality with which the poem ends (ll. 540–91) embeds the hoped-for union of man and woman within the context of natural eroticism. That the description begins with a single twenty-line sentence proves once more my earlier point that Shelley's style, reflecting his temperament, seeks to enumerate in syntactically convoluted ways the place he occupies within the external world and the control he can wield over it:

> Meanwhile
> We two will rise, and sit, and walk together,
> Under the roof of blue Ionian weather,
> And wander in the meadows, or ascend
> The mossy mountains, where the blue heavens bend
> With lightest winds, to touch their paramour;
> Or linger, where the pebble-paven shore,
> Under the quick, faint kisses of the sea
> Trembles and sparkles as with ecstasy,—
> Possessing and possest by all that is
> Within that calm circumference of bliss,
> And by each other, till to love and live
> Be one:—or, at the noontide hour, arrive
> Where some old cavern hoar seems yet to keep

> The moonlight of the expired night asleep,
> Through which the awakened day can never peep;
> A veil for our seclusion, close as Night's,
> Where secure sleep may kill thine innocent lights;
> Sleep, the fresh dew of languid love, the rain
> Whose drops quench kisses till they burn again.
>
> (ll. 540–59)

The sentence is richly hypotactic and paratactic simultaneously: it accumulates a list of possibilities ("We two will . . . or . . . or") within which it elaborates a system of subordinations. It seems initially random ("We will rise, and sit, and walk together" suggests a pattern of thoughtless, nonsequential actions, where one might expect "sit and rise and walk") yet deliberate in its metaphoric connections (e.g., "the roof of blue Ionian weather" recapitulates the previous minglings of art and nature). It focuses attention equally on the actions of the lovers and the erotic possibilities within the natural setting. By the time the sentence reaches its climactic middle (ll. 549–52), it has with seeming deliberateness confused the referents of its participles: it is the lovers who are "possessing and possest" although it may as well be the "kisses of the sea" against the "pebble-paven shore," for the antecedent pronoun ("we") has long since been lost amid the syntactic tendrils. Likewise, as the list regathers its force, we may justly wonder about the cave to which they wander. Does "the awakened day" never peep *through* the cavern or through the night? Can the moonlight, if kept asleep, properly belong to an "expired night"? Is the "veil for [the lovers'] seclusion" the moonlight or the cavern?[18]

In a world where lovers simultaneously "possess" and are "possessed by" their environment, the grammatical difficulties of the lines just quoted serve a legitimate function. As the remainder of the passage attests, Shelley and his lover are about to enter a passionate state far transcending both the representability and even the effort of language, as "thought's melody" approaches language and then "live[s] again in looks . . . harmonizing silence without a sound," while the lovers use their mouths for eloquence other than that of words: they are at last "confused in passion's golden purity" (l. 571). Shelley again uncharacteristically resorts to a bilingual Latinate pun to remind us of the connection between outpouring and intellectual uncertainty. And, we might infer, to remind us subtly of the connection between the lovers' passion and the innocence of the first golden age, here reinvented—or repurchased—by the aristocratic lover at whose command books and music may be sent abroad, instruments may be summoned to "call / The future from its cradle," and true taste will not stoop to hire luxury as its minion.

"Epipsychidion" mingles two kinds of wishful fantasies. The first is the source of the poem's dominant imagery, and it centers on the theme of erotic and personal fulfillment. It is a fantasy of escape and of evaporation, the self-in-love losing itself in the lover and amid a congenial, equally erotic natural setting. The second, that which I have been stressing, is domestic and sophisticated but also ironic and social. The ironies are implicit from the strange opening "Advertisement," which pretends that the poem is posthumous and intended as a "dedication to some longer [work]." Shelley portrays the author as having bought an island in the Sporades, which he was preparing to visit when he "died at Florence." The grimly proleptic anticipation of Shelley's actual death is mitigated by his elegant fictive self-portrayal as a modern cavalier, adjusting the *dolce stil nuovo* of love and art to a nineteenth-century setting. And just as Shelley has enticed Emilia Viviani with his promise of a tasteful modern pastoral that reproduces the golden age within the actual possibilities of contemporary life, he insists in the poem's envoi upon the socially ennobling force of his primary vision. He bids his "weak verses" to

> haste
> Over the hearts of men, until ye meet
> Marina, Vanna, Primus, and the rest,
> And bid them love each other and be blest:
> And leave the troop which errs, and which reproves,
> And come and be my guest,—for I am Love's.
>
> (ll. 599–604)[19]

Another way of describing the poem's double focus is to label it simultaneously centrifugal and centripetal: the lovers flee from the world in order to establish their self-sustaining love within an appropriately self-supporting natural framework. Once ensconced in their retreat, comfortable amid the necessary tastefulness, they generously bid others of their immediate coterie (Mary Shelley, Jane and Edward Williams, and "the rest") to join them. They have formed the center of a new circle. The pastoral, with all its backward-looking implications, heralds a utopia, with the forward-looking aspirations of social harmony as well as individual fulfillment. Shelley has daringly converted his little group not only into an Epicurean circle of friends living in *ataraxia* but also into semi-divinities.[20] It is this aspect of Shelley's pastoral that informs the middle section, all easy discursive couplets, in lines 147–89, the section that so inspired Bloomsbury (e.g., Forster's *Longest Journey*), with its anti-matrimonial, idealistic version of a "free" love that liberates those who are worthy of understanding and embracing it.

In this section, yet once more, Shelley's vision of freedom combines the adolescent heroics so enticing to the young Clarissa Dalloway ("Thy wisdom . . . bids me dare / Beacon the rocks on which high hearts are wreckt") and contempt for "those poor slaves . . . / Who travel to their home among the dead" with a philosophical appropriation of the medieval droit du seigneur. The aristocratic temper takes all things to itself and rationalizes its amassings by an appeal to the commonweal. Since "true love" (like understanding) can only be enlarged, never reduced, it "differs from gold and clay"; but Shelley bases his figurative depiction of love's infinity on a sense of bounty that, far from countering a mere economic enrichment, seems to duplicate it:

> If you divide pleasure and love and thought,
> Each part exceeds the whole; and we know not
> How much, while any yet remains unshared,
> Of pleasure may be gained, of sorrow spared:
> This truth is that deep well, whence sages draw
> The unenvied light of hope; the eternal law
> By which those live, to whom this world of life
> Is as a garden ravaged, and whose strife
> Tills for the promise of a later birth
> The wilderness of this Elysian earth.
>
> (ll. 178–89)

The nursery school enumerations of this verse are matched by Shelley's discursive "middle" tone, which he adopts whenever trying to explain, to rationalize, or to persuade. In this case his earlier aphorism, "to divide is not to take away" (l. 161), provides a starting point for further mathematical calculations even though they are nominally deployed to prove the paradoxical point that expenditures (the dividing of love) do not diminish one's erotic capital but instead augment it. The deep well of truth is the source of communal pleasures, universal (and therefore unenviable) hopes, and labor that culminates in a rebirth of Elysian perfection. Love becomes the quintessential georgic activity whose agency will restore a pastoral life.

It has, of course, often been noted that Shelley seeks to have his cake and eat it, too; his vision of erotic bliss and its promises is at once exclusive and general. If, as the bulk of "Epipsychidion" seeks to prove, Emilia Viviani is the "Being whom [his] spirit oft / Met on its visioned wanderings" (ll. 190–91), it should hardly be necessary for Shelley to embed a defense of free love in the middle of his rapt, ecstatic addresses to her. If he hopes to escape with her to an island hideaway, it comes as something of a surprise that he wishes to include there his extended community of friends and relatives.[21] The Shelleyan impulse toward utopian living may legitimately be read as the outgrowth of the spoiled child's accumulative urges or, equally, as the nobleman's sense of inherited privilege. Without psychoanalyzing Shelley himself, we can sense in his pastoral poems his poetic habits of appropriation: appropriation of persons, of property, and even of poetic styles (his own stylistic variety testifying as much to the magpie in him as to the intrepid experimenter with inherited forms). If the child is father of the Shelleyan man, the hero of these poems certainly has a streak of petulance that only barely disguises itself beneath a cloak of passivity: "Twin Spheres of light who rule this passive Earth, / This world of love, this *me*" (ll. 345–46) simultaneously diminishes and exaggerates the status of the single man who conceives of himself as an entire world. In Shelley's case we might profitably expand Irving Babbitt's old charge that Romantic love is merely an *égoisme à deux* to include a lazily sublime sense of self that,

Whitman-like, contains and controls multitudes.[22] *Prometheus Unbound,* especially in those passages that deliberately glorify the social dimension of erotic union, or that offer a vision of an extended family, provides the fullest version of Shelley's pastoral longings, his states of possession and of being possessed.

Yeats implicitly understood Shelley's yearnings. In his early twenties (the time of the fictional Clarissa Dalloway's adolescence), Shelley societies offered a substitute for "the orthodox religion, as our mothers had taught us . . . [and for] humanitarian or scientific pursuit."[23] Shelley's legacy fed into Yeats's glorification of that supreme triumvirate of countrymen, aristocrats, and artists ("Three types of men have made all beautiful things. . . . Aristocrats have made beautiful manners, because their place in the world puts them above the fear of life") and into his Wildean epigram, "All the most valuable things are useless."[24] Most important was Yeats's understanding of the social but hieratic dimension of Shelley's aspirations. If Shelley could follow the "images" in which "wisdom speaks," according to Yeats, they "would lead his soul, disentangled from unmeaning circumstances and the ebb and flow of the world, into that far household where the undying gods await all whose souls have become simple as flame, whose bodies have become quiet as an agate lamp."[25] What to another temperament—Leslie Stephen's, for example—was Shelley's mere escapism was for Yeats a reintegration into his proper, though distant, "household," an Epicurean compound where the gods greet and promote chosen mortals to their company.[26] Such a haven provides what Harry Berger, Jr., refers to as "the green world" of pastoral, but with a new twist: unlike Renaissance versions of the pastoral world, which represent either a positive because temporary withdrawal or a negative manifestation of "the urge of the paralyzed will to give up, escape, work magic, abolish time and flux and the intrusive reality of other minds,"[27] Shelley's peculiar paradises abolish neither time nor mortality, nor do they offer a temporary middle state; the body retreats as well as the mind, and the solitary self shares the company of congenial peers, often relatives. Far from dissolving all traditional ties, as Stephen or more hostile readers imply, Shelley always manages to transform and strengthen them.

I would like to examine some of the salient moments in *Prometheus Unbound* in order to support my hypothesis about Shelley's aristocratic reworking of pastoral tropes and about his stylistic habits. The end is a proper place to begin; Demogorgon's speech proclaims a new political order and a new personal one:

> This is the Day which down the void Abysm
> At the Earth-born's spell yawns for Heaven's Despotism,
>   And Conquest is dragged Captive through the Deep;
> Love from its awful throne of patient power
> In the wise heart, from the last giddy hour
>   Of dread endurance, from the slippery, steep,

And narrow verge of crag-like Agony, springs
And folds over the world its healing wings.

Gentleness, Virtue, Wisdom and Endurance,—
These are the seals of that most firm assurance
   Which bars the pit over Destruction's strength;
And if, with infirm hand, Eternity,
Mother of many acts and hours, should free
   The serpent that would clasp her with his length—
These are the spells by which to reassume
An empire o'er the disentangled Doom.

To suffer woes which Hope thinks infinite;
To forgive wrongs darker than Death or Night;
   To defy Power which seems Omnipotent;
To love, and bear; to hope, till Hope creates
From its own wreck the things it contemplates;
   Neither to change nor falter nor repent:
This, like thy glory, Titan! is to be
Good, great and joyous, beautiful and free;
This is alone Life, Joy, Empire and Victory.

                          (4. 554–78)

Like so much of Shelley's most characteristic verse, this lyric moves beyond will, effort, and exertion to praise passivity, endurance, and a heightened sense of being. Coming both as the climax of a play in which all action has been minimized (many earlier critics felt that the action moves downhill from lines 58–59, when Prometheus "recalls"—either revokes or remembers—his curse on Jupiter), and at the end of the structurally supererogatory but lyrically justifiable fourth act, an extended epithalamion, Demogorgon's closing paean to Prometheus and the new world created by his release epitomizes both Shelleyan versions of pastoral and Shelleyan stylistic maneuvers.[28]

The timeless infinitives of the last stanza are appropriate to an idealized utopian world in which time has stopped—or has only appeared to stop. Shelley inserts his own skeptical notes in the second stanza, bracketing them between the more elevated and hopeful stanzas that surround them; the possibility for a renewal of tyranny, like the suggestion in the famous lyrics from *Hellas* that history may re-begin its recurrent patterns, means that for Shelley paradises are never pure and seldom eternal. Tyranny may be repressed, covered, and defused, but it is never killed.[29] Such skepticism might derive from many sources, but certainly one possible origin is Shelley's echoing of Virgil's imagery for repression in the opening books of the *Aeneid*.[30] If Eternity should ever accidentally release the serpent of Destruction, *then* Gentleness, Virtue, Wisdom, and Endurance would suffice to combat it. The possibility of pain, evil, and oppression cannot be erased.

A second prominent feature of this lyric, related to the suppression or bracketing of Destruction within the middle stanza, is its series of variations on verbs of mere being. As befits a celebration of a new, peaceful order, the song is an experiment in static definition. "To be" sounds the loudest chords. Thus, the first stanza opens with Wordsworthian nakedness: "This is the Day." The second defers its predication until after the listing of antecedent abstractions: "Gentleness, Virtue . . . / These are the seals." And the third defers even more its statement of being until the antepenultimate line, which, when it comes, is itself subject to an interruption in the form of a simile: "To suffer . . . / To forgive . . . / This, like thy glory, Titan! is to be / Good." And it is also subject to the extension of an enjambment: the last definition, in other words, is the longest in coming within its own stanza, and the most difficult to articulate.

In all three stanzas active verbs are relegated to secondary, almost invisible levels. "Yawns . . . springs / And folds" (st. 1); "bars . . . free . . . clasp" (st. 2): these are subordinate to the formal demands of definition. As an appropriate climax to Shelley's stylistic experiments, the infinitives of the third stanza move along a scale from transitive verbs explicitly taking objects ("suffer," "forgive," "defy"), through transitive verbs with possible or implicit objects ("To love, and bear"), to intransitive (and negative) constructions: "Neither to change nor falter nor repent." In addition, the stanza's opening infinitives precede and enclose the simple present-tense "thinks" and "seems," and the implied future-tense, transitive "creates" and "contemplates," before settling into the climactic definition, which itself moves from a verbal to a nominal form: "This . . . is to be / Good" and "This is . . . Life." Shelley presents his utopianism within a lyric, in other words, that has forgone action in favor of stasis, gradually reducing verbs and verbal constructions to a bare minimum. Transitive action, like the possible renewal of Destruction's power in the middle stanza, is implied but bracketed; even in the third stanza the strongest indicative verbs ("creates," "contemplates") occupy a marginalized future status.

Time, as much as is poetically possible, has appropriately disappeared from the last lyric. By reaching to infinity through infinitives, and by adding a ninth line to his third stanza, Shelley seems to stretch through time to eternity. In order to praise his Titan's former long-suffering endurance, to offer it as a model for all human will, and to proclaim the new post-Olympian order, Shelley has devised a lyric and syntactic structure that minimizes action and accentuates states of permanence.

If this lyric were unique in the play, we could claim it as a vision of the new world order effected by Jupiter's fall and Prometheus' triumph. But such stylistic procedures characterize so much of the play's poetry that we must take them, instead, as what I have labeled Shelley's typical longing for stasis and his (at least partly) aristocratic impulse to furl his own wings. For example, he gathers together several of the work's persistent tropes and methods within a single speech:

Thy steeds will pause at even—till when, farewell.
The loud Deep calls me home even now, to feed it
With azure calm out of the emerald urns
Which stand forever full beside my throne.
Behold the Nereids under the green sea,
Their wavering limbs borne on the windlike stream,
Their white arms lifted o'er their streaming hair
With garlands pied and starry sea-flower crowns,
Hastening to grace their mighty Sister's joy.
                    [*A sound of waves is heard*]
It is the unpastured Sea hungering for Calm.
Peace, Monster—I come now! Farewell.

                                                    (3.2.40–50)

Ocean's leave-taking from Apollo appears at the end of a short, super-
fluous, ornamental scene in which the sun god reports the fall of Jupiter,
which has just occurred. Why, we may legitimately wonder, does Shelley
bother to include this brief encounter? In part, as I shall argue, the exchange is a prelude to Prometheus' grander speech in the next scene, and
prepares the reader for the Titan's more leisurely expatiation on the themes
of rest, seclusion, and recovery. Still more, it clarifies the largely aesthetic
nature of Shelley's treatment of revolution.

For the gods, work is effortless, and the natural world harmonious and
abundant. Ocean's divine pastoral solicitude derives from his cosmic regal
status. The pasturing of his marine flock is, linguistically at least, a tautology, as the "loud Deep" demands to be fed with an "azure calm" that exists
boundlessly in its own depths. The calm for which it hungers is provided
by a shepherd–deity, but it actually sustains itself. Ocean replenishes and
calms itself from its own infinite stores, but such restoration is depicted
figuratively as a willed effort. For a god, work only *seems* to exist, perhaps
even as an aesthetic possibility. In Marxist terms we might label it unalienated rather than alienated: work done exclusively for the worker, not for
another. The aesthetic frame of the scene extends into the detail of the sea
nymphs, objects of the gods' gaze, and solely ornamental in the marine
topography depicted in the speech. Female eroticism—the unnumbered
Nereids as buoyant ladies-in-waiting around their "mighty Sister"—
provides the ultimate "grace" note to the scene.

Apollo's report to Ocean concerning Jupiter's defeat makes of the cosmic revolution a radical aesthetic spectacle. Everything has been distanced.
The very frame of the dialogue suggests a repetition even within the re-
portage that aestheticizes the action. Apollo seems to be detailing the
events not for the first time but for the second, in reponse to Ocean's
incredulous requests: "He fell, thou sayest, beneath his conqueror's
frown?" (3.2.1); "He sunk to the abyss? to the dark void?" (l. 10). The
implied repetition evokes the leisurely pace of storytelling in which questions about previous details are not out of place. Shelley augments such

repetition with his almost inevitable similes: Jupiter falls "like the last glare of day's red agony" (l. 7), like "an eagle . . . caught in some bursting cloud / On Caucasus" (ll. 11–12). Such depiction removes action from our direct vision to the realm of indirect discourse and the quasi-resemblances that similes provide. This removal is inherently related to the prospective world of pastoral leisure and indolence, as Ocean implies in his prediction of the imminent calm of his "Heaven-reflecting sea" (l. 18):

> like plains of corn
> Swayed by the summer air; my streams will flow
> Round many-peopled continents and round
> Fortunate isles; and from their glassy thrones
> Blue Proteus and his humid Nymphs shall mark
> The shadow of fair ships, as mortals see
> The floating bark of the light-laden moon
> With that white star, its sightless pilot's crest,
> Borne down the rapid sunset's ebbing sea.
>
> (ll. 20–28)

Ocean and Apollo, shepherds of reflecting realms, prepare us for the longer, more leisurely depiction of utopian indolence framed in the following scene by Prometheus himself in pastoral terms.

Unbound by Hercules (3.3), Prometheus descends from a triumphal chariot piloted by the Spirit of the Hour. The allegorical significance of the descent (Mind liberated by Strength from Time) pales in comparison to Prometheus' sixty-line address to Asia, the equivalent of Shelley's invitations at the end of "Lines Written Among the Euganean Hills" and "Epipsychidion." Here we see the full force of Shelleyan pastoral as an aesthetic redemption of history and politics. Just as he had, in his preface, declared his unwillingness to "dedicate [his] poetical compositions solely to the direct enforcement of reform," and equally declared his "abhorrence" of didactic poetry, so within the drama he makes good his aristocratic promise "to familiarise the highly refined imagination of the more select classes with beautiful idealisms of moral excellence." For Prometheus a reunion with Asia promises a new order through an aesthetic retreat to a pastoral realm:

> Henceforth we will not part. There is a Cave
> All overgrown with trailing odorous plants
> Which curtain out the day with leaves and flowers
> And paved with veinèd emerald, and a fountain
> Leaps in the midst with an awakening sound;
> From its curved roof the mountain's frozen tears
> Like snow or silver or long diamond spires
> Hang downward, raining forth a doubtful light:
> And there is heard the ever-moving air
> Whispering without from tree to tree, and birds,

> And bees; and all around are mossy seats
> And the rough walls are clothed with long soft grass;
> A simple dwelling, which shall be our own,
> Where we will sit and talk of time and change,
> As the world ebbs and flows, ourselves unchanged.
>
> (3.3.10–24)

This is a catalogue not so much of pastoral commonplaces but of tropes out of others' books. Its echoes of Shakespeare (*A Midsummer Night's Dream*'s "I know a bank where the wild thyme blows," and Lear's invitation to Cordelia, "Come, we'll away to prison"); Coleridge (the leaping fountain from "Kubla Khan," the downward-hanging "spires" from "Frost at Midnight"); and Milton (whose "happy rural seat of various view" is here rendered as a "simple dwelling") testify to the literary artifice of the new world.[31]

As he does in "Euganean Hills" and "Epipsychidion," Shelley invents a dwelling that magically mingles architecture and nature: the cave is also something of a house, bejeweled but "rough"; dark, but richly and artificially illuminated; removed from but granting access to natural phenomena (literally the birds and the bees). Themselves unchanged, the Promethean family will make of human mutability its sole subject, like those Homeric gods who have woven ruin into human affairs merely to make a story of it. Matching the allusive, literary density of the speech is its own syntax: lines 30–56 consist of richly hypotactic clauses which detail the sensuous harmonies and activities of the Promethean family in its newfound domesticity. At the climax of this section and of these activities comes the note of a heightened aestheticism. The winds, claims Prometheus, will bring them

> lovely apparitions dim at first
> Then radiant—as the mind, arising bright
> From the embrace of beauty (whence the forms
> Of which these are the phantoms) casts on them
> The gathered rays which are reality—
> Shall visit us, the progeny immortal
> Of Painting, Sculpture and rapt Poesy
> And arts, though unimagined, yet to be.
>
> (ll. 49–56)

Less important than the genetic allegory of artistic creation implied by these lines (Prometheus-as-Mind embraces Asia-as-Beauty, illuminates the phantom forms, and makes them grow through some process of intellectual photosynthesis) is the equation of Prometheus and Asia with art itself. For if the "lovely apparitions" derive from the embrace of Mind and Beauty, they arise as well from arts as yet unborn. Shelley has devised a double principle of origination, comparable to the tautological feeding of the sea by its own infinite richness (3.2), which I have already noted:

Prometheus has all but explicitly equated himself and his family with the painting, sculpture, poesy, and yet unimagined arts whose "progeny immortal" will visit, delight, and enrich an audience that is also a creator. Love, mediated by art, beautifies, improves, and tames man, from whom "evil and error" will fall: "Such virtue has the cave and place around" (l. 63), announces the landlord of his new property.

As if in fulfillment of the new Promethean aestheticism, the Spirit of the Hour, who essentially ends the play proper (3.4) with his announcement of a new heaven and new earth, proclaims a world without labor. Of all the Romantic renditions of pastoral, Shelley's is the least tainted by a georgic impulse, in spite of his radical political leanings. Whereas in Keats we find reminders of gleaning and cider pressing as time runs down ("To Autumn"), whereas in Wordsworth the playfulness or "majestic indolence" of children and childlike adults alternates with their moments of hard labor, and whereas even in Coleridge, the most purely "spectatorial" of poets, aesthetic observation is compounded by a sense of its sinfulness, in Shelley we witness the unmitigated triumph of art as the symbol of the new order. It is an order depicted later in the century by Oscar Wilde, proposing the "aesthetic" as the goal of political change: "[C]ultivated leisure . . . not labour, is the aim of man—or making beautiful things, or reading beautiful things, or simply contemplating the world with admiration and delight."[32] The coursers of the Spirit of the Hour "sought their birthplace in the sun / Where they henceforth will live exempt from toil, / Pasturing flowers of vegetable fire" (3.4.108–10). The Hour himself will retire his chariot:

> And where my moonlike car will stand within
> A temple, gazed upon by Phidian forms,
> Of thee, and Asia and the Earth, and me,
> And you fair nymphs, looking the love we feel,
> In memory of the tidings it has borne,
> Beneath a dome fretted with graven flowers,
> Poised on twelve columns of resplendent stone
> And open to the bright and liquid sky.
>
> (ll. 111–18)

This heavenly garage contains the ennobled, or petrified, sculpted forms of the drama's primary actors. Whether this statuary represents their ultimate metamorphosis or merely an additional, separate incarnation is unknowable.

Shelley's depiction of the end of an old order and the beginning of a new one concludes with the Spirit's description of his final trip to earth. His catalogue of the changes wrought within political and social institutions, and within the mind of man, speaks for the millenarian side of Shelley's vision. Thrones are kingless, hypocrisy has evaporated, envy and shame have been replaced by love: such is the picture Shelley paints. And it is *as a picture* that he wishes us to retain this scene. The "mighty change" (l. 129) that the Spirit discovers has come about in an apparently bloodless coup.

All "thrones, altars, judgement-seats and prisons" (l. 164), we read, "[s]tand, not o'erthrown, but unregarded now" (l. 179). The convoluted sentence that separates verb from subject by sixteen lines, and fills those lines with appositives and subordinations galore, brings the play to an end by affirming the fact as well as the principle of aesthetic transformation. People and society have replaced their foul disguises, their ugly masks, with the radiant truth that burns beneath: "The painted veil . . . is torn aside" (ll. 190–92), and "The loathsome mask has fallen" (l. 193). A deliberately theatrical metaphor carries the weight of Shelley's transformation scene. What exists is what is *regarded;* when the old order is no longer witnessed, it no longer has force to threaten or control.

That the emblems of tyranny are merely "unregarded" rather than overthrown indicates not the airy Platonism of which Shelley has been accused, with reason, ever since Mary Shelley's note ("Shelley believed that mankind had only to will that there should be no evil, and there would be none"), but the deeper sense that a political revolution against Jupiter that resorts to the techniques of force and fraud would merely replicate the tyranny it sought to undo.[33] As Blake well knew, Orc and Urizen form a pair entwined in each other's destinies, and even Jupiter recognized in Demogorgon a progeny that would fall with him ("We two will sink in the wide waves of ruin / Even as a vulture and a snake outspent / Drop, twisted in inextricable flight" [3.1.71–73]). In order to avoid becoming Jupiter, the next order must evade everything that belongs to his patriarchal realm. It must not resort to force or violence, to action of any sort. The only genuine revolution is spiritual, and for Shelley, we might observe, "spiritual" and "aesthetic" seem synonymous. He maintains an aristocrat's belief in the innate superiority of certain states, places, and persons in order to sanction his belief in the saving grace and graceful salvation of pastoral landscape and poetry. To the radical aristocrat, a passion for reforming the world involves improving its taste and transforming its politics into spectacle.[34]

Excepting "Rosalind and Helen," subtitled "A Modern Eclogue," the title poem of Shelley's 1819 volume, and certainly one of the worst poems ever written by a major poet, *Adonais* is the most conventionally pastoral of Shelley's poems, in spite of the inventive changes it works on the tradition. These poems share at least one major feature in addition to exemplifying Shelley's continual stylistic experimentation: they both presuppose a sense of identity that is twinned rather than single. In this regard they maintain the social dimension of poems otherwise diverse, like *Prometheus Unbound* and "Euganean Hills." "Rosalind and Helen" is cast as a narrative dialogue in which the two friends tell their lengthy, confusing, and preposterous tales of woe to each other while a narrator occasionally interrupts to locate the characters and their stories in a pseudo-Wordsworthian vein. The story is action-packed, but great changes occur suddenly and causelessly, or are merely reported. Shelleyan motifs—atheism, incest, love, murder, revenge, drowning, illegitimacy—abound with predictable violence. After the two friends rehearse their autobiographies, we learn that henceforth they will live together as sisters in their pastoral retreat by Lake Como, having escaped from domestic tragedy and social abuse; their two children will grow up together and marry.[35]

"Rosalind and Helen" contains a density of narrative detail by which Shelley packs the substance of a pathetic romance into the form of a pastoral dialogue. *Adonais* accumulates the conventional tropes of pastoral elegy in order to commemorate Keats and to prepare Shelley, as his bene-ficiary, for his own deathly salvation. Many of these tropes might encourage a view of pastoral as the preeminent genre of doubleness, for example, the dialogues or singing contests that fill the eclogues of Theocritus and Virgil as well as those of their modern descendants, and the aural echoes and other sorts of mirroring that inhabit the traditional pastoral landscape. Whether as nostalgic glances toward a golden age or proleptic images of a utopian ideal, pastoral poems unavoidably concern themselves with themes and images of origins and destinations, and in Shelley's elegy for Keats the question of both beginnings and endings is entwined with the poet-narrator's concern for his own vocational and personal destiny. Within this destiny the poet's passivity—call it inaction, weakness, or indolence—overcomes all aspects of the will.

The tropes of Virgilian pastoral provide important precedents, although not genuine sources, for Shelley's poem.[36] Aside from the obvious pastoral tropes adumbrated by critics such as Renato Poggioli and Thomas Rosen-meyer, Shelley might have found congenial the way Virgilian pastoral (especially Eclogues 1, 4, and 9) occasionally touches on public and political issues; its interest in issues of ownership (Eclogues 1 and 3); its use of the catalogue as structural organization (2 and 6); the amoebean singing contests that often end mysteriously or arbitrarily (3, 5, and 7); and perhaps, above all, the Virgilian habit of construing *otium* as a condition preferable to heroism, to action of any kind, especially in Eclogue 4, where even reading leads to heroic aspiration tainted by sin, and where masculine aspiration is always suspect. The combination of ownership (in life) and passivity (in death) marks the Daphnis elegy (Eclogue 5) as one that Shelley might have found persuasive, especially the aesthetic encomium inscribed on Daphnis' tomb ("formosi pecoris custos, formosior ipse") and the way Daphnis "marvels" at the beauty of the heaven to which he has been translated. The passivity of the miraculous child (Eclogue 4), for whom the earth gives its bounty untilled, and the invitations to sit in the shade and observe, rather than take part in, a singing contest (Eclogue 7), remind us that pastoral *as a genre* sanctifies the condition of watching, of *being* an audience, at the same time that it establishes connections among artists, the living with the dead, the present with the absent.

This is especially true in Eclogue 10, where the human and the inanimate worlds alike respond to the plight of lovesick Gallus. "Neget quis carmina Gallo?" asks Virgil, the precursor to Milton's "Who would not sing for Lycidas?" To which he notes, "[N]on carmina surdis, respondent omnia silvae." And just as Shelley, at the end of *his* poem, goes off heroically to imitate and follow the fate of Adonais, so Virgil, at the close of Eclogue 10, gives us a double perspective on the limitations as well as the consolations of pastoral. Inflamed and thwarted by love, Gallus wishes to exchange his fealty to one god for an attachment to a more daring one. All the while ruefully admitting that love conquers all ("omnia vincit Amor: et nos cedamus Amori"), he would more happily serve a sterner master ("nunc insanus amor duri me Martis in armis / tela inter media atque adversos detinet hostis"). But the Virgilian speaker offers a second perspective following Gallus' plangent self-abnegation. Sitting idle beneath a tree, the poet–singer confesses his love for Gallus but then gently turns away, suggesting that danger lurks even in the shade. The motif of exit here— prelude to the successively more daring leave-takings at the ends of "Lycidas" and *Adonais*—is both a homecoming for the poet's flocks and a suggestion of some possible longer flight for the poet himself:

> surgamus: solet esse gravis cantantibus umbra,
> iuniperi gravis umbra, nocent et frugibus umbrae.
> ite domum saturae, venit Hesperus, ite capellae.

(Let's leave: the shade is usually harsh for singers. The juniper's shade is also harmful; and shadows damage the grain. Go home, my well-fed goats, the evening star is rising. Go.)

The peculiarities of this ending raise many questions. Specifically, what are we to make of the respective fates of Gallus and his narrator–friend? Who is going where? Who is staying? What satisfactions and what dangers attend upon staying and going? What solace and what frustrations derive from pastoral performance, and what potentially salutary effects may an audience expect from such laments and commands as mark the end of the last Eclogue?[37] Performance, rather than nature or shepherds or the Empsonian formula of complexity through simplicity, may be the defining trope of all pastoral.[38] It certainly might explain Shelley's interest in how all of his pastoral predecessors, beginning with Virgil, developed ways of observing—both taking part in and witnessing—a pastoral spectacle. The modern pastoral artist exaggerates the leisure of performance that we find inherent in his ancient sources.

Shelley may have found in his Latin precursor a sanction for his own radical aesthetic—that is, stylistic and generic—experiments. It is worth pondering why Shelley chose to construct his peculiar pastoral elegy in Spenserian stanzas, conflating as it were his multiple homages to Milton's "Lycidas" within a pseudo-Spenserian allegory containing abstractions as well as the more expected personifications of classic pastoral.[39] To say that the choice of a stanza pays homage to the Keats of "The Eve of St. Agnes" is in part to beg the question; Shelley might have chosen equally well otherwise. It is the sheer artifice of *Adonais* that astonishes. Just as the poet–shepherds can foresee their fate in Adonais' (l. 300), Shelley tackles his subjects through the voice and styles of others. The first pastoral elegy, practically the first major elegy of any sort since "Lycidas," the poem constitutes a stylistic palace of art. No other poem since Milton's elegy to King so flagrantly, deliberately espouses the capacity of pastoral to absorb multiple influences, to engage in contests with several defunct singing masters, and to submit the variousness of Virgilian pastoral to the demands of a modern temperament that is at once aristocratic and theatrical.

Everything in Keats's life, according to Shelley's preface, has been scripted. Of Keats he says that "the poor fellow seems to have been hooted from the stage of life," and of Joseph Severn, Keats's deathbed companion, that "I should have been tempted to add my feeble tribute of applause to the more solid recompense." Such (dare we say) seriously playful artifice seems to have escaped the notice of the three contemporary reviews, two hostile and one appreciative, that treated the poem, although the vitriolic attack in *Blackwood's* at least implicitly understood the fictiveness of pastoral elegy by developing a satiric series of whining, bathetic parodies with which to cudgel both Keats and Shelley.[40]

With all its artifice, the intentionally heightened pathos of the poem allows Shelley to stress a theatrical, rather than a "merely" pastoral, event. The processions, abstractions, roles, doublings, and masks that dominate the elegy's enactments of grief betray an exaggerated self-consciousness even in this most self-conscious of artificers. The famous self-depiction in the middle of the poem (which one critic labels "virtually a caricature of grief")[41] suggests, among other things, the distance of this poem from "Lycidas" and other pastoral elegies, in the (only) apparently confessional mode with which the poet introduces himself:

> Midst others of less note, came one frail Form,
> A phantom among men; companionless
> As the last cloud of an expiring storm
> Whose thunder is its knell; he, as I guess,
> Had gazed on Nature's naked loveliness,
> Actaeon-like, and now he fled astray
> With feeble steps o'er the world's wilderness,
> And his own thoughts, along that rugged way,
> Pursued, like raging hounds, their father and their prey.
>
> (st. 31)

This complex piece of self-aggrandizement and self-diminution makes of Shelley an extreme version of the self with which his readers were familiar in poems as early as "Alastor" and as recent as "Epipsychidion." Barely material ("frail," "phantom," "last cloud"), anonymous, outcast, and pursued, he reaches a level both abstractly Platonic ("Form") and mythically Ovidian ("Actaeon-like"). The self is simultaneously extended and reduced in order to create a role at once larger and smaller than an ordinary human one. For his sin or error, he is punished; for thinking, he is pursued by the thoughts he has created. He is bound on a wheel of his own devising.

Whereas earlier the thoughts of Adonais were said to mourn *their* father (st. 14), now mental productions return to haunt and torment. The contrast exists together with the implicit comparison.

Amid the procession of mourners, Shelley himself embodies those personified abstractions that make the Spenserian stanza an appropriate vehicle for the conveyance of lament:

> A pardlike Spirit beautiful and swift—
> A Love in desolation masked;—a Power
> Girt round with weakness;—it can scarce uplift
> The weight of the superincumbent hour;
> It is a dying lamp, a falling shower,
> A breaking billow;—even whilst we speak
> Is it not broken? On the withering flower
> The killing sun smiles brightly: on a cheek
> The life can burn in blood, even while the heart may break.

> His head was bound with pansies overblown,
> And faded violets, white, and pied, and blue;
> And a light spear topped wih a cypress cone,
> Round whose rude shaft dark ivy tresses grew
> Yet dripping with the forest's noonday dew,
> Vibrated, as the ever-beating heart
> Shook the weak hand that grasped it; of that crew
> He came the last, neglected and apart;
> A herd-abandoned deer struck by the hunter's dart.

> (st. 32–33)

Far from being the gratuitous piece of self-pity that an anti-Romantic reader might deem it, Shelley's self-presentation makes the strongest case for the inevitable complexities of his pastoral experiments. Things are seldom what they seem: strength is masked by weakness, love by desolation. The self is dehumanized and simultaneously elevated to become a "Spirit," a "Power," an "it." The central metaphors ("dying lamp," "falling shower," "breaking billow") reduce the subject to a man-made or natural object, while the final metaphor and synecdoche ("withering flower," "a cheek") return it to semihuman status.

The panoramic experiment continues most daringly in stanza 33, where Shelley himself becomes, through a sequence of metonymic substitutions, the floral procession of conventional elegy. Not only does the mourning self turn into the apparatus of mourning; Shelley also gently inscribes himself within Keats's own poems, or inscribes Keats's within his own, by his reference to the "fast fading violets"—now thoroughly faded—of the "Ode to a Nightingale." Shelley's complex fate, twinned with Keats's, has begun to emerge. Just as he is *of* a crew but *apart* from it, and just as he is simultaneously weak and strong, so Shelley is also both subject and object. The curious syntax depicting the thyrsis he carries exemplifies the dilemma of this pseudo-Dionysos, part victim, part deity. "A light spear . . . / vibrated": the verb is deliberately distanced from its noun in order to heighten suspense, and the subsequent clause ("as the ever-beating heart") continues the sense of tenuous connections, this time depicting the movement of power from heart to hand to shaft. Heart shakes hand; hand grasps spear; spear vibrates. The verbs diminish from transitive to intransitive ones, as the human figure, by stanza's end, has been himself victimized and reduced as the "herd-abandoned deer struck by the hunter's dart." The return from Dionysos to Actaeon, and *his* metamorphosis into a deer, has been completed, and along with this there continues the identification with Adonais, the poet who earlier was described as "pierced by the shaft which flies / In darkness" (ll. 11–12).

The sense of an identity both separate and social reaches its climax in the last stanza of Shelley's self-portrait:

> All stood aloof, and at his partial moan
> Smiled through their tears; well knew that gentle band
> Who in another's fate now wept his own;
> As in the accents of an unknown land,
> He sung new sorrow; sad Urania scanned
> The Stranger's mien, and murmured: "who art thou?"
> He answered not, but with sudden hand
> Made bare his branded and ensanguined brow,
> Which was like Cain's or Christ's—Oh! that it should be so!
>
> (st. 34)

The revelation of Shelley as sacrificial outcast (as well as potential savior) through the sudden, heightened melodrama of self-exposure is perhaps less important than the stanza's opening lines, which place him as both tangential and central to the process of mourning and to the procession of mourners. Whereas for three stanzas he has been the separate creature, now it is all the others who stand "aloof." Familiarity mingles with foreignness: Shelley sings new sorrow in unknown accents, which everyone seems to understand. Most curious of all is the grammatical collapse surrounding the enjambment between lines 2 and 3. By omitting a specific pronomial direct object ("that gentle band knew *him* who wept his own fate through another's"), the clause reduces the distance among the various mourners and the objects of their laments. Everyone within the band weeps his own fate in weeping for Adonais. The individual and the collective stand sentinel together in the "who" that straddles the two lines.

By focusing on Shelley's self-portrait I have tried to show how his separation from the procession of mourners strangely cements his connections with it, just as the paradoxes of his strength-in-weakness complicate our sense of his role in the poem. Allegory, by one way of construing it, is at least etymologically a way of saying one thing *through* another, and by weeping for Adonais, or by adopting Keats's language, Shelley has created a vehicle for his own presentation. Such doubling seems inevitable in both allegory and pastoral, and consequently justifies Shelley's choice of the Spenserian stanza. Representation through reflection is the common coin of allegory; a sense of universal destiny that of any elegy; echoes and reflections the constitutive tropes of pastoral. For Shelley in *Adonais* these translate into theatrical representations of self and of human thought. The procession of human mourners in the middle of the poem merely repeats, after all, an earlier procession (st. 9–14), in which Keats's flocks, now construed as his "Dreams" and "Splendours" ("All he had loved, and moulded into thought," [l. 118]), come forth to lament the loss of their maker:

> And others came . . . Desires and Adorations,
> Winged Persuasions and veiled Destinies,
> Splendours, and Glooms, and glimmering Incarnations
> Of hopes and fears, and twilight Phantasies;
> And Sorrow, with her family of Sighs,
> And Pleasure, blind with tears, led by the gleam
> Of her own dying smile instead of eyes,
> Came in slow pomp;—the moving pomp might seem
> Like pageantry of mist on an autumnal stream.
>
> (st. 13)

Just as later the members of the human community mourn their common lot by mourning Adonais, so in stanza 10 one of Adonais' dreams mistakes one of her own tears for a sign of life from the poet's corpse. Mistaken identities and confused alliances are as much a part of Shelley's pastoral as of Spenserian allegory. If outer and inner dimensions can exchange places—Keats's thoughts both past and as yet unborn participate in lamenting his demise—so can abstraction assume a human role in the dramatic pageant. Thus, Urania represents not only a mighty mother—a heavenly Venus and a Miltonic muse—but also the presiding saint of thought itself. She is the allegorical personification of allegory, of poetic figuration, come forth to mourn the death of him who would rightly do her service:

> *He* will awake no more, oh, never more!
> "Wake thou," cried Misery, "childless Mother, rise
> Out of thy sleep, and slake, in thy heart's core,
> A wound more fierce than his with tears and sighs."
> And all the Dreams that watched Urania's eyes,
> And all the Echoes whom their sister's song
> Had held in holy silence, cried "Arise!"
> Swift as a Thought by the snake Memory stung,
> From her ambrosial rest the fading Splendour sprung.
>
> (st. 22)

Although much of this must have seemed, even to Shelley himself, like an archaic exercise by which to externalize thought, his own self-consciousness about his procedure becomes part of the spectacular drama: "Of what scene [are we] / The actors or spectators?" he has just asked (st. 21), and the whole process of figuration throughout *Adonais* has implicitly made a similar demand. The pastoral frame permits through its very fictiveness the doubled perspective of *observing* (as I have noted earlier) as both participation and witnessing. There is no better way to enjoy such doubleness than through the medium of a self-conscious drama in which one is aware of playing a part, watching oneself as a functionary in a larger scene.[42]

Shelley places himself at the center of his poem but keeps himself distanced from the other mourners at the funeral, and he also maintains a Cartesian fiction concerning the self-seeing and the self-seen; thus the phrase "he, as I guess" (st. 31), with its self-portrayal beneath the transparent fiction of objectivity. Such self-presentation opens the larger question of the progressive treatment of the poem's eponymous hero and that of its narrator as the latter comes to imitate and thereby to replace the former as the main character in the pastoral drama. What Dr. Johnson condescendingly referred to as the fiction of pastoral has at least one important connection to the reality of death, sacrificial or otherwise: both death and pastoral make of a human subject a passive object of or within a greater spectacle. The actor cons a part that has been written for him. Not only does Adonais gradually disappear from the poet's focus during the last third of his poem, as grief is replaced by consolation among the living, but Keats himself is gradually subsumed by passive constructions, while Shelley, who has so far virtually forsworn mentioning himself, comes to the front as joint subject and object of the action.

For Shelley, Romantic indolence means absorption within either a domestic economy or a cosmic one. Thus the aristocratic, Epicurean *ataraxia* in "Euganean Hills," "Epipsychidion," and *Prometheus Unbound,* and the last lyrics to Jane Williams. In *Adonais* both Keats and Shelley are passively distilled into finer versions of themselves. As the poem rises to its triumphal close in stanzas 38–55, Shelley converts Adonais' passivity into a virtue. Transitive verbs, even active forms of verbs, essentially vanish, and their subject along with them. Thus:

> Our delight is fled . . .
> He wakes or sleeps . . .
> He is sitting . . .
>
> (st. 38)

> He is not dead, he doth not sleep—
> He hath awakened from the dream of life . . .
>
> (st. 39)

> He is made one with Nature: there is heard
> His voice in all her music . . .
> He is a presence to be felt and known . . .
>
> (st. 42)

> He is a portion of the loveliness
> Which once he made more lovely. . .
>
> (st. 43)

Adonais significantly evaporates from the poem at this point. Equally important is the fact that within these pivotal stanzas active verbs are kept to a minimum: "He has outsoared the shadow of our night" (st. 40) is the notable exception to the rule. Another active construction is mitigated by its being negative: he "now can never mourn / A heart grown cold" (st. 40). And in the dependent clause from stanza 43, action has been relegated to a past tense. Finally, the last active construction for Adonais returns him (and us) to the theatricality of death:

>   he doth bear
> His part, while the one Spirit's plastic stress
> Sweeps through the dull dense world, compelling there,
> All new successions to the forms they wear;
> Torturing th'unwilling dross that checks its flight
> To its own likeness, as each mass must bear . . .
>
> (st. 43)

Adonais makes a powerful reappearance in the poem's final stanzas as an enticement to Shelley to meet him: "'Tis Adonais calls" (l. 476) and, at last, "The soul of Adonais, like a star, / Beacons from the abode where the Eternal are" (ll. 494–95). Having successfully borne his own part, Adonais directs others, aurally and visually, calling and beaconing to Shelley, who has now assumed the role of hero in a drama of passivity.

Shelley's own appearance in the poem has been late in coming, and reticent all along, in spite of the classic passive-aggressive performance he gives in stanzas 31–34. The poem has kept first-person pronouns to an absolute minimum until the very end. (Likewise, in "Euganean Hills," first-person deictics in the opening 285 lines are minimal.) Shelley's personal pronouns would themselves make an interesting subject of study; as he admits in *On Life,* they are "grammatical devices invented simply for arrangement, and totally devoid of the intense and exclusive sense usually attached to them."[43] For so deeply personal a poem, by a poet normally thought so monomaniacal, *Adonais* is curiously devoid of first-person deictics. We have only the opening "I weep for Adonais," the formulaic "Ah woe is me!" (l. 154), the self-dividing and self-referential "he, as I guess" (l. 274), a brief homage to Leigh Hunt ("Let me not vex . . ." [l. 315]), plus a handful of expected first-person plural phrases that contrast Adonais with *our* collective plight. By stanza 47 Shelley has shifted gears, now addressing his imagined self in the second person: "Who mourns for Adonais? oh come forth / Fond wretch!" This self-distancing continues through stanza 51, reaching a momentary stay as Shelley objectifies the specific loss of his own infant son, and in one stanza equates second- and first-person-plural pronouns:

> Here pause: these graves are all too young as yet
> To have outgrown the sorrow which consigned
> Its charge to each; and if the seal is set,
> Here, on one fountain of a mourning mind,
> Break it not thou! too surely shalt thou find
> Thine own well full, if thou returnest home,
> Of tears and gall. From the world's bitter wind
> Seek shelter in the shadow of the tomb.
> What Adonais is, why fear we to become?

The rhetorical question prepares the ground not only for the suicidal movement of the last four stanzas but also, and more particularly, for Shelley's new self-involvement within the drama. The combination of intense pronominal shifting, scriptural allusiveness, and a climactic sense of Shelley as both hero and victim, subject and object, radically changes the very nature of pastoral elegy, as has long been observed, but perversely honors the letter and the spirit of the genre as well.

From the memorable contrast between heaven's light and earth's shadow ("The One remains, the many change and pass"), life's "dome of many-coloured glass" and "the white radiance of Eternity" (ll. 460–63), through to the end of the poem ("The soul of Adonais, like a star, / Beacons from the abode where the Eternal are" [ll. 494–95]), these stanzas may be construed as an experiment in the nature of singularity and plurality. As such they remind us of the radically extensive view of the self that exists everywhere in Shelley's pastoral poetry, stressing as it always seems to do the community of selfhood rather than its isolated or atomic existence. At the start of stanza 52, white radiance figures forth divine wholeness, while the prismatic kaleidoscope of colors stands for division and impure plenitude. By the end, however, and in something of a reversal, Adonais becomes both a terminal beacon *and* one among many in the heavenly abode of the (plural) Eternal. Just as the "solemn troops and sweet societies / That sing" *entertain* Lycidas as they receive him into a highly social and theatrical version of heaven, so here Shelley mitigates the heroic dangers of following Adonais' beacon with a sense of the receptive community that awaits at the adventure's end.

The divine parody of the marriage ceremony—"No more let Life divide what Death can join together (l. 477)—makes of the suicidal compact with Adonais a heavenly wedding. Under the apparent guise of escape, Shelley is seeking here the same kind of community he sought with Emilia Viviani and his other intimate friends at the end of "Epipsychidion." (In stanza 54 the ongoing allusions to the beginning of Dante's *Paradiso* support the sense of aristocratic privilege with which Shelley toyed in his earlier poem.) More important is the deliberate, almost willful, perversity of the pronomial confusion that attends Shelley's depiction of "that sustaining Love"

> Which through the web of being blindly wove
> By man and beast and earth and air and sea,

> Burns bright or dim, as each are mirrors of
> The fire for which all thirst; now beams on me . . .
>
> > (ll. 481–85)

Each thing *is* a mirror of the fire for which *all things* thirst, although in differing degrees. Everything longs for what it most resembles, not (as in the Spenserian and Platonic "Sensitive Plant") for what it lacks. Opposites do not attract; resemblances do. Thus the importance for Shelley of echoes, mirrors, incest, and of his stylistic preference for strings of similes: what things have in common is ultimately more important, as earnests of community, than what separates them. Even within this stanza the relationship of singleness and plurality suggested by "each are" merely reverses an earlier pattern, in which Shelley piles appositions together to suggest plurality and then reduces them to singleness:

> That Light whose smile kindles the Universe,
> That Beauty in which all things work and move,
> That Benediction which the eclipsing Curse
> Of birth can quench not, that sustaining Love
> Which through the web of being . . .
>
> > now beams on me . . .
> >
> > (ll. 478–85)

Things in common—the designated Light, Beauty, Benediction, and the ultimate Love—*are* the same, as the several nouns subside or build to a single verb, uniting them under the control of the Love that is the final name for all of them.

In the drama of syntax, apposition, and agreement that reaches its climax in the poem's last two stanzas, Shelley as hero comes to center stage, in several figurative ways. The lines just quoted from stanza 54 submit him to the scrutiny of the "beams" of love, spotlighting him as it were for his future role in the movement of discovery and adventure he may yet follow. The final stanza puts him on an equal footing with Adonais, but at the same time he is all object, submitting himself passively to those forces beyond his control and his will:

> The breath whose might I have invoked in song
> Descends on me; my spirit's bark is driven,
> Far from the shore, far from the trembling throng
> Whose sails were never to the tempest given;
> The massy earth and sphered skies are riven!
> I am borne darkly, fearfully, afar:
> Whilst burning through the inmost veil of Heaven,
> The soul of Adonais, like a star,
> Beacons from the abode where the Eternal are.

Active participation is relegated to past creative activity ("I have invoked in song"); everything else related to the subject of the lines makes him either a grammatical object ("Descends on me") or the subject of a passive verb ("is driven," "borne darkly"). Separating himself from *hoi polloi* as he had done in "Epipsychidion," Shelley embarks not only upon an ultimate, internalized quest romance, but also upon a quest for the final pastoral *locus amoenus*.[44] Having shunted aside the "unprofitable strife" (l. 346) of secular *negotium*, he now follows Keats into the perfect pastoral of death. "Seek[ing] shelter in the shadow of the tomb" (l. 458), he passes beyond all effort and even will as he renders himself up, first to the beams of love, then to the fearful waves of transcendence that bear him onward and upward to a new home among the Eternal. As the literary vehicle of such transport, pastoral—with its conventional artifice, its theatricality, and its ventriloquisms—has served him powerfully.

6

Our American Cousins

We do not know today whether we are busy or idle. In times when we thought ourselves indolent, we have afterwards discovered, that much was accomplished, and much was begun in us. All our days are so unprofitable while they pass, that 'tis wonderful where or when we ever got anything of this which we call wisdom, poetry, virtue.

—Emerson, "Experience"

What was the fate of indolence after the English Romantics took hold of it? One might be tempted to continue the study of the theme, and the tropes, of indolence through the languors of Tennyson's Lotos-Eaters, the world-weary measures of Swinburne, the aestheticism of William Morris's "idle singer of an empty day," the civilized nostalgia of *A Shropshire Lad*, or the decadents of the eighties and nineties who paved the way for Yeats. A more interesting path would involve a trans-Atlantic crossing. In the poetry of Whitman and Frost we may discover the truest confirmation of the legacy of the English Romantics. These two utterly different poets confirm and transform all of the positive manifestations of indolence that I have examined in the preceding chapters: the symbiotic connections between work and play; the pleasures of mere looking; the physiological and psychological grounds for relaxing contemplation; the reconfigurings of pastoral as a genre; and the elevation of "the aesthetic" to the level of a necessity. Although they lack, understandably, Shelley's aristocratic pretensions as well as Coleridge's numbing dejection and Oblomovian torpor, Whitman with his loafing and cruising, and Frost with his insistence on the play element in labor prolong Romantic indolence in all its majesty. The American lilies of the field toil not, but neither are they entirely idle.

This does not mean that what we characterize as fin-de-siècle malaise has no American manifestations:

> There is no dearer lover of lost hours
> Than I.
> I can be idler than the idlest flowers;
> More idly lie
> Than noonday lilies languidly afloat,
> And water pillowed in a windless moat,
> And I can be
> Stiller than some gray stone
> That hath no motion known.
> It seems to me
> That my still idleness doth make my own
> All magic gifts of joy's simplicity.[1]

We might easily dismiss S. Weir Mitchell's "Idleness" as a tired rendition of an old theme, did it not come from the pen of the man who proposed the rest cure for neurotics of both sexes, and who refers in another poem to "the noble waste of lazy hours."[2] Laziness and waste in his dictionary have entirely positive, Emersonian valences, with none of the puritanical distrust of idleness that we might expect, and little of the sybaritic, self-indulgent escapism that we find in poems by his English contemporaries. The "gray stone" echoes, of course, Wordsworth's "Expostulation and Reply," but by way of the intermediary of Emerson's "Waldeinsamkeit":

> See thou bring not to field or stone
> The fancies found in books;
> Leave authors' eyes, and fetch your own,
> To brave the landscape's looks.
>
> Oblivion here thy wisdom is,
> Thy thrift, the sleep of cares;
> For a proud idleness like this
> Crowns all thy mean affairs.[3]

"Noble waste" (which certainly sounds like an equivalent of *pourriture noble,* the noble rot needed for a rich, sweet wine) and "proud idleness" echo Wordsworth's "majestic indolence" more straightforwardly than anything in the poetry of his English followers. Emerson requires us to put down the dull and endless strife of books and goes Wordsworth one better: Emerson equates the *appearance* of the still earth with its animated "looking" at his interlocutor. It is a daring and a brave thing to be able to respond to the landscape's looks. One must have eyes with which to see and to know that one is being looked at. Their American cousins and heirs appropriated and transformed the legacy of the English Romantics.

Walt Whitman did not invent loafing, but it is the one word that most readers remember from *Leaves of Grass*. He did not invent the word, either, though it seems to come from the period of his youth and is more distinctly American than British.[4] Whitman loafed first and loafed loudest. At the end of the century Santayana characterized his mind as "a rich, spontaneous, absolutely lazy fancy," with a technique apposite to his temperament: "[A] multiplicity of images pass before him and he yields himself to each in turn with absolute passivity."[5] Indolence functions as the paradoxical mainspring of Whitman's actions, just as his "absolute passivity" results in the heroic assertions of his accumulated lists. Whitman learned the art of spectatorship—overt looking as well as covert voyeurism—from Coleridge and Keats, and his passive reflection (in both senses) of others is his version of Wordsworth's Lockean empiricism. In the apparent waste of loafing he discovers the bounty of his own productions.[6]

The youthful Whitman—whether posing or in earnest—made a good case for the "genuine, inbred, unvarying loafer . . . your calm, steady, philosophick son of indolence" in a trifling piece of early journalism that calls for "a nation of loafers," a political party to represent their best interests, and even a landscape appropriate to their needs: "Imagine some distant isle inhabited altogether by loafers. Of course there is a good deal of sunshine, for sunshine is the loafer's natural element. All breathes peace and harmony."[7] This twenty-year-old flaneur sounds a distinctly un-English note; he gives us no pastoral shade here, no crepuscular sadness, no shame or hiding. This is a full-bodied, robustly self-conscious American idleness that parades its own virtues assertively and unneurotically. Certainly Whitman absorbed some of the ideas of Charles Fourier (even if at second hand through Margaret Fuller, Horace Greeley, and the enterprise of Brook Farm), central to which was the hope that play might save society from the numbing despair of the industrial revolution. But Whitman's commitment to loafing had a somatic basis even before any political or ideological ones; a recent biographer has noted "his luxuriating, easeful body, tending to voluptuousness," and additionally refers to Whitman's placing a photograph of himself beside one of William Cullen Bryant and asking Horace Carpenter whether "this loafer, this lubber, could ever be transmuted into that gentleman?"[8]

Whether flirting with his readers or spying unseen on the people of his world, Whitman lifts the role of spectator to dramatic heights. In this act, composed in equal parts of the aesthetic and the erotic, he clearly moves beyond both Coleridge and Keats, and in the passiveness with which he augments his identity, accumulating everything within him, he likewise elevates Wordsworth's empiricism in unprecedented ways. "There Was a Child Went Forth" is in this regard the quintessential Whitman poem, a list of all those things and persons that the child first perceives and then becomes. Ego formation is essentially passive. Like a phantom, absorbed,

arrested, or curiously floating, the Whitmanesque self both contains multitudes, as he puts it with bravura, and is contained by them. Never has such
a king of languor composed such a heroic poem.

Even acknowledging the secrecy, reticence, and perpetual self-editing as
the price that Whitman paid for the psychosexual daring of his poem,
readers tend to come away from *Leaves of Grass* with a sense of its author's
grand confidence.[9] Whitman hardly ever expresses guilt or shame about
lolling, loafing, staring, or cruising. He never experiences those admonitory moments by which Wordsworth, to pick a forebear both comparable
and distinct, is educated: encounters with leech gatherer, discharged soldier, starving fisherman. The gazing self in Wordsworth, initially unseen,
steps out to confront the impoverished, pitiable object of his gaze, who
then schools him in human suffering or the facts of economic and political
realities. Whitman simply evades such meetings in the first place, preferring
to address the others in his world from a position of complete safety.[10]
Since he is not a poet of dramatic encounters, Whitman can never be
corrected (although he is fully capable of self-contradiction). The solitary
singer has a monarchic largesse and is, accordingly, never alone. This is due
in part to his passivity, taking all in, and at the same time to the aggressive
and compulsive list making that accumulates a self and a poem by acts of
incorporation. Whitman's "central man," to use Stevens's term, is bodily
rather than political. And the animating force of his body is its stasis. Thus,
the fête champêtre to which Whitman invites his soul in the famous opening of "Song of Myself" represents a reduction of heroic aspiration to
pastoral eroticism (or the conflation of the latter with the former). The
resolute tones of Virgilian epic ("I celebrate . . . and sing") are applied to
the "self," and Virgil's battle theme devolves into a celebration of splendor
in the grass: "I loafe and invite my soul, / I lean and loafe at my ease
observing a spear of summer grass." Whitman moves apparently down-
ward along the generic ladder, even as he invites the soul—the internal, the
feminine, the anima—to join the body—the external, the male, the
writer—in celebration.

Before returning to "Song of Myself," or to any of Whitman's earlier
poems, I want to take a glance at the *terminus ad quem,* the final lyrics in the
Annexes, "Sands at Seventy" and "Good-Bye My Fancy," which critics
usually slight. Here Whitman repays his lifelong debt to the Romantics,
unveiling a resemblance that he had obscured for most of his career. Nowhere do we see so clearly his reliance on deep Romantic, especially Keatsian, tropes. These poems work through accumulation and enumeration,
like the odes to Psyche and Autumn, but without dramatic encounters or
extended meditations. Everything tends to the paratactic, as befits the poet
of the endless list. Indolence is observed and stated rather than enacted:

Not from successful love alone,
Nor wealth, nor honor'd middle age, nor victories of politics or war;
But as life wanes, and all the turbulent passions calm,

As gorgeous, vapory, silent hues cover the evening sky,
As softness, fullness, rest, suffuse the frame like freshier, balmier air,
As the days take on a mellower light, and the apple at last hangs really
    finish'd and indolent-ripe on the tree,
Then for the teeming quietest, happiest days of all!
The brooding and blissful halcyon days!

("Halcyon Days")

Whitman is both a belated Keatsian and a contemporary of Whistler, whose soft-focus impressionism he seems to be imitating here. The framing of the scene, and the replacement of life's masculine, heroic accomplishments by sensuous, mellow abstractions culminate in the antepenultimate line, which equates the moment of perfect growth with absolute laziness. Becoming something of an imagist poet here (as in "Twilight," a three-line miniature depicting the dissolution of day and of self into the apathy of nirvana), Whitman uses his observed data to depict the day rather than himself. Although he claims with heightened, desperate jocularity that he is "so loth to depart! / Garrulous to the very last" ("After the Supper and Talk"), the poems of the two Annexes convey both a slowing down and a depiction of the embryonic possibilities for growth and new beginning. He does not merely wait for death, nor does his physical breakdown portend only life's termination.

In his last two poems, "Unseen Buds" and "Good-Bye My Fancy!," he invokes indolence as the condition that precedes work and life rather than as the reward that follows them. Here is Whitman's true legacy from Keats: the waste that looks like idleness is actually a token of future labors.[11] "Unseen Buds" is entirely fragmentary, a titular subject in the first line developed through participial and other adjectival constructions, but forbidden altogether any verb of action even to the end: "Unseen buds, infinite, hidden well, / . . . Urging slowly, surely forward, forming endless, / And waiting ever more, forever more behind." This eternal vigilance, moving forward to new birth and simultaneously backward to an implied (but surely a falsely imagined) death, belongs to a purgatorial state between two solider ones, as though Whitman had combined Keats's sense of natural growth with the frozen presence of the figures on the Grecian urn, forever young and forever piping. Even the music here, relying on a Romantic mellifluousness that Whitman largely spurned in his earlier poetry, joins ideas through assonance and alliteration: "forward," "forming," "forever more." Earlier ("So Long!" in *Songs of Parting*) Whitman had proclaimed, "I am as one disembodied, triumphant, dead," but especially as death approaches, he tropes it as a transient condition, a way station en route to new birth. (This must be what Lawrence referred to when he called Whitman "a very great post-mortem poet, of the transitions of the soul as it loses its integrity.")[12] His indolence is always restless. Closer to the end such farewells, as in the two poems titled "Good-Bye My Fancy!," accommodate greetings: the *vale* of Whitman's last line ("Good-bye—and hail! my Fancy") itself constitutes an invitation.

These hospitable gestures encourage us to return to the invitations to loaf with which "Song of Myself" begins. Just as the end promises a new beginning, the beginning already contains suggestions of the harvest. Whitman even momentarily assumes the pose of a Keatsian worker–deity when, in part 9 of "Song of Myself," he is "stretch'd atop of the load," riding amid the harvest he has (we assume) participated in. Like Marvell's Damon, Whitman-as-farmhand reaps himself as part of his labors—so much so that at the end of "Song of Myself" Whitman repeats his opening invitation, but with a difference. Now, Walt departs into the air along with the hawk, who has complained "of [his] gab and [his] loitering," and into the ground, where he is subsumed by the elements. He is now the object of our quest:

> Failing to fetch me at first keep encouraged,
> Missing me one place search another,
> I stop somewhere waiting for you.

This game of cosmic hide-and-seek epitomizes Whitman's strategies throughout "Song of Myself": playing peek-a-boo, inviting us to join him in his idling, and then mysteriously evading our grasp. Even his grammar and syntax support the fluidity of his sense of self; the last sentence strings together as equivalent elements two imperatives and one simple declarative, just as it mingles motifs appropriate to epic (the quest as heroic labor) and pastoral (the stasis of mere "waiting").

Whitman's rhetorical and syntactic maneuvers can often catch us off guard, as though he himself has leapt from behind the bushes where he had hidden himself. In part 4, having denied that the "me myself" might be other people, "the fever of doubtful news, the fitful events," Walt places the real self on the periphery:

> Apart from the pulling and hauling stands what I am,
> Stands amused, complacent, compassionating, idle, unitary,
> Looks down, is erect, or bends an arm on an impalpable certain rest,
> Looking with side-curved head curious what will come next,
> Both in and out of the game and watching and wondering at it.

Whitman gives us two views of himself. The first is as the "unitary" (true?) self, the "what I am" apart from the hurly-burly, an aesthete contemplating the comings and goings of others. The essential self has no center; it is all circumference. But the famous last line suggests a duplicity that partially obscures or undoes what precedes it. If he is *both* in and out of the game, he figures as a participant as well as a spectator, like a member of a wrestling tag team. Moreover, the first half of the line is complicated still further by the second half, which ought rhetorically to say something like "and watching and playing at it" in order to keep a parallelism with Whitman's implied doubleness—unless, that is, Whitman wants us to hear the second half of the line as antithetical rather than parallel to the first half, for example, "Although I play the game by coming into and going out of it alternately, I *also* simply stand in the audience as a perpetual spectator." From such passages we may hope for a final balance, but they disorient us, never permitting us certain knowledge of where or when Whitman may reenter the lists from the sidelines. We experience the poem as a sequence of quicksilver moods, the poetic equivalent of those epigrams of Emerson's that are difficult to arrange within a paragraph. "Only a language experiment," Whitman's famous estimate of his poem, means *playing* with the language in order to give the appearance, but perhaps not the essence, of a unified self.

Leaves of Grass variously depicts the rhythms of Whitman's game of spectatorship and sexuality, of passivity and assertion, femininity and masculinity, pastoral and epic, and absorption and projection. "Spontaneous Me" (*Children of Adam*) equates the real self ("lusty lurking masculine poems") with the phallus, currently "drooping shy and unseen." Elsewhere, it's not the tumescent and detumescent phallus that contains Whitman's double focus but the bi-gendered or bisexual nature of his speaker, such as the man–woman figure in the bathing scene of section 11 in "Song of Myself." This figure watches and waits, as does the languorous, metaphorically femininized Coleridge of "The Eolian Harp" and "Dejection: An Ode," and the passive Shelley of "Epipsychidion." The effort "to feel the puzzle of puzzles, / And that we call Being" (section 26) is gamesmanship of the highest order, as the "puzzle" of this line is refigured, in the opening of section 27, as a serious ontological question: "To be in any form, what is that?" Everywhere it comes down to this: Is life a game or different from one? Is the real me a participant or an observer? Along the spectrum from indolence, absorption, and witnessing to activity, assertiveness, and participation, where does Walt Whitman wish to place himself?

Life is a game one observes, in the double sense of watching and performing a ritual. Section 33, the longest in "Song of Myself," starts with an anatomy of indolence:

Space and Time! now I see it is true, what I guess'd at,
What I guess'd when I loaf'd on the grass,
What I guess'd while I lay alone in my bed,
And again as I walk'd the beach under the paling stars of the morning.

There follows a catalogue of Walt's activities—of inspection, visiting, and doing ("I am the man, I suffer'd, I was there")—culminating in a battle scene that features a dying general who heroically urges his comrades to mind the entrenchments. A passionate aria, the entire section starts with loafing and builds toward heroic sacrifice; it combines Keatsian empathy with Shelleyan self-theatricalizing:

Agonies are one of my changes of garments.
I do not ask the wounded person how he feels, I myself become the
  wounded person,
My hurts turn livid upon me as I lean on a cane and observe.

Whitman's enterprise, as a character in his poem and the maker of that poem, involves the simultaneous observation of and participation in a scene whose reality is created and compromised by his relationship to it: "I take part, I see and hear the whole." Likewise, in the later "Song of the Broad-Axe" self-creation and poetic composition (as well as nation building) move from an acknowledgment of quietude ("Resting the grass amid and upon, / To be lean'd and to lean on") to heroic exclamations: "Muscle and pluck forever!"

Looking occupies the middle ground between leaning–loafing and muscular doing. The specularity of "Crossing Brooklyn Ferry," with its equation of the living people Whitman watches on the boat with the generations of gazers and readers to come, hinges on the coincidence of vision ("Just as you look, I look'd") which allies Whitman with prior Romantic poets such as Coleridge ("This Lime-Tree Bower My Prison") and later ones such as Elizabeth Bishop (from "Poem": "Our 'visions' coincided"). Idling, loafing, and peeping have a single purpose—the discovery of the other, the lover—which Alan Helms has referred to as "cruising the reader."[13] This goal is not merely aesthetic, but neither does it preclude the aesthetic. The "faint indirections" ("Among the Multitude") by which Whitman and his reader–lover will recognize each other foretell the modernist insistence on difficulty, allusiveness, and remoteness as constituents of poetic substance. "Cautiously peering, absorbing, translating" ("Out of the Cradle Endlessly Rocking") describes the work of the Whitmanesque self and poet. For Whitman (as in "Sometimes for One I Love") poetry is the sole compensation for unrequited love. We might speculate that all of Whitman's work, even more than that of other artists, constitutes a wish fulfillment. Although we think of him as the poet who speaks on behalf of an entire continent, Whitman was, like Wallace Stevens, a great stay-at-home. His New Orleans trip of 1848, his years in Washington during the Civil War, his excursions to Colorado, Ontario, and Boston (1879–81) represent his only real physical explorations. But like Thoreau, who traveled much in Concord, and like Stevens, who imagined a Europe of the mind, Whitman accumulated in *Leaves of Grass* a history, a travelogue, a diary of imagined activity. Writing was the substitute for physical adventures, whether touristic or erotic.

Multifaceted Whitman greatly contains multitudes and reflects (upon) the scenes he witnesses. Absorption and projection seem, in the end, to be pretty much the same because the self is always and invariably multiple. The child goes forth and "becomes" everything he witnesses. The self accumulates. But it is also existentially alone and isolated. Whitman's sense of speaking for, as well as listening to, all Americans counters his claim of being a watching, waiting, idly loitering, isolated particle. Even indolent loafing exists in two forms, one in solitude, the other in companionship. Loitering alone or lingering with comrades, Whitman learns from the animals, who always exist as ensembles, a collective composure that he lacks in himself: "serene-moving animals teaching content" he calls them in *Drum-Taps*. Whitman can write so movingly about the "dear love of comrades" because he must strive for it, as for an unrealizable goal. At the conclusion of "Song of Myself," when he stops, he stops only for a moment, "waiting for" the fulfillment of desire.

Frost inherited Whitman's need for loafing, but he often called it work, absorbing it more directly into the tradition of pastoral, albeit an American version of that most aristocratic of genres.[14] Whereas Whitman is at heart a modern urban flaneur, the journalist as boulevardier, Frost wears the guise of the country mouse following the rhythms of nature, not those of man. Because American pastoral is democratic, and because *all* pastoral has a social dimension, Whitman's loafing often poses as an invitation. Frost's hospitality ("You come, too") is at its most generous when it appears in those poems that treat the identity of play and work. In "Mending Wall" and "Two Tramps in Mud Time" other people are foils for the poem's speaker; in "Rose Pogonias," "The Tuft of Flowers," and "The Wood-Pile" absent workers have bequeathed a landscape to present admirers. Some poems ("After Apple-Picking," "The Silken Tent") consider only a single subject. In all of these play as work, or play as indolent evasion, comes to signify the stillness and contemplation necessary for the creation or appreciation of art. Rest allows looking; play, a momentary cessation of work or a reimagining of it, is the proof of human freedom. Both result in "the aesthetic," that which we experience in waiting, and in working or playing *deliberately*.

Frost would subscribe in part to Thoreau's famous formulation: "The mass of men lead lives of quiet desperation. . . . A stereotyped but unconscious despair is concealed even under what are called the games and amusements of mankind. There is no play in them, for this comes after work."[15] Some poems, it is true, depict leisure as a release—however troubled—after work ("After Apple-Picking," "Waiting," "A Time to Talk," "The Wood-Pile," "Unharvested"). Just as often, however, Frost's speakers perform their labors for the fun of it as well as for the need to do so. Play and work are simultaneous or equivalent in "Mending Wall," "The Mountain," "A Hundred Collars," "Birches," "A Lone Striker," "Two Tramps in Mud Time," "The White-Tailed Hornet." In all cases, however, work and play exist in a healthy, harmonious relation to each other, whether equated or opposed.

In Frost work partakes of the aesthetic, and dreamy indolence ("The fact is the sweetest dream that labor knows," as he puts it in "Mowing")—or its appearance—is essential to life. Such idling opens up the larger paradox that Frost, as well as other American poets who have inherited the mantle of the Romantics, embodies in his work. We can label it the necessity of the supplement.[16] To be an ornament (as I will suggest in my discussions of "The Investment" and "A Young Birch") is to be in one way inessential and extraneous. But throughout American poetry, in spite of its strongly puritanical and doggedly didactic streak, there flows another current, one that asks us to see the extraneous, the peripheral, the ornamental as the equivalents as well as the opposites of the essential, the central, the necessary. Just as Whitman gives us the "real me," his central man, as a peripheral figure, this aesthetic current depicts art, like play, as both what is *not* required and what is *also* required (as Wallace Stevens puts it, "as a necessity requires"). Contingency heightens our sense of necessity.

Emerson neatly embodies such a paradox in his lines from "The Poet" that immediately follow the oft-quoted formula that "not meters, but a meter-making argument" creates a poem, which is itself "a thought so passionate and alive that like the spirit of a plant or an animal it has an architecture of its own, and adorns nature with a new thing." Emerson's own troping violently mixes metaphors: the poem is both an organism and a constructed artifact. It occupies a site *within* nature, rather like Stevens's jar upon a hill, slightly awkward, out of place, and comic. As an adornment it is at once necessary and supererogatory. It combines the natural (plant or animal), the spiritual indwelling within the natural, and finally the artificial. By the end of the sentence Emerson has rendered the poem as "a new thing" but also in a peculiar way as the creator, or at least benefactor, of that adornment ("it adorns . . . *with*"). This is an odd defense of the place of art. The paradox of the poem as organism and thing, object and benefactor, material and spirit, partakes of the essence of pastoral, the genre that best represents the duplicities of and within art.

In his genial collection of essays on gardening, Michael Pollan mentions the traditional American prejudice against fences, citing as a starting point Anne Bradstreet's English garden ode, which removes the wall, that staple of all European gardens. If, says Pollan, we conceive of land or landscape as moral and spiritual, then "ornamental gardening becomes problematic." In fact, before 1894 no writer on gardening in this country seems to have made mention of either color or fragrance, according to Allen Lacy's anthology *The American Gardener*. Usefulness, political symbolism, and spiritual well-being predominate. The garden was (as it always has been, but under different disguises) a trope of cosmic order: "We gardened for a variety of reasons—moral, spiritual, therapeutic, and economic—but aesthetic pleasure was not one of them." At the end of the book Pollan returns to the same point, the American puritanical aversion to pleasure, here equated with aesthetics, which in landscaping is symbolized by fences: "We . . . still feel uncomfortable talking about aesthetics—about the *look* of our gardens, and how that is achieved."[17]

We have descended from a race of garden destroyers, more at home with the usefulness of agriculture than the elegance of floral borders; even

Thomas Jefferson replaced his ornamentals with fruit-bearing trees. Likewise, we often demand of literature a heightened sense of purpose that ought to transcend the "merely" pleasurable or ornamental.[18] But Frost can have it two ways: this is the poet, after all, whose most famous critical epigram reminds us that a poem begins in delight and ends in wisdom. It is significant that he began writing at exactly the time when, according to Lacy, color and fragrance first entered the garden and gardening literature as organizing principles. As in classic aesthetics the *dulce* and the *utile* coincide. Such a twinning returns me to one of the points in my first chapter, the antagonism in Kant, and within the legacy to Romanticism of Plato and Aristotle, between work and play, craft and art, necessity and freedom, or morality and pleasure. As Frank Lentricchia and, especially, Richard Poirier have pointed out, Frost tears down these particular walls even as he builds up other, perhaps unnecessary fences.[19] Art is the only province in which the law of the excluded middle does not hold sway: a thing can be work and play, x and not-x simultaneously.[20]

At play in the fields of the mind, Frost has democratized the tropes of aristocratic pastoral, the genre that, according to hostile critics, gives pleasure to idle spectators at the expense of actual workers. In the new American version laborer, observer, and fun lover are rolled into the single figure of the working poet. Like Whitman, Frost is both in and out of the game, or in and out of the field where the work–game takes place. But whereas Whitman uses his poetic lists as hymns to passivity, collection, and absorption, and loafing as the means of building a self, Frost either narrates or dramatizes the playfulness of work. Like Whitman, Frost takes up the Romantic trope of looking (not just seeing, but Wordsworth's "I gazed and gazed") to establish contact between person and landscape or person and person. In such looking (as in the early poems "The Vantage Point" and "The Tuft of Flowers" or the late "Two Look at Two") Frost portrays those moments necessary for aesthetic revelation and enjoyment.

Such enjoyment occupies the heart of the matter. Frost's poetry encourages a reconsideration of the relationship of art to life, leisure to ardor, indolence to work. In "The Investment" a hungry worker digging for potatoes is stopped by the sound of a piano coming from an old house "renewed with paint." The scene depicts the rural poverty of both the observer and the observed: "Over back where they speak of life as staying / ('You couldn't call it living, for it ain't')." The music provokes contemplation and questioning:

> All that piano and new paint back there,
> Was it some money suddenly come into?
> Or some extravagance young love had been to?
> Or old love on an impulse not to care—
>
> Not to sink under being man and wife,
> But get some color and music out of life?
>
> (ll. 9–14)

The digger's questions put us in mind of the meanings of "extravagance" for Frost (especially since this is the longest word in the sonnet); in this case it unites the foolishness of the unthinking young with the desperation of the uncaring old. The idioms of the couplet are tense and complementary: "being" (l. 13) can be heard as either participle or gerund, and "get . . . out of life" goes well beyond its colloquial origin in "let's get some fun out of life" to remind us of the work of extraction or excavation that the couple, whether young or old, are presumably engaged in. The work, in other words, is derived *from* life, but it exists in order to embellish life with the aesthetic harmonies of the inessential. An investment is both economic—the principal from which one derives interest—and ceremonial, like an investiture, a laying on of an obligation normally symbolized by some material object (cloak, crown, medallion). The workers add the aesthetic dimension *to* life as a supplement, but they also derive it "out of" life and labor themselves.

I take "The Investment" as a response to "I Wandered Lonely as a Cloud," that earlier Romantic poem about the economic systems of memory and aesthetics. Another relatively obscure poem by Frost, "A Young Birch," which opens the 1942 *Steeple Bush* and makes a didactic statement about aesthetics at a time of international disaster, can be heard as an echo of an even greater range of Romantic aestheticism, ending as it does with what had become after more than a century the cliché of the opening of Keats's *Endymion*. The poem opens as arboreal observation, a study of natural growth: "The birch begins to crack its outer sheath / Of baby green and show the white beneath." Even here we sense an act of dramatic self-exposure, a striptease, contained within the image of tree-as-embryo emerging from its own shell. Soon it will be all white, save for its tuft of "leafy green," an emblem of continuing delicacy, fragility, and simultaneous bravery. It is "the only native tree that dares to lean." Becoming a tree, it also impresses its essence upon any would-be destroyer, as the poem ends with a revelation of this tree's authentic purpose:

> But now at last so obvious a bole
> The most efficient help you ever hired
> Would know that it was there to be admired,
> And zeal would not be thanked that cut it down
> When you were reading books or out of town.
> It was a thing of beauty and was sent
> To live its life out as an ornament.

The ornamental is, in fact, a divine edict, the essence of the tree's life. To cut it down would be an error of judgment, or just a mistake, on the part of the hired help (Frost gets in a sly cut at absentee landlords, gentleman farmers, abstracted or bookish intellectuals, all of whom are often unavailable to witness nature's bountiful presentation). Ornament, in short, is purposefulness.

Frost emphasizes the tree's passiveness (it "was sent") *after* its opening action of self-exposure. Only at the end does it grow into what it was meant to become, an object of pure being, ornamental *and* essential. Frost plays cunningly with his infinitives: sometimes we cannot tell whether he intends purpose or merely result. "It was there to be admired" and "It . . . was sent / To live its life out." By whom? we may legitimately ask. Likewise, we have the discomfiting opening of "The Need of Being Versed in Country Things" ("The house had gone to bring again / To the midnight sky a sunset glow"), and the even more sinister end of "Never Again Would Birds' Song Be the Same" ("And to do that to birds was why she came"). Although the objects in Frost's nature are fully animated, they are also curiously will-less.

The young birch resembles another passive object in Frost's landscape, the unspecified woman who is the subject of "The Silken Tent," a celebration equating pure being, metaphor, and elegant ornamentation with stasis, inaction, and the abandonment of will:

> She is as in a field a silken tent
> At midday when a sunny summer breeze
> Has dried the dew and all its ropes relent,
> So that in guys it gently sways at ease,
> And its supporting central cedar pole,
> That is its pinnacle to heavenward
> And signifies the sureness of the soul,
> Seems to owe naught to any single cord,
> But strictly held by none, is loosely bound
> By countless silken ties of love and thought
> To everything on earth the compass round,
> And only by one's going slightly taut
> In the capriciousness of summer air
> Is of the slightest bondage made aware.

However one may feel about the sexual politics inherent in Frost's depiction of woman, "She" embodies indolence, becoming herself a Spenserian pastoral figure whom surrounding masculine courtiers, the cords, both hold in place and pay homage to. An embodiment of the soul as well as of leisure, she reminds us that freedom itself is always a chosen illusion, that it is contingent on the "slightest bondage" (of body, control, community), of which it is often unaware. The silken tent, that protection from the noonday sun, depends literally on connections to the sometimes capricious will of others. In its swaying and relenting, it lets go its own presumed will to offer us an object of beauty as well as a haven from the sun. Guy lines "merely" (in both the older and newer senses of that word) support it; they frame the female–tent ("it") as if it were a painting. This delicate depiction suggests that we ignore such scaffolding at our own peril. Freedom is only apparent, and the seeming stasis of pure being ("she is") can be rendered only metaphorically ("as in a field"). Finally, the poem asks which is primary, which secondary: the woman who is the grammatical subject but who is never mentioned after her position at the start of the sentence, or the titular tent, which receives the bulk of the attention but which, we tend to forget, exists only as a metaphor of descriptive support for the poem's real subject. Ornament and essence, like the other paired opposites I have mentioned (worship and control, stasis and movement, freedom and contingency, action and indolence) can appear more as synonyms than as antonyms.

As part of his glorying in ornament and leisure, Frost has a powerful feeling for leftovers, for what drops by the wayside, abandoned, forgotten, or unharvested. From early lyrics such as "Rose Pogonias" (with its prayer that "in the general mowing / That place might be forgot") and "The Tuft of Flowers" (in which an unseen mower has apparently spared or ignored "a leaping tongue of flame"), through "The Wood-Pile," to "Unharvested" (with an equivalent prayer: "May something go always unharvested!"), Frost develops a subgenre within the larger pastoral and georgic fields he normally plows. These poems demand neither an end to labor nor a holier-than-thou ecological self-righteousness that puts man and nature everywhere at strife. Rather, they prefer nature—some of it, some of the time—to be left alone, for aesthetic rather than moral or practical reasons. Aesthetic wonder leads to a sudden influx of grace in these chance discoveries, more welcome for having come unsought. Frost's speakers do not strive to find the spared flowers, the unmown meadow, the abandoned and wrapped woodpile. Such striving would constitute willed labor, and it would, more important, rival in a minor key the real labors of the absent, forgetful workers. These poems commemorate places presided over by a tutelary genius of negligence, a cousin, we might say, of idleness. Human forgetfulness and error, not laziness per se, receive Frost's highest praise. Confusion has its purposes, on both the human and the natural planes. "None should mow the grass there / While so confused with flowers" ("Rose Pogonias"): here is literal and figurative confusion overwhelming a human mower and a field of grass. These extraneous, economically useless flowers have inundated and undone a worker and the field in which he labors.

Like art, nature requires labor to render its bounties available. The unseen axeman (in "The Wood-Pile") who mistakenly leaves a cord of maple to sit in the snow-filled woods, where the wandering poet discovers it several years later, does so only because he "lived in turning to fresh tasks" and thus "[c]ould so forget his handiwork on which / He spent himself, the labor of his ax, / And leave it there far from a useful fireplace." Other tasks called him away from this one, the speaker thinks; *we* naturally think of the axeman as a pastoral poet like the Milton of "Lycidas," veering off to "fresh woods and pastures new."[21] His gesture implies a generous wastefulness, but as so often happens in Frost, this apparent dichotomy between purpose and accident, or between use and waste, is undone by the poem's last two lines, where we learn that the woodpile serves a purpose: "To warm the frozen swamp as best it could / With the slow smokeless burning of decay." Frost wants us, I think, to take the ending as a purely ironic comment as well as a deep truth about the usefulness of composting, which nature performs with or without human interference. Man has intervened in nature and has accidentally left behind a marker. Wrapped now by the twining clematis, the woodpile is Nature's gift to herself and to the man who has come upon it. (Compare Thoreau in "House-Warming": "Every man looks at his wood-pile with a kind of affection" [*Walden,* p. 522].) As in "A Young Birch" Frost saves result—if not purpose or intention—for the very end.

Frost keeps finding in will and its opposite a cogent poetic subject. Like labor and fun ("vocation" and "avocation" he calls them in "Two Tramps in Mud Time"), these two are sometimes difficult to disentangle. Frost treats both pairs of opposites in "Birches," an inspired reponse to Wordsworth that brings together the Boy of Winander, the rowboat thief of *The Prelude,* book 1, and the young spoiler of "Nutting" into a single American figure: Huckleberry Finn as caught by Winslow Homer. The young boy plays in nature but seeks to subdue it to his will. Frost calls attention to the ambivalent status of "bending" as both transitive and intransitive. At the beginning ("When I see birches bend to left and right"), the sight of trees bending without apparent cause sets him to wondering. He would "like to think some boy's been swinging them." But then truth breaks in ("with all her matter of fact about the ice storm") and disrupts his dream, which then resumes by reinvigorating the poem's major verb: "I should prefer to have some boy bend them." He wants visible human causation rather than be left, as he was at the poem's start, with a natural effect that only suggests a cause. Frost also wants us to see the boy's action as a powerful act of symbolic castration. His efforts to subdue his father's trees, "[taking] the stiffness out of them" until they hang limp, is Oedipal drama revised for country life. Such play is childhood's serious work. Frost would agree with Thoreau in "What I Lived For" (*Walden,* p. 398): "Children, who play life, discern its true law and relations more clearly than men." The speaker projects a human cause upon the scene and then reimagines himself back into it, and into his own past, hoping to be able to imitate the boy he once was and swing far away from earth, with the proviso that he be able to return. Moving "toward heaven" and then earthward by choice and gravity, riding the tree and being returned by it, the dreaming speaker subjects nature to his will and submits to natural forces. Just as he wishes to return to dreaming from "considerations" (the poem's longest word and the symbol of the burdens of adult consciousness), he also understands that life requires a metronomic rhythm between extremes. Tethering matches extravagance. To "be a swinger of birches" means both to ride and to control them and to be carried by them, to force them up only to be delivered down by them. To exert one's will means knowing when to abandon it.

Frost braces his poems between such tense contraries as these: will and passivity, labor and leisure, even looking and being looked at (as in the remarkable "Two Look at Two"). One of the principles of poststructuralist thought has been the iron rule that binaries always establish hierarchies, but in poetry, at least, this does not necessarily obtain. And it is especially unhelpful in appreciating the particular tendencies in American poetry of the sort I have been examining here, where opposites attract and merge rather than maintain divisions. In Frost, as in Emerson and Keats, indolence comes as a reward or gift after work, but it also prepares the way, as gestation, for work to come. Most of all it can be said to constitute, sometimes invisibly, work itself. Like Wordsworth, Frost hardly ever reckons play as the mortal enemy of adult responsibility or labor. Any critical or philosophical appraisal of life's necessities that fails to account for its supplements cannot be credited as adequate. Need alone, as King Lear puts it, will not explain our nature, behavior, or purposes. Paradoxically, something more is needed. Like the "old, old house renewed with paint" in "The Investment," human beings require a renovation that one might easily mistake for mere decoration. Such renovation preserves (as the paint protects the wood beneath) by laying on something additional to the existing structure.

Another word for such renovating protection is art, and its realm is what we designate "the aesthetic." I have tried in this book to defend this realm by examining its implicit formulations in the work of several major poets, and by connecting it to the general theme of indolence in the work of the Romantics. American poetry of the past one hundred years looks like the natural or inevitable continuation of this work. (This trans-Atlantic crossing should encourage a revision of Harold Bloom's theories of influence for the peculiar reason that separations through nationality, more than those through time and space, tend to diminish rather than augment the possible anxieties of such influence.) Even contemporary poets whom we would not normally think of as Romantic heirs embrace indolence as the sine qua non of work and aesthetics as a portion of ontology.

I give the last word to two contemporary American poets, who do not directly treat indolence per se but who strongly if implicitly argue for the role of the aesthetic as central rather than peripheral to our life. In "Filling Station" Elizabeth Bishop takes a look at a dirty, seemingly squalid, oil-soaked family-run filling station. Her bemused speaker is led to a condition of aesthetic wonder as she observes anomalous details among the gas pumps:

> Some comic books provide
> the only note of color—
> of certain color. They lie
> upon a big dim doily
> draping a taboret
> (part of the set), beside
> a big hirsute begonia.
>
> Why the extraneous plant?
> Why the taboret?

> Why, oh why, the doily?
> (Embroidered in daisy stitch
> with marguerites, I think,
> and heavy with gray crochet.)
>
> Somebody embroidered the doily.
> Somebody waters the plant,
> or oils it, maybe. Somebody
> arranges the rows of cans
> so that they softly say:
> ESSO—SO—SO—SO
> to high-strung automobiles.
> Somebody loves us all.[22]

Bishop leaves her principal question ("Why?") unanswered. It's as if she had broached a serious speculation about the purpose of art but then shunted it aside in favor of a consideration of the art's maker. If we didn't know that Bishop wasn't particularly interested in philosophy, we might suspect her of slyly suggesting Kant's definition of art as purposefulness without purpose: the speaker implicitly realizes that she cannot answer the *why* directly and turns instead to the *who* of the matter. The hand of an unknown but guessable artist belongs no doubt to the absent mother, who is otherwise invisible but for her handiwork. Work and domesticity coincide peculiarly ("Do they live in the station?" the speaker has asked a moment before), just as "the extraneous" turns out to be more than merely frivolous ornamention. Instead, embroidery, supplementing in daisy stitch the living plant beside the table, evinces the work of maternal love.

With hindsight we may realize that Bishop's great theme was not the relationships between travel and domesticity, or North and South, or even the consolations offered to a timid, repressed person by her famous seeing eye. Rather, it is the necessity of the extraneous, the useless. In chapter 1 I quoted Bishop's casual articulation of an *ars poetica*: "What one seems to want in art, in experiencing it, is the same thing that is necessary for its creation, a self-forgetful, perfectly useless concentration."[23] Such concentration informs her late poem "The End of March," in which a rickety cabin by the sea, a "crypto-dream-house," embodies the locus for a life simultaneously indolent and creative:

> I'd like to retire there and do *nothing,*
> or nothing much, forever, in two bare rooms:
> look through binoculars, read boring books,
> old, long, long books, and write down useless notes,
> talk to myself, and, foggy days,
> watch the droplets slipping, heavy with light.
>
> (*Complete Poems,* pp. 179–80)

Do we hear in the last line a recollection of Coleridge's "Frost at Midnight"? I suspect we should. Retirement contains pleasures impossible to realize: Bishop can never reach her dream-house in her walk down the beach, let alone get the chance to inhabit it. Indolence must be worked for.

Purposeless gazing and the making of useless notes may parody the academic life that Bishop was leading at Harvard, unhappily, at the end of her life; they also inspired her finest poems, in *Geography III*. Apparent uselessness may characterize an artist's, or an aesthete's life, but creative rewards derive from labors unwitnessed and perhaps unknown. In "Poem" (also referred to in chapter 1), Bishop rounds at the end to the economic language with which she began. The painted "piece of Bristol board" which brings together "life and the memory of it" becomes "the little that we get for free, / the little of our earthly trust. Not much" (*Complete Poems*, p. 177). Useless, free, unregarded from time to time, but worthless, value-less, meaningless? Bishop refrains from moralizing, but her sense of the artist's effort and labor goes without saying.

In a poem dedicated to Bishop, James Merrill makes a comparable point. The titular hero of "The Victor Dog" has no choice but to endure, revolve, and listen:

> Bix to Buxtehude to Boulez,
> The little white dog on the Victor label
> Listens long and hard as he is able.
> It's all in a day's work, whatever plays.

For such a character work and game coincide; the little fellow "earnestly" pays attention to "whatever plays." Attention has as its reward another kind of attending: he dreams he goes to "the première of a Handel / Opera long thought lost—*Il cane Minore*." The dog is both vanquished and vic-tor, captive and hero, listener and title character:

> Its allegorical subject is his story!
> A little dog revolving round a spindle
>
> Gives rise to harmonies beyond belief,
> A cast of stars. . . . Is there in Victor's heart
> No honey for the vanquished? Art is art.
> The life it asks of us is a dog's life.[24]

This "dog's life" gives a new spin to the old cliché, since the Victor dog neither hunts nor serves. He merely waits and listens; like most cossetted house pets he leads the canine life of Riley and is rewarded for patience by stellification. As Ephraim, Merrill's guardian spirit in the earliest part of *The Changing Light at Sandover,* admonishes his earthly charges, who are about to intervene in heavenly affairs that do not concern them:

> WILL
> U NEVER LEARN LOOK LOOK LOOK LOOK YR FILL
> BUT DO DO DO DO NOTHING.[25]

Looking, listening, and doing nothing: such is the aesthete's labor and at least part of the artist's. The true allegorical subject of "The Victor Dog" is the life of any person dedicated to art, whether as a creator or as an audience. Even in the case of the latter, receptivity demands patience of a high, heroic order. When we least expect it, as Emerson sweetly suggests in "Experience," much *is begun* in us. Such beginnings have little to do with the will, conscious or otherwise. We acquire wisdom, virtue, and especially poetry through the ordeals of our indolence.

Appendix A

Shelley's Last Lyrics

As a continuation of my thoughts on Shelley, I add here a brief commentary on his last lyrics, which have already profited from the attentions of Judith Chernaik, Richard Cronin, Donald Davie, G. M. Matthew, and more recently William Keach.[1] For my purposes the group contains the four poems to Jane Williams ("The Invitation," "The Recollection," "With a Guitar," "The Fair Stars Were Twinkling") plus the thematically and personally related pair "The Serpent Is Shut Out from Paradise," and "Lines Written in the Bay of Lerici." In addition to their expression of Shelley's difficult, intense but generous, and occasionally barely articulable feelings for Jane Williams, and in addition to the "urbanity" that Davie long ago identified as their salient characteristic, these poems elaborate in interesting ways many of the versions of Shelleyan pastoral that I discuss in chapter 5. With their pastoral allusiveness they also embody new but not unexpected versions of Shelleyan or aristocratic indolence, distinct from yet perhaps cousin-german to the other Romantic manifestations of indolence that we have seen in Wordsworthian play, Keatsian watchfulness, and Coleridgean dejection.

Shelley here combines three habits: his enduring interest in role playing; the simultaneously centripetal and centrifugal movements of his desire; and his sophisticated, not to say haughty, sense of entitlement, especially in matters of aesthetic taste. For poems at once so intensely personal, Shelley maintains a curious distance—call it urbanity, politeness, or fear of self-exposure—with regard to both his thematic material and his addressee. A reader has the sense of observing another act in Shelley's "mental theater," with its protagonist donning one mask after another.[2] First he is a courtly Ariel, then the serpent; first a Maying cavalier, then a distanced observer of the happiness of others; first someone on holiday, then, at last and most pathetically, a Coleridgean stay-at-home who watches while others sail off to Cytherea or Elysium. Where *Adonais* unknowingly anticipates Shelley's death by drowning, these last lyrics present an image of a man for whom even the act of being "borne darkly, fearfully afar" demands more will than he can allow himself.

The four longer works which I have already considered—"Euganean Hills," "Epipsychidion," *Prometheus Unbound,* and *Adonais*—all end with the poet–speaker or the Titan–hero among a new community to which he has escaped (cf. "On Life": "Each is at once the centre and the circumference; the point to which all things are referred, and the line in which all things are contained" [*Shelley's Poetry and Prose,* p. 476]). Flinging himself to a point on a perimeter, he establishes there the center of a new circle, in which both a sexual pairing and an elite society stimulate thoughts of pastoral nostalgia and utopian perfectability. The late lyrics, by contrast, surround an absent or inarticulable center. Either "the serpent is shut out from Paradise" and cannot reenter it, or else a moment of shared bliss with Jane Williams, whether real or imagined, literally or only metaphorically erotic, exists as the unspoken hiatus between two poems ("The Invitation" and "The Recollection") which were originally one. Anticipation and memory, in other words, bracket the climactic center from which the reader, perhaps like the newly embarrassed or fragile poet, is excluded. "The Recollection," with its self-naming unique among Shelley's poems, also attests most strongly to the delicacy of his refusals.

Beginning with an invocation to "Memory" to arise to its "wonted work" and to "trace / The epitaph of glory fled" (ll. 1–8), Shelley relives a prior experience by representing it. Tracing the epitaph, however, dims and distances more than it enlivens and reproduces, since the tracing renders but a less visible version of the original experience. Shelley has taken Wordsworth and turned him on his head. In the Wordsworthian myth, the evaporated "glory" of childhood blessedness is replaced by the "abundant recompense" of "the philosophic mind" or the recreative, metaphor-making power that figuratively recaptures past evanescence.[3] The reliving of an original experience, as at the end of "I Wandered Lonely as a Cloud," strengthens and augments an originary one. For Shelley, repetition through the work of memory does no such thing. The legitimacy of hearing "The Recollection" as a response to Wordsworth as much as to the fragile ties of Shelley's marriage in his last months comes from the double allusion to the Intimations Ode: not only "glory fled" but also a "flower beneath [their] feet" suggests the way in which this experience is Shelley's equivalent of a Wordsworthian schema. The beauty of the recollected scene with Jane Williams, depicted in lines 9–80, ends abruptly with a double ruination, one at the time of the original walk (January 2, 1822) and one at the time of composition (February 2).

The seventy intervening lines look like a familiar Shelleyan catalogue. A reflecting *locus amoenus*—"on the bosom of the deep / The smile of Heaven lay"—provides the natural setting for the would-be lovers' own mingling. The "inviolable quietness" (l. 37) is rendered, paradoxically, even more still by the work of the "busy woodpecker." As in "Epipsychidion," sound and silence are harmonious equals. And the lovers' breath, as a corollary to the woodpecker's sound, "made not less / The calm that round us grew" (ll. 39–40). Shelley is not a poet usually given to litotes as a rhetorical device, so the unusual "made not less" suggests a delicate reluctance, or even a fear, to articulate the experience. He remarks the unreality of the event even though its site resembles those of earlier Shelleyan unions:

> There seemed from the remotest seat
>   Of the white mountain-waste,
> To the soft flower beneath our feet
>   A magic circle traced,
> A spirit interfused around
>   A thrilling silent life,
> To momentary peace it bound
>   Our mortal nature's strife;—
> And still I felt the centre of
>   The magic circle there
> Was one fair form that filled with love
>   The lifeless atmosphere.
>
> (ll. 41–52)

The "magic circle traced" around the would-be lovers is as ephemeral as the epitaph that Shelley had earlier ordered to be retraced by memory itself. Its effect, like its peace, is only "momentary," in part because its origin seems to come from without and within. The lovers are "bound" by an "inter-fusing" spirit—interfusing them with each other and with their sur-round—but the "centre" of the circle, the figure of Jane Williams, provides not just a focus but also a causal principle. She, or it, "fill[s] with love" an atmosphere that otherwise would remain lifeless.

Shelley returns in part 4 of his recollection to continue the familiar picture of his standard pastoral pleasance, the mirroring landscape in which he situates the lovers. Every element reflects its opposite; all are equal partners in the whole. The last section, however, essentially undoes all that has gone before:

> Sweet views, which in our world above
>   Can never well be seen,
> Were imaged in the water's love
>   Of that fair forest green;
> And all was interfused beneath
>   With an Elysian glow,
> An atmosphere without a breath,

A softer day below—
Like one beloved, the scene had lent
    To the dark water's breast,
Its every leaf and lineament
    With more than truth exprest;
Until an envious wind crept by,
    Like an unwelcome thought
Which from the mind's too faithful eye
    Blots one dear image out.—
Though thou art ever fair and kind
    And forests ever green,
Less oft is peace in S[helley]'s mind
    Than calm in water seen.

(ll. 69–88)

Shelley's insistent repetition (e.g., the recurrence of "interfused" in line 73, and the earlier "trace," and "magic circle") is as atypical as his litotes. Such moving down previously untrod stylistic paths signals other kinds of uncertainties. Even in a poet whose characteristic landscapes and moments are marked by shimmering ephemerality, there is something disquieting in the distancing of pastoral bliss that occurs here. *That* fair forest green is triply removed from us: by time, space, and by its status as reflection in the water below. As he does in "The Serpent Is Shut Out from Paradise" and even more touchingly in "Lines Written in the Bay of Lerici," Shelley here brings Elysium into his poem only for the purpose of refusing himself a genuine admittance to it. Paradise is but a glow, reflected in waters themselves unapproachable. Though that reflection is "more than" true, it is also inaccessible, and easily destructible. "More than truth" means, ironically, "with less than the force of solid reality."

The principle of harmony derived equally from an external and a human source, and its destruction comes from an "envious wind" twinned to a human "unwelcome thought." Shelley's mind pathetically hungers for a peace it may not have, just as the stillness of a pool is easily, naturally disturbed by any passing breeze. The ready dissolution of calm all but obliterates the jaunty eagerness of "The Invitation," the pendant poem, with its carpe diem dismissal of Reflexion, Sorrow, Despair, Care, and even Hope, those personified distractions that Shelley sends packing as he heads for the "woods . . . plains . . . [and] pools" with Jane Williams. Like his other pastoral retreats, the site in "The Invitation" brings to nature an architectural ornamentation and a sense of reflective oneness that turns out, after "The Recollection," to have been momentary and delusive. At the conclusion of "The Invitation" Shelley paints his lovers into a pastoral retreat at noon, responsive to both light and shade, water and earth, when

the blue noon is over us,
And the multitudinous
Billows murmur at our feet

> Where the earth and ocean meet,
> And all things seem only one
> In the universal Sun.—
>
> (ll. 64–69)

Having somehow transported the lovers from the pine forest to the ocean, and from covert to full sunshine, Shelley anticipates a climactic mingling—"all things *seem only one*"—that he can never fully affirm or accept. Peace, mingling, "universality," all conditions to be wished for, are precisely what Shelley denies himself in these poignant lyrics.

Aside from Byron, Shelley is the most self-dramatizing of the Romantic poets. As a means of self-definition, playing a part comes more naturally to him than analyzing the autobiographical subject, "seek[ing] the origin" (as Wordsworth does in the opening books of *The Prelude*) of one's ego or character. Whether as the combined figure of Cain, Christ, Actaeon, and Dionysus (in *Adonais*), or as a cosmic "passive earth, this world of love, this *me*" ("Epipsychidion"), Shelley typically presents himself as performing in a script not of his own choosing. In "The Serpent Is Shut Out from Paradise," the self-pitying Satanic equation has been legitimately inspired by the punning reference to Shelley's name in his Pisan circle ("the snake" as a bilingual combination of "Bysshe Shelley" and *bischelli* [a little snake]). Shelley tries to name himself, stutteringly and punningly; he cannot really do it, just as he admits that he has been spoiled "for the task / Of acting a forced part in life's dull scene" (ll. 27–28). No longer able to play the role—in his "cold home"—of husband or lover, he blames Jane Williams for destroying his part and with it his equanimity. He is no longer capable, he says,

> Of wearing on my brow the idle mask
> Of author, great or mean,
> In the world's carnival. I sought
> Peace thus, and but in you I found it not.
>
> (ll. 29–32)

The ambiguous "but" and double negative of line 32 show Shelley hedging: either "I found peace nowhere, *except* in you" or "I found peace *everywhere,* except in you." There is a hint here of Shelley as petulant child, a role he has played often and not always pleasantly in his poetry. But more poignantly, the entire poem, like the final lyric sequence that contains it, represents Shelley as the would-be angel desperate for quietude, for furling his wings, for the calm of either love or home or death: "Doubtless there is a place of peace / Where *my* weak heart and all its throbs will cease" (ll. 47–48). For Shelley, such calm is always figured as a place of pastoral seclusion, of erotic and social happiness.

Just as Coleridge in *his* dejection often displaces all hope for happiness upon another, either a better version of himself (the infant Hartley in "Frost at Midnight") or a simpler one (Sara Hutchinson in "Dejection: An

Ode"), so Shelley also derives vicarious pleasure from another's joy. In his case, however, that pleasure seems to derive specifically from an aristocratic graciousness. His self-presentation as Ariel in "With a Guitar. To Jane" continues the elegant sophistication of "Epipsychidion"; now he dons the mask of Shakespeare's noble sprite and enacts his fictive role with light-hearted gusto. This Ariel finds his own happiness by pursuing Miranda's, and only through the double agency of his gift giving and her artistry. It all comes down, as the groom says in *Dark Victory,* to a matter of breeding. Ariel is both responsive servant ("When you die, the silent Moon / . . . is not sadder . . . / Than deserted Ariel") and controlling principle ("Like an unseen Star of birth / Ariel guides you o'er the sea / Of Life from your nativity"). Serving the will of Miranda, the airy spirit finds himself "Imprisoned for some fault . . . / In a body like a grave"; he wishes only a smile and a song to redeem "his service and his sorrow" (ll. 23–26, 28–30, 38–39, 41).

The longest section of the poem, its second verse paragraph (ll. 43–90), details the construction and the fate of the gift guitar from a piece of wood that was once alive, then died, and was then reborn into art. These lines form a single sentence, with all of the typical resting places that Shelley inserts into such sentences, and even though there is a period at the end of line 86, the last four lines begin with an adversative "But" and may be legitimately considered a logical part of the entire semantic and grammatical unit. (The first paragraph was divided in half by a period after line 22.) The etiology of the object is presented in largely hypotactic clauses, reaching a climax at the end:

> it knew
> That seldom heard mysterious sound,
> Which, driven on its diurnal round
> As it floats through boundless day
> Our world enkindles on its way—
> All this it knows, but will not tell
> To those who cannot question well
> The spirit that inhabits it:
> It talks according to the wit
> Of its companions, and no more
> Is heard than has been felt before
> By those who tempt it to betray
> These secrets of an elder day.—
> But, sweetly as its answers will
> Flatter hands of perfect skill,
> It keeps its highest holiest tone
> For our beloved Jane alone.
>
> (ll. 74–90)

Several aspects of this verse call attention to Shelley's graciousness. For one thing, after the first half of the poem, Ariel–Shelley has all but disappeared.

(The procedure differs from that of *Adonais,* in which Shelley replaces the disappearing Keats as the central focus.) Here, the very fact of the speaker's attention to his object—both the object he is presenting and the person to whom he is giving it—establishes the genteel self-abnegation that is the positive counter to the more extreme banishments represented by figures such as Actaeon or Christ. Shelley's model, like the poem's tone, is entirely secular. For another, the spiritual superiority that belongs to the aristocratic circle at the end of "Euganean Hills," "Epipsychidion," and *Prometheus Unbound* here devolves entirely upon the benign figure of Jane Williams. And, last of all, the relation of agent to instrument that exercised Shelley through *Adonais* as well as *A Defence of Poetry* here centers on a sequence of gracious deferrals that lead backward to origins (the etiology of the guitar) and forward to the conclusion of artistic performance. Just as "each are mirrors of / The fire for which all thirst" (*Adonais,* ll. 484–85), so here one gets from the guitar—either as player or as listener—only what one is already capable of knowing and feeling. The noble flattery that the guitar makes reproduces the very compliment that Shelley, himself now nameless and unself-regarding, pays to his muse, the goddess of performance. The guitar, as a principle of music, is all potential, requiring the actualizing force of the singer–player. In "The Keen Stars Were Twinkling" Shelley takes this motif one step farther by requiring Jane's voice, as well as her fingers, to animate (literally: he says her tender voice "to the strings without soul had then given its own") the guitar.

As servant, as vicarious recipient of Miranda–Jane's own happiness, this Ariel–Shelley neither plays nor sings himself but commits himself entirely to the passive role of audience. "Imprisoned . . . in a body" (ll. 38–39) as the soul of the guitar is imprisoned in a wooden artifact, Shelley-as-sprite seems doubly cut off from the source of harmony and delight, except as a lucky recipient. Not only will no one animate him as physically and directly as Jane animates the strings of the guitar, but in both of these poems the "highest holiest tone" (l. 89) issues from a world to which his own relationship is merely contingent. In "The Keen Stars Were Twinkling" Shelley enjoins his muse, as he earlier invoked his skylark, to grant him access to a diviner world:

> Though the sound overpowers
> Sing again, with your dear voice revealing
> A tone
> Of some world far from ours,
> Where music and moonlight and feeling
> Are one.

> (ll. 19–24)

One way of measuring the distance Shelley has come between the relative confidence of "To a Sky-Lark" and the muted sadness of the 1822 poem is to notice how in the earlier (1820) lyric he returns to himself as beneficiary and then imitator of the bird's song:

> Teach me half the gladness
>   That thy brain must know,
> Such harmonious madness
>   From my lips would flow
> The world should listen then—as I am listening now.

The reciprocity of listening and singing has been replaced in the second poem by a sense of exile from the land of unity, "[w]here music and moonlight and feeling / Are one," and the poet no longer claims for himself the privilege or the ability to match even *half* the gladness of his inspiring singer. Himself an entirely passive audience, he has abandoned his active role in the singing contest.

Whereas in earlier poems possession and the state of being possessed defined Shelley's position with regard to his audience, his lover, or his world, at the end his passiveness seems to overwhelm the poetry, leaving him the vicarious participant in the happiness of another, the audience for another's song, the actor who has replaced more demanding roles with that of the exiled serpent. The final lyric, "Lines Written in the Bay of Lerici," is unfinished, like *The Triumph of Life;* it is tantalizing but unproductive to imagine how it might have ended. As it stands, it gives us a Shelley (appropriately) in a state of virtual paralysis. Indolence, with its potential pastoral pleasures, has metamorphosed into a state of garish abandonment and a solitude in which the standard Shelleyan images of contentment have been reduced to their negative parodies.

Addressing the moon ("fair coquette of Heaven"), he laments the bitterly ironic fact that Jane, a "guardian angel" who is "far more true" than the wandering moon, has nevertheless left him. Able to sustain himself only by reconstructing her presence in memory, he still feels incapable of articulating dangerous thoughts, resorting instead to a reminiscence in which he performs an entirely spectatorial function:

>   disturbed and weak
> I sate and watched the vessels glide
> Along the ocean bright and wide,
> Like spirit-winged chariots sent
> O'er some serenest element
> To ministrations strange and far;
> As if to some Elysian star
> They sailed for drink to medicine
> Such sweet and bitter pain as mine.
> And the wind that winged their flight
> From the land came fresh and light,
> And the scent of sleeping flowers
> And the coolness of the hours
> Of dew, and the sweet warmth of day
> Was scattered o'er the twinkling bay;
> And the fisher with his lamp

And spear, about the low rocks damp
Crept, and struck the fish who came
To worship the delusive flame:
Too happy, they whose pleasure sought
Extinguishes all sense and thought
Of the regret that pleasure [   ]
Destroying life alone not peace.

(ll. 36–58)

For once Shelley is going nowhere; he merely watches the vessels setting sail for paradise. That they have a mission to return with heavenly salves to minister to him makes him seem, if possible, even more passive. Where the daring detail of the night-hunting fisherman might have led the poem we can only conjecture: if the victimized fish has been duped by a delusive flame, what does this say about Shelley and his response to the "twinkling bay"? The poem's two remaining, aborted couplets will not answer this question. In his last lyric Shelley almost equates watching and the passivity of appreciation with sickness, self-deception, and self-destruction. No motion has he now, no force; he *only* hears and sees.

Appendix B

The Text of Coleridge's "Dejection: An Ode"

[WRITTEN APRIL 4, 1802]
Late, late yestreen I saw the new Moon,
With the old Moon in her arms;
And I fear, I fear, my Master dear!
We shall have a deadly storm.
Ballad of Sir Patrick Spence

I

WELL! If the Bard was weather-wise, who made
  The grand old ballad of Sir Patrick Spence,
  This night, so tranquil now, will not go hence
Unroused by winds, that ply a busier trade
Than those which mould yon cloud in lazy flakes,   5
Or the dull sobbing draft, that moans and rakes
Upon the strings of this Æolian lute
    Which better far were mute.
  For lo! the New-moon winter-bright!
  And overspread with phantom light,   10
  (With swimming phantom light o'erspread
  But rimmed and circled by a silver thread)
I see the old Moon in her lap, foretelling
  The coming-on of rain and squally blast.
And oh! that even now the gust were swelling,   15

And the slant night-shower driving loud and fast!
Those sounds which oft have raised me, whilst they awed,
    And sent my soul abroad,
Might now perhaps their wonted impulse give,
Might startle this dull pain, and make it move and live!   20

II

A grief without a pang, void, dark, and drear,
    A stifled, drowsy, unimpassioned grief,
    Which finds no natural outlet, no relief,
      In word, or sigh, or tear—
O Lady! in this wan and heartless mood,   25
To other thoughts by yonder throstle woo'd,
    All this long eve, so balmy and serene,
Have I been gazing on the western sky,
    And its peculiar tint of yellow green:
And still I gaze—and with how blank an eye!   30
And those thin clouds above, in flakes and bars,
That give away their motion to the stars;
Those stars, that glide behind them or between,
Now sparkling, now bedimmed, but always seen:
Yon crescent Moon, as fixed as if it grew   35
In its own cloudless, starless lake of blue;
I see them all so excellently fair,
I see, not feel, how beautiful they are!

III

    My genial spirits fail;
    And what can these avail   40
To lift the smothering weight from off my breast?
    It were a vain endeavour,
    Though I should gaze for ever
On that green light that lingers in the west:
I may not hope from outward forms to win   45
The passion and the life, whose fountains are within.

IV

O Lady! we receive but what we give,
And in our life alone does Nature live:

Ours is her wedding garment, ours her shroud!
   And would we aught behold, of higher worth,   50
Than that inanimate cold world allowed
To the poor loveless ever-anxious crowd,
   Ah! from the soul itself must issue forth
A light, a glory, a fair luminous cloud
     Enveloping the Earth—   55
And from the soul itself must there be sent
   A sweet and potent voice, of its own birth,
Of all sweet sounds the life and element!

V

O pure of heart! thou need'st not ask of me
What this strong music in the soul may be!   60
What, and wherein it doth exist,
This light, this glory, this fair luminous mist,
This beautiful and beauty-making power.
   Joy, virtuous Lady! Joy that ne'er was given,
Save to the pure, and in their purest hour,   65
Life, and Life's effluence, cloud at once and shower,
Joy, Lady! is the spirit and the power,
Which wedding Nature to us gives in dower
   A new Earth and new Heaven,
Undreamt of by the sensual and the proud—   70
Joy is the sweet voice, Joy the luminous cloud—
     We in ourselves rejoice!
And thence flows all that charms or ear or sight,
   All melodies the echoes of that voice,
All colours a suffusion from that light.   75

VI

There was a time when, though my path was rough,
   This joy within me dallied with distress,
And all misfortunes were but as the stuff
   Whence Fancy made me dreams of happiness:
For hope grew round me, like the twining vine,   80
And fruits, and foliage, not my own, seemed mine.
But now afflictions bow me down to earth:
Nor care I that they rob me of my mirth;
    But oh! each visitation
Suspends what nature gave me at my birth,   85

My shaping spirit of Imagination.
For not to think of what I needs must feel,
　　But to be still and patient, all I can;
And haply by abstruse research to steal
　　From my own nature all the natural man—   90
　　This was my sole resource, my only plan:
Till that which suits a part infects the whole,
And now is almost grown the habit of my soul.

VII

Hence, viper thoughts, that coil around my mind,
　　　Reality's dark dream!   95
I turn from you, and listen to the wind,
　　Which long has raved unnoticed. What a scream
Of agony by torture lengthened out
That lute sent forth! Thou Wind, that rav'st without,
　　Bare crag, or mountain-tairn, or blasted tree,   100
Or pine-grove whither woodman never clomb,
Or lonely house, long held the witches' home,
　　Methinks were fitter instruments for thee,
Mad Lutanist! who in this month of showers,
Of dark-brown gardens, and of peeping flowers,   105
Mak'st Devils' yule, with worse than wintry song,
The blossoms, buds, and timorous leaves among.
　　Thou Actor, perfect in all tragic sounds!
Thou mighty Poet, e'en to frenzy bold!
　　　What tell'st thou now about?   110
　　　'Tis of the rushing of an host in rout,
　　With groans, of trampled men, with smarting wounds—
At once they groan with pain, and shudder with the cold!
But hush! there is a pause of deepest silence!
　　And all that noise, as of a rushing crowd,   115
With groans, and tremulous shudderings—all is over—
　　It tells another tale, with sounds less deep and loud!
　　　A tale of less affright,
　　　And tempered with delight,
As Otway's self had framed the tender lay,—   120
　　　'Tis of a little child
　　　Upon a lonesome wild,
Not far from home, but she hath lost her way:
And now moans low in bitter grief and fear,
And now screams loud, and hopes to make her mother hear.

VIII

'Tis midnight, but small thoughts have I of sleep: 126
Full seldom may my friend such vigils keep!
Visit her, gentle Sleep! with wings of healing,
  And may this storm be but a mountain-birth,
May all the stars hang bright above her dwelling,   130
  Silent as though they watched the sleeping Earth!
    With light heart may she rise,
    Gay fancy, cheerful eyes,
  Joy lift her spirit, joy attune her voice;
To her may all things live, from pole to pole,   135
Their life the eddying of her living soul!
  O simple spirit, guided from above,
Dear Lady, friend devoutest of my choice,
Thus mayest thou ever, evermore rejoice.

Notes

Chapter 1

1. For an extensive bibliography for and analysis of the New Historicism, see Alan Liu, "The Power of Formalism: The New Historicism," *ELH,* 56 (1989):721–71. Liu sensibly distinguishes those New Historicists working from a Marxist base (old-style British "cultural materialism") from those whose primary, if unspoken, allegiance is to a heightening of formalism. In addition, I would stress a connection between what might be labeled the "new asceticism"—particularly with regard to high culture—and aesthetics in general. I am reminded of Max Weber's remark that the "ascetic aversion of pious Jews toward everything esthetic was *originally* based on the second commandment of the Decalogue. . . . But another important cause of aversion to things esthetic is the purely pedagogic and jussive character of the divine service in the synagogue, even as it was practiced in the Diaspora, long before the disruption of the Temple cult." See Max Weber, *The Sociology of Religion,* trans. Ephraim Fischoff (Boston: Beacon Press, 1963), p. 256. In the current atmosphere of "cultural studies," which prefers ideological to aesthetic examination, we have a modernized version of the "purely pedagogic and jussive character" of Hebrew observances.

2. Terry Eagleton, *The Ideology of the Aesthetic* (Oxford: Basil Blackwell, 1990), attempts to redeem the aesthetic, both in its relation to the body and for its potentially liberating personal effects, even though he still gives no credence to an autotelic work of art. Nor does he—deliberately, according to his own admission— deal with specific works of art. He thereby thwarts an empirical literary critic's desire to see how poetry itself might constitute and be constituted by the philosophical category that Eagleton derives from the ideology of the Enlightenment bourgeoisie.

3. Raymond Williams, *Problems in Materialism and Culture* (London: Verso Editions and NLB, 1980), p. 44. Although Williams had earlier rejected "the aesthetic . . . as a separate abstract dimension and as a separate abstract function," he also emphasized the need to acknowledge those intentions and responses "that have been grouped as aesthetic in distinction from other isolated intentions and responses." See Raymond Williams, *Marxism and Literature* (Oxford: Oxford University Press, 1977), p. 156.

4. Jerome McGann, *Social Values and Poetic Acts: The Historical Judgment of Literary Work* (Cambridge, Mass.: Harvard University Press, 1988), p. 98. Later in the book McGann reasserts the communal basis of all literary activity. Throughout his scholarly career he has tried to re-embed literature within a social and political context in order to understand the ideological component that critics of Romanticism in particular have ignored: "Writing and reading are social acts with public and transpersonal agencies and consequences. The question is, whether as citizens of an imperial world, as 'imperial intellects,' we have yet any desire, or capacity to discover our insularities" (p. 114).

5. In response to Schiller's *Aesthetic Letters,* and their origin in Kantian aesthetics, Babbitt remarks: "[B]y encouraging the notion that it is possible to escape from neo-classical didacticism only by eliminating masculine purpose from art, [Schiller] opens the way for the worst perversions of the aesthete, above all for the divorce of art from ethical reality. In art, according to Schiller, both imagination and feeling should be free and spontaneous, and the result of all this freedom, as he sees it, will be perfectly 'ideal.'" Irving Babbitt, *Rousseau and Romanticism* (Boston: Houghton Mifflin, 1919), p. 43.

6. Friedrich Schiller, *The Aesthetic Letters, Essays, and the Philosophical Letters of Schiller,* trans. J. Weiss (Boston: Charles C. Little and James Brown, 1845), pp. 72–74.

7. Even so trenchant a Marxist critic as Louis Althusser excepts art from ideology: "I do not rank real art among the ideologies." His exception should prove truest, I think, in regard to lyric poetry. See Louis Althusser, *Lenin and Philosophy and Other Essays* (New York: Monthly Review Press, 1971), p. 221. We might even say that Walter Benjamin's remark that "[c]ommunism responds by politicizing art" is the historical rather than the necessary sequel to his earlier observation that "the logical result of Fascism is the introduction of aesthetics into politics. . . . All efforts to render politics aesthetic culminate in one thing: war." See Walter Benjamin, "The Work of Art in the Age of Mechanical Reproduction," in *Illuminations,* ed. Hannah Arendt (New York: Harcourt Brace, 1968), pp. 243–44. When both communism and fascism no longer exist, might we return to "the aesthetic" in good faith?

8. See especially Harold Bloom, *The Anxiety of Influence* (New York: Oxford University Press, 1973), and *A Map of Misreading* (New York: Oxford University Press, 1975). The more recent anthologies and critical histories of Sandra Gilbert and Susan Gubar now constitute something of a locus classicus for the tradition of women's writing.

9. Hugh Sykes Davies, *Wordsworth and the Worth of Words,* ed. John Kerrigan and Jonathan Wordsworth (Cambridge: Cambridge University Press, 1986), p. xi. See also W. R. Johnson, *Momentary Monsters: Lucan and His Heroes* (Ithaca, N.Y.: Cornell University Press, 1987), pp. ix–x. Such aesthetic presuppositions put one in a position easily assailable by the most nitpicking of the hermeneuticists, but literature is a circle that does not easily admit entry or else admits one all *too* easily.

The self-referentiality of language within a single writer's oeuvre is an assumption whose truth, and practicality, I have invoked in a commentary on two approaches to "A Slumber Did My Spirit Seal" by M. H. Abrams and J. Hillis Miller. See Willard Spiegelman, "Romanticism and the 'New' Critics," *Salmagundi,* nos. 76–77 (1987–88): 257–65.

10. The evidence derives from the following concordances: Lane Cooper, *A Concordance to the Poems of William Wordsworth* (London: Smith, Elder & Co., 1911); Ione Dodson Young, *A Concordance to the Poetry of Byron* (Austin: Pemberton Press, 1965); Sister Eugenia Logan, *A Concordance to the Poetry of Samuel Taylor Coleridge* (St. Mary-of-the-Woods, Ind.: privately printed, 1940); Michael Becker, *A Concordance to the Poems of John Keats* (New York: Garland, 1981); F. S. Ellis, *A Lexical Concordance to the Poetical Works of Percy Bysshe Shelley* (London: Bernard Quaritch, 1892).

11. My hunches about the transformation of sloth from deadly sin to pleasurable and even salutary activity resemble the thesis of John Cuddihy concerning the transformation of avarice into the bureaucratic forms that Marx labeled the wheels of capitalism, and the upward revaluation and institutionalization of lust by Freud. See John Cuddihy, *The Ordeal of Civility: Freud, Marx, Lévi-Strauss, and the Jewish Struggle with Modernity* (New York: Basic Books, 1974).

12. Montaigne, "On Idleness," *Essais* 1.8.

13. Jean-Jacques Rousseau, *The Reveries of the Solitary Walker,* trans. and ed. Charles E. Butterworth (New York: New York University Press, 1979), p. 66.

14. George Eliot, *The Mill on the Floss,* ed. Gordon Haight (Oxford: Clarendon Press, 1980), p. 410.

15. Quoted in Richard Ellmann, *Oscar Wilde* (New York: Knopf, 1988), p. 422, and in relation to the subtitle of Wilde's "Artist as Critic": "With Some Remarks on the Importance of Doing Absolutely Nothing." Both Schlegel and Wilde, before and after the English Romantics, inherited Winckelmann's idea of divine ease, itself a borrowing from Lucretius and other Epicurean writers, which may constitute the most important aspect of Romantic classicism.

16. Lore Metzger, *One Foot in Eden* (Chapel Hill: University of North Carolina Press, 1986), gives a full treatment of this Romantic genre. Annabel Patterson, *Pastoral and Ideology: Virgil to Valéry* (Berkeley: University of California Press, 1987), treats the Romantics passim.

17. Siegfried Wenzel, *The Sin of Sloth: Acedia in Medieval Thought and Literature* (Chapel Hill: University of North Carolina Press, 1960). The locus classicus for compilations of the appearances of sloth in medieval literature is Morton W. Bloomfield, *The Seven Deadly Sins* (Michigan: State College Press, 1952), esp. p. 219.

18. Wenzel takes Petrarch's *Secretum* or *Discourses on the Contempt of the World* as indication of a consciousness closer to that of the Renaissance. Acedia here is a "tenacious plague" rather than an acute attack: "It springs from the cumulative discouragement which the consideration of the miseries of the human condition, the memory of past hardships, and the fear of the future jointly produce" (Wenzel, p. 157).

19. For a discussion of the presentation of melancholia in art, see Sander Gilman, *Seeing the Insane* (New York: John Wiley & Sons, 1982). Gilman shows how cultural stereotypes and artistic renderings mutually affect one another.

20. As a footnote to the "ordering" of the sins, which Bloomfield treats extensively, one might note a late eighteenth-century children's book, by the pseud-

onymous Solomon Winlove (perhaps Oliver Goldsmith), *Moral Lectures on the Following Subjects* (London: E. Newberry, 1787), which removes indolence from among some of the seven deadly sins that begin the table of contents—pride, envy, avarice, and anger—and places it after hypocrisy, charity, generosity, and compassion and before mankind, credulity, contempt, and modesty. Lust has been eliminated (possibly because this is a book for children), as has gluttony. There seems to be both method and randomness in the treatment of the subjects. Indolence gets one of the largest entries; the four deadly sins that open the book receive shorter shrift. The reader is given the Franklinesque advice to look after himself: "[I]f we are our own enemies through laziness, we shall never have a friend, and, indeed, we can never deserve one" (p. 60). A spiritual sin has been transformed into an economic one, and three times the author admonishes: "Go to the ant, thou sluggard! Consider her ways, and be wise." The ant is always female, the lazy reader a male. Busyness has assumed its rightful place as a domestic virtue.

21. Robert Burton, *The Anatomy of Melancholy* (New York: Dutton, Everyman's Library, 1964), p. 88. For a discussion of the "Saturnine temperament," see Rudolf and Margot Wittkower, *Born Under Saturn* (New York: Random House, 1963), pp. 102–8, who discuss the topos from Aristotle through Ficino, noting the traditional distinction between positive melancholy (or contemplation) and its relation to genius, and clinical depression. They also observe that the category had a pseudo-life of its own: "By and large, together with the 'proto-Bohemian,' the melancholic artist had gone out of fashion in the seventeenth century. The great masters of the period, Bernini and Rubens, Rembrandt and Velasquez, were never described as melancholic and showed no trace of the affliction. It was not until the Romantic era, with artists like Caspar David Friedrich, that melancholy appears once again as a condition of mental and emotional catharsis" (p. 106). What was true for the visual arts on the Continent obviously did not obtain in England, especially in literature. See also Raymond Klibansky, Erwin Panofsky, and Fritz Saxl, *Saturn and Melancholy: Studies in the History of Natural Philosophy, Religion, and Art* (New York: Basic Books, 1964).

22. Ruth A. Fox, *The Tangled Chain: The Structure of Disorder in "The Anatomy of Melancholy"* (Berkeley: University of California Press, 1976), p. 257.

23. Aldous Huxley, "Accidie," in *On the Margin* (London: Chatto & Windus, 1923), pp. 21–22.

24. J. H. Plumb, *Georgian Delights* (Boston: Little, Brown, 1980), pp. 15–16 and passim. See also Esther Moir, *The Discovery of Britain: The English Tourists, 1540–1840* (London: Routledge, 1964). For a more recent, genial discussion of modern habits of leisure, see Witold Rybczynski, *Waiting for the Weekend* (New York: Viking, 1991).

25. J. H. Plumb, "The Commercialization of Leisure," in Neil McKendrick, John Brewer, and J. H. Plumb, *The Birth of a Consumer Society: The Commercialization of Eighteenth-Century England* (Bloomington: Indiana University Press, 1982), pp. 265–85.

26. Norbert Elias and Eric Dunning, *Quest for Excitement: Sport and Leisure in the Civilizing Process* (London: Basil Blackwell, 1986), p. 121.

27. Philip Barrough, *The Methode of Phisicke* (1583). This information is contained in the invaluable encyclopedia of Richard Hunter and Ida Macalpine, *Three Hundred Years of Psychiatry, 1535–1860* (1963; rpt. Hartsdale, N.Y.: Carlisle, 1982), p. 28.

28. Hunter and Macalpine, pp. 191, 240–43.

29. Richard Blackmore, in the 1726 edition of *A Treatise of the Spleen and Vapours,* says that in southern countries hysteria predominates, whereas in mist-ridden England the spleen is most affected. George Cheyne, in *The English Malady* (1733), also blames the moisture of the English air, the climate, the soil, and the rich diet, all of which contribute to emotional heaviness and torpor. See Hunter and Macalpine, pp. 319–54.

30. See Roy Porter, "'The Hunger of Imagination': Approaching Samuel Johnson's Melancholy," in *The Anatomy of Madness: Essays in the History of Psychiatry,* ed. W. F. Bynum, Roy Porter, and Michael Shepherd (London: Tavistock, 1985), pp. 63–88.

31. E. L. McAdam, Jr., *Samuel Johnson: Diaries, Prayers, and Annals* (New Haven: Yale University Press, 1958), p. 77; see also p. 257 and passim.

32. Samuel Johnson, *The Rambler,* vol. 3, ed. W. J. Bate and Albrecht B. Strauss, *Yale Edition of the Works of Samuel Johnson* (New Haven: Yale University Press, 1969), 5:64. Cf. "Idleness can never secure tranquility" (ibid., 4:348). In one of his last letters Johnson refers to indolence as "that voluntary debility [which] if it is not counteracted by resolution . . . will render in time the strongest faculties lifeless" (*Letters,* ed. R. W. Chapman [Oxford: Clarendon Press, 1952], 3:182).

33. Roy Porter locates Johnson's fear of indolence specifically within his obsessive phobias concerning damnation, although Johnson paradoxically never looked to his religion as a possible source of comfort or remedy. There was apparently no way out: "Unable, through poverty, situation, and temperament, to assimilate himself to the *bourgeois gentilhomme*'s ease, unable to fuse learning and sociability in Addisonian moderation, he lurched from melancholy toil to melancholy indolence, fearing all the time that way madness lay" (Porter, p. 77).

34. S. Weir Mitchell, *Doctor and Patient,* 4th ed. (Philadelphia: J. P. Lippincott, 1904), p. 161.

35. James Engell, *The Creative Imagination* (Cambridge, Mass.: Harvard University Press, 1981), offers the fullest treatment of the historical changes in the philosophical conception of imagination during the early modern period. The chimeras of fancy somehow have given way, through the intervening philosophy of Locke and other empiricists, to an ennobling conception of the importance of general passivity in mental alertness. Rousseau's *Rêveries du promeneur solitaire* glories in the passiveness that Wordsworth, in *Lyrical Ballads,* and later Maggie Tulliver in *The Mill on the Floss* enjoy.

36. Roy Porter, *Mind-Forg'd Manacles: A History of Madness in England from the Restoration to the Regency* (Cambridge, Mass.: Harvard University Press, 1987), pp. 61–62 and passim.

37. Michel Foucault, *Madness and Civilization: A History of Insanity in the Age of Reason,* trans. Richard Howard (New York: Random House, 1965), p. 58.

38. See Amariah Brigham, *Remarks on the Influence of Mental Cultivation upon Health* (Hartford, 1832); and Sir Andrew Halliday, *A General View of the Present State of Lunatics, and Lunatic Asylums* (London, 1828), cited in Hunter and Macalpine, pp. 821–25 and 785–88.

39. See E. S. Turner, *Taking the Cure* (London: Joseph, 1967), for a history of eighteenth-century spas; see also Michel Foucault and Richard Sennett, "Sexuality and Solitude," *London Review of Books,* May 21, 1981, pp. 3–5, on the recommendation of solitude as an antidote to urban torpor.

40. Samuel Taylor Coleridge, "On Revisiting the Sea-Shore, After Long Absence, under Strong Medical Recommendation Not To Bathe," dated August 1801

and first published in the *Morning Post* on September 15, 1801. Coleridge's subtitle, as well as his decision in the poem to take the plunge, indicates the controversy attending sea bathing among contemporary medical experts. Suffering from a swollen knee, Coleridge had visited the Hutchinsons in Durham in July. His doctor had advised against sea bathing and "horse exercises," but with a "Faith in the Ocean," Coleridge plunged and frolicked in the waves (*CL*, 2:751).

41. Richard Holmes, *Coleridge: Early Visions* (New York: Viking, 1990), p. 60.

42. Alexander Morison, *Outlines of Lectures on Mental Diseases* (1824), cited in Porter, *Mind-Forg'd Manacles*, p. 161.

43. Raymond Williams, *The Country and the City* (New York: Oxford University Press, 1973), p. 128.

44. See John Barrell, *The Idea of Landscape and the Sense of Place, 1730–1840: An Approach to the Poetry of John Clare* (Cambridge: Cambridge University Press, 1972). For studies in the relationship, later in the century and in France, between art and society, see Robert L. Herbert, *Impressionism: Art, Leisure, and Parisian Society* (New Haven: Yale University Press, 1988), which theorizes that the new bourgeois classes in Haussmann's Paris created the vogue for the Sunday world of impressionist painting. As the Seine was built up and gradually industrialized in the 1860s and 1870s, Monet, Renoir, and Manet dealt with the transformation of the actual landscape by retreating to their real or metaphorical Givernys. See also T. J. Clark, *The Painting of Modern Life: Paris in the Art of Manet and His Followers* (New York: Knopf, 1985), which opens with a quotation from Meyer Schapiro's 1937 essay "The Nature of Abstract Art" published in the *Marxist Quarterly*. Both books invoke Veblen's theory of class, leisure, and the organized commercialization of recreation.

45. Ann Bermingham, *Landscape and Ideology: The English Rustic Tradition, 1740–1860* (Berkeley: University of California Press, 1986), p. 9. See also James Turner, *The Politics of Landscape: Rural Scenery and Society in English Poetry, 1630–1660* (Cambridge, Mass.: Harvard University Press, 1979). See also Patterson in regard to the political background of pastoral literature.

46. Louis Hawes, *Presences of Nature: British Landscape, 1780–1830* (New Haven: Yale Center for British Art, 1982), p. 82. Hawes discusses the relationship between "working landscape" pictures and the more established genres: mountain, coastal, ruin, rural, and townscape pictures. By 1821 Turner was showing a preference for working scenes over recreational ones, especially in his watercolors. See also Francis Klingender, *Art and the Industrial Revolution* (1947), rev. ed. (London: Evelyn, Adams & Mackay, 1968); and Peter Quennell, *Romantic England: Writing and Painting, 1717–1857* (New York: Macmillan, 1970).

47. Alan Liu, *Wordsworth: The Sense of History* (Stanford: Stanford University Press, 1989), pp. 1–137 and passim.

48. Hugh Sykes Davies's chapter "Wordsworth and the 'Picturesque,'" in *Wordsworth and the Worth of Words*, pp. 189–260, traces the origins of Wordsworth's interest in *nakedness* of landscape as a rebellion against the inanities of much picturesque theorizing, which Sykes Davies argues became associated in Wordsworth's mind with the excesses of Godwinism. At the same time, Sykes Davies offers interesting reminiscences of a late Edwardian boyhood that involved many travels of the officially sanctioned sort, from "station" to "station" along a picturesque trailway. "It was rather like being in church" (p. 225), he drily summarizes.

49. The standard operating definitions of the sublime come, of course, from Edmund Burke, *A Philosophical Enquiry into the Origin of Our Ideas of the Sublime*

and Beautiful, ed. J. T. Boulton (New York: Columbia University Press, 1958). The most important modern commentary is Thomas Weiskel, *The Romantic Sublime: Studies in the Structure and Psychology of Transcendence* (Baltimore: Johns Hopkins University Press, 1976).

50. *Notebooks,* 1:760. See, also, his reference to a "Gold-headed Cane on a pikteresk Toor" (ibid., 1:508); here the instruments of the tour have completely taken over from their agents.

51. Wallace Stevens, *The Collected Poems of Wallace Stevens* (New York: Knopf, 1957), p. 372.

52. Ernest de Selincourt, ed., *Journals of Dorothy Wordsworth* (London: Macmillan, 1959), 1:131–32. One of the major differences, of course, between Dorothy's account and her brother's recreation is his invention of the motif of capital returns, of which an original, on-the-spot rendering would tend to be ignorant.

53. For a discussion of the river tour and related phenomena, see Malcolm Andrews, *The Search for the Picturesque: Landscape Aesthetics and Tourism in Britain, 1760–1800* (Stanford: Stanford University Press, 1989), which stresses the way theorists of the picturesque suppressed a viewer's moral responses to scenes of poverty—the hovel, the ruin—by emphasizing purely visual values. For Andrews, "the Picturesque eye . . . is anti-Georgic" (p. 64). For Wordsworth, as we shall see, it is never so simple.

54. Kurt Heinzelman, "Wordsworth's Labor Theory: An Economics of Compensation," in *The Economics of the Imagination* (Amherst: University of Massachusetts Press, 1980), pp. 196–233, writes suggestively about Wordsworth's economic language and themes, but does not mention "I Wandered Lonely as a Cloud." For a general anatomy of literature's relationship to, and grounding in, economics, see Marc Shell, *Economy of Literature* (Baltimore: Johns Hopkins University Press, 1978). Well before the recent interest among literary scholars in economics, Donald Hall somewhat playfully proposed the money connection in "I Wandered Lonely." See his piece in the *New York Times Book Review,* October 9, 1966.

55. Immanuel Kant, *The Critique of Judgement,* trans. James Creed Meredith (Oxford: Clarendon Press, 1952), pp. 50, 122.

56. Stephan Körner, *Kant* (Baltimore: Penguin Books, 1955), p. 189. A new aestheticism may be on the way in. As a counter to Terry Eagleton's Marxist discussion of the bourgeois discourses of aesthetics, one could cite Charles Wegener's *Discipline of Taste and Feeling* (Chicago: University of Chicago Press, 1992), an admittedly "somewhat bizarre commentary on certain parts of Kant's third critique" (p. xi). Wegener's book is an "inquiry into the normalities of aesthetic functioning" that differentiate it from other forms of human activity. His refreshing conclusion—at once startling and, *sub specie aeternitatis,* thoroughly classical—is that "aesthetic sensibility is as much a characteristically human kind of functioning as are knowing and doing" (p. 215); it invites us to consider, amid the conflicting ideologies and discursive maneuvers of much recent criticism, the principle of beauty as a universal phenomenon. In addition, see Frances Ferguson, "Romantic Studies," in *Redrawing the Boundaries: The Transformation of English and American Literary Studies,* ed. Stephen Greenblatt and Giles Gunn (New York: Modern Language Association of America, 1992), pp. 100–129, for a discussion of the recent revival of interest in Kantian aesthetics among scholars of Romanticism.

57. The quotations are from, respectively, Anne Stevenson, "Letters from Elizabeth Bishop," *Times Literary Supplement,* March 7, 1980, pp. 261–62; and Eliz-

abeth Bishop, *The Complete Poems, 1927–1979* (New York: Farrar Strauss, 1979), pp. 176–77.

Chapter 2

1. Mikhail Bakhtin, *Rabelais and His World* (Cambridge, Mass.: Harvard University Press, 1968), p. 7. See also C. L. Barber, *Shakespeare's Festive Comedy* (Princeton: Princeton University Press, 1959).

2. Few critics have attempted to ascertain why so much of Wordsworth's poetry (though not that which appeals to modern tastes) from *all* stages in his career could be characterized as "light" verse, in both its formal and metrical manner and its thematic and emotional matter. The brooding, apocalyptic, self-conscious poet whom Geoffrey Hartman characterized for one generation of readers in *Wordsworth's Poetry, 1787–1814* (New Haven: Yale University Press, 1964), and the evasive, history-haunted one whom Alan Liu has created in *Wordsworth: The Sense of History* (Stanford: Stanford University Press, 1989), are often hard to square with the author of "The Waterfall and the Eglantine," "The Oak and the Broom," "Written in Germany on One of the Coldest Days of the Century," and "Rural Architecture," all from the 1800 *Lyrical Ballads*. Critics inevitably sweep under the carpet evidence that does not fit the poet to their stereotypes; still, for forty years Wordsworth wrote much that we would now haughtily dismiss as mere "verse," or perhaps as verse more suited to genteel, especially female, readers. And yet Wordsworth, despite his puritanical leanings, and unlike Coleridge and Keats, seldom seems troubled by potential charges of "unmanliness" or of being un-manned by the *kind* of poetry he writes. See chap. 5, "Romantic Theory and English Reading Audiences," in Jon P. Klancher, *The Making of English Reading Audiences, 1790–1832* (Madison: University of Wisconsin Press, 1987), pp. 135–71, for a discussion of the relationship between Romantic ideology and audience building. Class rather than gender is Klancher's main focus.

3. "I griev'd for Buonaparte," a contemporary poem, offers another example of Wordsworth's use of nominal lists in a quasi-allegorical way. The sestet is a miniature study in Wordsworthian habits of figuration and syntax:

> Wisdom doth live with children round her knees:
> Books, leisure, perfect freedom, and the talk
> Man holds with week-day man in the hourly walk
> Of the mind's business: these are the degrees
> By which true Sway doth mount; this is the stalk
> True Power doth grow on; and her rights are these.

The paradoxical combinations within these abstractions (for example, "leisure" and "week-day . . . business") are deployed in an attempt to define the origins of true power in ordinary life. This effort parallels the similar combinations in "Resolution and Independence."

4. As I have pointed out in *Wordsworth's Heroes* (Berkeley: University of California Press, 1985), pp. 95–99, the fact that "the whole Body of the man did seem / Like one whom I *had met* with in a dream" (ll. 116–17; emphasis added) suggests that the leech gatherer had been at least imaginatively predicted at an earlier time.

5. In book 7 Wordsworth stresses the historically sanctioned but nevertheless spiritually corrupt Bartholomew Fair, which, according to its first historian, began by uniting the ties of religion, trade, and pleasure, and which gradually was loosed

from the first two in succession; by Wordsworth's time pleasure reigned. See Henry Morley, *Memoirs of Bartholomew Fair* (London: Chatto and Windus, 1880), especially the final chapter, "Last Years of the Condemned," which traces the gradual demise from 1752 to 1855.

6. *The Collected Works of William Hazlitt,* ed. A. R. Walker and Arnold Glover (London: J. M. Dent, 1904), 12:51–59. The quotations from the essay come from pp. 51, 52, and 58.

7. Lucy Newlyn, "Wordsworth, Coleridge, and the 'Castle of Indolence' Stanzas," *Wordsworth Circle,* 12 (1981): 106–13; and *Coleridge, Wordsworth, and the Language of Allusion* (Oxford: Clarendon Press, 1986), pp. 109–13. Newlyn observes that Matthew Arnold's notorious confusion of the two portraits (he mistakenly thought the first man, rather than the second, was Wordsworth's vision of Coleridge) "is not only justifiable, but imaginatively right" ("Wordsworth, Coleridge," p. 106). For Newlyn, both pictures are a composite of details, "made to resemble Thomson's indolent poet-companions. . . . [B]ecause of the confidence that is his alone, Wordsworth turns out to have written two self-portraits" (p. 111).

8. For a discussion of the "pleasance" or the *locus amoenus,* see Thomas G. Rosenmeyer, *The Green Cabinet: Theocritus and the European Pastoral Lyric* (Berkeley: University of California Press, 1969), pp. 179–203.

9. See my analysis of the scope of Wordsworth's sentences in "Some Lucretian Elements in Wordsworth," *Comparative Literature,* 37 (1985): 27–49.

10. Donald Davie, "Dionysus in *Lyrical Ballads,*" in *Wordsworth's Mind and Art,* ed. A. W. Thomson (Edinburgh: Oliver & Boyd, 1969), pp. 120, 138.

11. Among discussions of Romantic irony, even that of Anne K. Mellor, *English Romantic Irony* (Cambridge, Mass.: Harvard University Press, 1980), few critics stress the healthy aspects of Wordsworth's playfulness. One exception is the suggestive essay by Richard Gravil, *"Lyrical Ballads* (1798): Wordsworth as Ironist," *Critical Quarterly,* 24.4 (1982): 39–57, which insists on the healthy irony (Kierkegaardian "mastered irony") of the volume rather than Hegelian "infinite absolute negativity."

12. See John Turner, *Wordsworth: Play and Politics, A Study of Wordsworth's Poetry, 1787–1800* (London: Macmillan, 1986). Turner's thesis is developed from D. W. Winnicott, *Playing and Reality* (New York: Basic Books, 1971).

13. The relation between child's play and aesthetic playfulness in Kant's aesthetics is discussed by Terry Eagleton (e.g., "[A]esthetic judgment is then a kind of pleasurable free-wheeling of our faculties"), in *The Ideology of the Aesthetic* (Oxford: Basil Blackwell, 1990), p. 85 and passim.

14. For an evaluation of leisure as a version of energy and of idleness as a moral category, see Jeffrey Baker, "Idleness and Deliberate Holiday," in *Time and Mind in Wordsworth's Poetry* (Detroit: Wayne State University Press, 1980), pp. 113–43. Baker's main point is that deliberate holiday (like "majestic indolence" in *Prelude,* book 8) is always unneeded and signifies man's independence from nature and strict time.

15. See Friedrich Schiller, *The Aesthetic Letters, Essays, and the Philosophical Letters of Friedrich Schiller,* trans. J. Weiss (Boston: Charles C. Little and James Brown, 1845), pp. 72–74.

16. Eliot's famous put-down of Milton, that he wrote poetry as if it were merely "a solemn game," is one such formulation, ironic in that much the same charge may be directed back to Eliot himself. Auden's professed fondness for the sport of

poetry writing, his lifelong interest in puzzles, anagrams, and the other challenges on which a would-be poet might sharpen his or her skills, has inspired one whole line of postWar poetry.

17. The most important modern spokesman for play was the Dutch historian Johann Huizinga; see *Homo Ludens: A Study of the Play Element in Culture* (Boston: Beacon Press, 1955). The fact that the first German edition appeared in 1944, and that the foreword is dated 1938, in our century's bleakest time, gives added weight to the transhistorical need for, and belief in, leisure and play as universal human categories. For Huizinga the irrationality of play is connected to its "significant form" as well as to its status as a free and voluntary activity. That play operates according to rules and creates order is another indication of its intrinsic connection to art. His summary of the formal characteristics of play bears a significant resemblance to many Romantic and post-Romantic definitions of art: "a free activity standing quite consciously outside 'ordinary' life as being 'not serious,' but at the same time absorbing the player intensely and utterly. It is an activity connected with no material interest, and no profit can be gained by it. It proceeds within its own proper boundaries of time and space according to fixed rules and in an orderly manner. It promotes the formation of social groupings which tend to surround themselves with secrecy and to stress their difference from the common world by disguise or other means" (p. 13). On p. 132 Huizinga finally equates poetry and play (see pp. 119–35, "Play and Poetry").

18. See Jacques Derrida, *Of Grammatology*, trans. Gayatri Chakravarty Spivak (Baltimore: Johns Hopkins University Press, 1976), pp. 144–45, where he begins his famous discussion of "the supplement," a concept I pick up again in the concluding chapter of this book. An interesting, although historically prior, equation of ornament with truth comes in the last *Tatler* essay of Richard Steele, who states that his general purpose has been "to recommend truth, innocence, honour and virtue, as the chief ornaments of life." With truth and virtue as ornaments, one wonders what the essence of such a life might be. See *Tatler*, ed. George Aitken (London, 1899), 4: 375.

19. In "To the Memory of Raisley Calvert" (written between 1802 and 1804, printed in the 1807 volume), Wordsworth acknowledges the economic basis of his own "straying" and "freedom." He is careful (as many of his recent Marxist critics are not) to remind his audience and himself that his bequest from Calvert hardly allowed him untold riches: "I, if frugal and severe, might stray / Where'er I liked." In addition, the early frugal freedom will enable him to "meditate . . . lays / Of higher mood." This Virgilian note invites us to connect Wordsworth's generic progress to his actual economic conditions.

20. See William Empson, *Some Versions of Pastoral* (New York: New Directions, 1960), p. 5: "the waste even in a fortunate life, the isolation of a life rich in intimacy." This formulation is adduced as a universal human truth even though most of its articulations may be regarded as bourgeois. Empson knew to cover all the bases.

21. See James K. Chandler, *Wordsworth's Second Nature* (Chicago: University of Chicago Press, 1984), pp. 150–55, on Hazlitt's place in these conversation poems, where he acknowledges that William subversively triumphs by evading the issues. Mary Jacobus, *Tradition and Experiment in Wordsworth's Lyrical Ballads* (Oxford: Clarendon Press, 1976), p. 101, labels the poems "witty . . . almost epigrammatic," and deals in part with the odd humor of "Peter Bell" (pp. 262–72). Stuart Curran, *Poetic Form and British Romanticism* (New York: Oxford University Press,

1986), pp. 99–107, dealing with Wordsworthian pastoral, acknowledges the "baffling irresolvability in these comprehended perspectives" (p. 100) but adds, "and yet the singing contest must go on, even though one is doomed not to win it" (p. 101). Curran finds that the complex frames of the Matthew poems, as well as those of "The Brothers," "Michael," and "The Ruined Cottage," force "temporal concerns upon the timeless realm of pastoral and mak[e] us aware that art can contain what it allows to threaten it from within" (p. 103).

22. See Paul J. Alpers, *The Singer of the Eclogues: A Study of Virgilian Pastoral* (Berkeley: University of California Press, 1979); and Michael C. J. Putnam, *Virgil's Pastoral Art* (Princeton: Princeton University Press, 1970).

23. On liminal figures in Wordsworth—liminal in their physical stationing and in their ontological status—see Jonathan Wordsworth, *William Wordsworth: The Borders of Vision* (Oxford: Clarendon Press, 1982); and Hartman, esp. pp. 198–207.

24. Feminist critics have examined the role of Dorothy in these poems and, more generally, in the life of Wordsworth and his household at this point. It has become a commonplace that Wordsworth's creation depended on his too easy appropriation of Dorothy's perceptions (see Margaret Homans, *Women Writers and Poetic Identity* [Princeton: Princeton University Press, 1980], pp. 41–103), or that the life of the male poet was made possible by his presence amid a household of women helpers. Susan M. Levin, in *Dorothy Wordsworth and Romanticism* (New Brunswick, N.J.: Rutgers University Press, 1987), p. 63, supposes that "there must be some resentment in [Dorothy's] characterization of herself as having much to do, of being one of two 'able-bodied people in the house except the servant and *William,* who you know is not expected to do anything,'" but I suspect that the proposed resentment is a historical projection backward from a twentieth-century perspective. For Dorothy Wordsworth and labor, see Alan Liu, "On the Autobiographical Present: Dorothy Wordsworth's *Grasmere Journals," Criticism,* 26 (1984): 115–37. Much of Dorothy Wordsworth's writing, in letters and journals, supposes the equality of brother and sister during their shared experiences. See, for example, the Grasmere Journal entry for April 29, 1802 ("William lay, and I lay, in a trench under the fence"), in *Journals of Dorothy Wordsworth,* ed. Ernest de Selincourt (1941; rpt. London: Macmillan, 1959), pp. 139–40. Her *Recollections of a Tour Made in Scotland, A.D. 1803* is an important addition to the travel accounts of eighteenth-century women writers. Dorothy's own reports of walking *for leisure and exercise* bespeak a certain considerable degree of comfort (see, e.g., *EY*, pp. 46–47). Since all contemporary accounts—pictorial as well as literary—of Lake District tourism present male and female tourists in equal numbers, we must be wary of finding in Romantic indolence a too easy question of gender.

I think of Wordsworth as relatively untroubled by the kind of fears that beset both Coleridge and Keats (see my discussions in chapters 3 and 4), and which Frank Lentricchia conceives as central to a poet such as Wallace Stevens. See Frank Lentricchia, "Patriarchy Against Itself: The Young Manhood of Wallace Stevens," in *Ariel and the Police* (Madison: University of Wisconsin Press, 1988), pp. 136–95, for a discussion of the "feminization" of aesthetics in the trans-Atlantic crossing of such Romantic paradigms as Keatsian sensuousness and eroticism.

25. Don H. Bialastosky, *Making Tales: The Poetics of Wordsworth's Narrative Experiments* (Chicago: University of Chicago Press, 1984), passim, deals extensively with the mysteries and the uncertain incompleteness of many of Wordsworth's most typical poems. In my discussion in *Wordsworth's Heroes* of *The White*

Doe of Rylstone (pp. 166–89), I consider such epistemological mysteries within the genre of historical romance.

26. See Geoffrey H. Hartman, "Wordsworth, Inscriptions, and Romantic Nature Poetry," in *From Sensibility to Romanticism: Essays Presented to Frederick A. Pottle,* eds. Frederick W. Hilles and Harold Bloom (New York: Oxford University Press, 1965), pp. 389–414.

27. In the second volume of *Lyrical Ballads,* the other two poems labeled "pastoral" are "The Oak and the Broom," a simple didactic dialogue on the subject of tenacity and bending, and "The Pet Lamb," in which the poet translates his sympathy for a pretty girl and her animal into a projection of his own verse onto her. Recent criticism of Wordsworthian pastoral has centered on its supposed transmutation of politics and history into inwardness. For a good summary of the new criticism, see Annabel Patterson, *Pastoral and Ideology: Virgil to Valéry* (Berkeley: University of California Press), pp. 263–84. Patterson also stresses the combination of pastoral and georgic elements, but refers to "Michael" and "The Idle Shepherd-Boys" as "subtle contributions to the counter-revolutionary programs of the British government, promoting a conservative ideology based on the 'georgic' values of hard work (by others), land ownership . . . and, above all, the premise that hardship is to be countered by personal 'Resolution and Independence' rather than social meliorism" (p. 273). Rather than seeing "The Idle Shepherd-Boys" as imbued with class consciousness, it might be possible to reduce it to the cliché that boys will be boys. Other recent studies of "Michael" that deal with its stylistic innovations are Bruce Graver, "Wordsworth's Georgic Pastoral: *Otium* and *Labor* in 'Michael,'" *European Romantic Review,* 1.2 (Winter 1991): 119–34 (note especially the assertion that Wordsworth does *not* naively claim that poetic labor can "alleviate the plight of the working rural poor" [p. 131]); and Judith Page, "'A History / Homely and Rude': Genre and Style in Wordsworth's 'Michael,'" *Studies in English Literature,* 29 (1989): 621–36, which places the poem within the eighteenth-century tradition of responses to the pastoral genre and which treats Wordsworth's serious reconsideration of the original pastoral impulses in Theocritus.

28. See Brennan O'Donnell, "Numerous Verse: A Guide to the Stanzas and Metrical Structures of Wordsworth's Poetry," *Studies in Philology,* 86 (1989): 1–136. This monograph, an old-fashioned taxonomy, attests to the metrical and stylistic variety of Wordsworth's poetry. From this point of view he was the most experimental poet of his century. Only seven poems employ an eleven-line stanza; of these "The Danish Boy" most closely resembles "The Thorn" and "The Idle Shepherd-Boys" but for an opening *a b a b* quatrain. Wordsworth's own remarks on his choice of this form for "The Thorn" are among his most bewildering: "It was necessary that the Poem, to be natural, should in reality move slowly; yet I hoped, that, by the aid of the metre, to those who should at all enter into the spirit of the Poem, it would appear to move quickly" (*Lyrical Ballads,* p. 351). Exactly why "The Thorn" and "The Idle Shepherd-Boys" (along with "The Danish Boy") should share a stylistic base is a question worthy of attention.

29. Marjorie Levinson, *Wordsworth's Great Period Poems* (Cambridge: Cambridge University Press, 1986), p. 156, n. 56. Levinson's chapter "Spiritual Economics: A Reading of 'Michael'" (pp. 58–79) is one of the strongest Marxist readings of Romantic poetry. For a counter to such readings, see Mark Jones, "Double Economics: Ambivalence in Wordsworth's Pastoral," *PMLA,* 108 (1993):

1098–1113. In the name of Bakhtinian multivocality, Jones returns us to a conception of pastoral based on Empsonian ambiguity.

30. A similar unwillingness to describe a tragedy more fully occurs in the 1805 tale of Vaudracour and Julia in *Prelude*, book 9. Separated from his lover and caring for his baby son, who then dies "by some mistake / Or indiscretion of the father" (ll. 907–08), Vaudracour withers away, never again speaking. Not even the "voice of freedom" through the land rouses him from his torpor, "but in those solitary shades / His days he wasted, an imbecile mind" (ll. 934–35). Wordsworth refuses to *kill* this quasi-autobiographical representation, but what is more interesting is that he associates guilt and madness specifically with silence and indolent wastefulness.

31. Mary Moorman, *William Wordsworth: A Biography,* vol. 1, *The Early Years, 1770–1803* (Oxford: Oxford University Press, 1957), pp. 479–80.

32. Jonathan Wordsworth, *The Music of Humanity* (London: Thomas Nelson, 1969), p. 95, describes the introduction to "Michael" as "a clumsy address to the reader." If we take the pastoral to be a study of investments, sacrifices, legacies, and poetic as well as patrimonial bequests, the opening paragraph is indeed central. The relationship of the priest's opening speech to what follows is slightly more awkward, however.

33. An excellent summary of tourism in the Lakes is Malcolm Andrews, *The Search for the Picturesque: Landscape Aesthetics and Tourism in Britain, 1760–1800* (Stanford: Stanford University Press, 1989), esp. chap. 7, "The Tour to the Lakes" (pp. 153–95), which renders an account from Mrs. Piozzi's 1789 exclamation—"There is a *Rage for the Lakes*"—and from the picturesque handbooks of Thomas West (1778), which went through seven editions before the end of the century, and the more famous theories of William Gilpin and Uvedale Price.

34. The priest's condescension here resembles Wordsworth's own in a later letter to Lady Beaumont upon the publication of the 1807 *Poems in Two Volumes,* on the subject of bad readers and judges of poetry: "These people in the senseless hurry of their idle lives do not *read* books, they merely snatch a glance at them that they may talk about them" (*MY,* 1:150).

35. Motifs of suspension and liminality have been associated by many of Wordsworth's critics; he is the first to give them license to do so in his remarks about "hanging" in the 1815 Preface (*PrW,* 3:31), when, discussing examples from Virgil's first Eclogue, *King Lear,* and *Paradise Lost* (2:636–43), he uses "hanging" as an example of the imaginative, nonliteral use of language. See Paul Alpers, *The Singer of the Eclogues: A Study of Virgilian Pastoral* (Berkeley: University of California Press, 1979), pp. 93–95, for another commentary on the passage from the first Eclogue.

36. See Helen Vendler, "Lionel Trilling and the *Immortality Ode,*" *Salmagundi,* 41 (1978): 66–86.

37. Richard Baxter, *A Christian Dictionary,* 2nd ed. (London, 1678), bk. 1, p. 390. Cf. Edward Barry, *A Letter on the Practice of Boxing* (London, 1789), p. 31, for the truism that idleness is "the fruitful root of every vice." For Wordsworth and the other Romantic poets it is also the fruitful root of every creation. For Wordsworth's general indebtedness to the forms as well as the doctrines of radical Protestantism, see Frank D. McConnell, *The Confessional Imagination: A Reading of Wordsworth's Prelude* (Baltimore: Johns Hopkins University Press, 1974); and Richard Brantley, *Wordsworth's "Natural Methodism"* (New Haven: Yale University Press, 1975).

38. Henry Fielding, *An Enquiry into the Causes of the Late Increase of Robbers* (London, 1751), p. 7. For a recent study of political and religious attitudes toward leisure and entertainment during this period, see Robert W. Malcolmson, *Popular Recreation in English Society, 1700–1850* (Cambridge: Cambridge University Press, 1973).

39. Quoted in Hugh Cunningham, *Leisure in the Industrial Revolution* (London: Croom Helm, 1980), p. 12. Cunningham studies the "privatisation" of leisure as a concomitant to that of property during the industrial revolution in England, and the efforts of social, religious, and legislative reformers to counteract the growing privatization of working culture by restressing paternalism in the form of ancient games, recentering leisure in the home, and most of all by establishing "rational recreation" in the form of circulating libraries, subscription concerts, and public parks. See, especially, "Public Leisure and Private Leisure," pp. 26–109.

40. For the shape of *The Prelude,* see M. H. Abrams, *Natural Supernaturalism: Tradition and Revolution in Romantic Literature* (New York: W. W. Norton, 1971), esp. pp. 17–80 and 278–92. See also Herbert Lindenberger, *On Wordsworth's Prelude* (Princeton: Princeton University Press, 1971).

41. A recent Wordsworth biographer distinguishes between an escape and a pastoral haven: in 1799 Wordsworth "had chosen his home not as a negative retreat from the 'real world,' but as a positive commitment to an austere and dedicated life amidst the elemental forms of nature. His model was not Cowper, the stricken deer retiring from the herd [*The Task* 3.108–11], but Milton, seeking the quiet of Horton to equip himself through reflection and study for a life dedicated to high endeavour." Stephen Gill, *William Wordsworth: A Life* (Oxford: Clarendon Press, 1989), p. 174.

42. In ten appearances of "voluptuous" throughout his poetry, Wordsworth uses the adverb form only once. (The line is cited, in fact, in the *OED*.) Significantly, one of the adjectival appearances comes in the "wise restraint / Voluptuous" of "Nutting," which I discussed earlier. "Voluptuous indolence" shows up in *Ecclesiastical Sonnets* 1.23, where the phrase is opposed by the "toil stupendous" and "perpetual industry" of the Venerable Bede. At bottom Wordsworth tends to associate voluptuousness more with the generalized, almost aesthetic gratification of sense experience than with the domain of Eros.

43. Hartman, *Wordsworth's Poetry,* pp. 33–69, argues for such a triple organization of the poem. Nevertheless, as readers we are privy to only two of these parts and in them the arrangement of the material determines how we confront the facts of the reconstructible life.

44. *Correspondance complète de Jean-Jacques Rousseau,* ed. R. A. Leigh (Oxford: Voltaire Foundation at the Taylor Institution, 1978), 32:82 (my translation). See Jean-Jacques Rousseau, *The Reveries of the Solitary Walker,* trans. Charles E. Butterworth (New York: New York University Press, 1979), pp. 62–73, for the text of the fifth walk. Passages such as this abound in Rousseau's oeuvre. For a comparison of Rousseau and Wordsworth, see Margery Sabin, *English Romanticism and the French Tradition* (Cambridge, Mass.: Harvard University Press, 1976), pp. 3–124.

45. Irving Babbitt, *Rousseau and Romanticism* (Boston: Houghton Mifflin, 1919), p. 43. Babbitt also quotes, disapprovingly, from Rousseau: "I felt in the midst of my glory that my heart was not made for so much turmoil, and soon without knowing how I found myself once more among my beloved pastorals, renouncing forever the toils of Mars" (p. 73). Thus does the pastoral impulse seem always to provoke its enemies. Terry Eagleton traces the rise of aestheticism to the

rise of the bourgeoisie in the mid-eighteenth century. Although they express their disapproval in different registers (Babbitt theologically, Eagleton secularly) both critics exhibit a puritanical distrust of art that derives from leisure, escape, or the isolation of the artist. A self-justifying aestheticism (art for art's sake) is equally suspect.

46. See, for example, Bialastosky, pp. 161–84; Theresa M. Kelley, *Wordsworth's Revisionary Aesthetics* (Cambridge: Cambridge University Press, 1988), pp. 98–100; my own discussion in *Wordsworth's Heroes,* pp. 130–37; Jonathan Wordsworth, *William Wordsworth: The Borders of Vision,* pp. 10–16, among many other treatments.

47. This fact balances Wordsworth's earlier statement that the face of every neighbor at home is "a volume." It also balances his later vertiginous sense of loss in the hurly-burly of London, when he says to himself: "The face of every one / That passes by me is a mystery!" (*Prelude* 7.596–97). Paul Magnuson, in "'My Own Voice': 'The Ancient Mariner' and 'The Discharged Soldier,'" *Coleridge and Wordsworth: A Lyrical Dialogue* (Princeton: Princeton University Press, 1988), pp. 68–95, treats the relationship of the two poems and stresses the importance of dialogue, but he ignores the fact that Wordsworth does not give us the substance of the soldier's words until the very end, and then only in an admonitory epigram.

48. In book 8 Wordsworth modifies his commitment to the ornamental qualities of poetry when he reports that the "first poetic faculty / Of plain Imagination and severe [began] to put on / A visible shape." Even here, however, plain severity is balanced by the very fact of being externally clothed. In addition, he seems retrospectively embarrassed by "the shapes / Of wilful fancy grafted upon feelings / Of the imagination" (see 8.511–623).

49. Dorothy Wordsworth to Mrs. Thomas Clarkson, February 13, 1804 (*EY,* 440).

Chapter 3

1. Samuel Johnson, *Letters,* ed. R. W. Chapman (Oxford: Clarendon Press, 1952), 3:182.

2. Another interesting gloss on Coleridgean sloth comes in a letter of July 27, 1802, to Sara Hutchinson, on the subject of his mountaineering: "When I find it convenient to descend from a mountain, I am too *confident & indolent* [emphasis added] to look round about & wind about 'till I find a track or other symptom of safety; but I wander on, & where it is first *possible* to descend, there I go—relying upon fortune for how far down this possibility will continue (*CL,* 2:841).

3. For Coleridge in the mountains, see Richard Holmes, *Coleridge: Early Visions* (New York: Viking, 1990), pp. 330–34; William Ruddick, "'As Much Diversity as the Heart That Trembles': Coleridge's Notes on the Lakeland Fells," in *Coleridge's Imagination,* ed. Richard Gravil, Lucy Newlyn, and Nicholas Roe, (Cambridge: Cambridge University Press, 1985), pp. 88–101; and, especially, Molly Lefebure, *Cumberland Heritage* (London: Gollancz, 1970), who remarks his noticing "the ridiculous discrepancy between the exaggerated awe with which picturesque tourists treated the fells and the confident manner in which the dalesfolk lived and worked in these reputedly hair-raising regions" (p. 134). Unlike the early tourists, who came with books, or at least with guides, who were driven from station to station, and who, since the "high, empty, remote rockscapes were foreign to the aesthetic canons of the time . . . felt no desire to experience them"

(Ruddick, p. 89), Coleridge began to scamper, often recklessly, among the high places.

4. Peter L. Thorslev, Jr., *Romantic Contraries: Freedom Versus Destiny* (New Haven: Yale University Press, 1984), makes the strongest case for such "contrarieties" as the basis for Romantic art and philosophy.

5. I take this as a more acute version of what Paul De Man referred to as the absence at the center of *all* writing, that of the Word never present. See Paul De Man, *Blindness and Insight: Essays in the Rhetoric of Contemporary Criticism* (New York: Oxford University Press, 1971), pp. 117–19. Jean-Pierre Mileur, *Vision and Re-Vision: Coleridge's Art of Immanence* (Berkeley: University of California Press, 1982), reminds us that Coleridge always used the Bible as point of reference and of absence.

6. This is what Richard Holmes refers to when, discussing Coleridge's retreat to opium in early 1801 just as Wordsworth seems to have gained the upper hand in their relationship, he allows that Coleridge *uses* his frustrations for subject matter: "While Wordsworth gained the authority of poetic success, Coleridge found the authority of poetic failure" (p. 300). Even before the Dejection Ode, however, Coleridge worked his poems from a basis in indolence, construed either as observation and contemplation or as mere sloth.

7. For a sense of what has been purged from the earlier verse epistle in the construction of the final ode, see Gene Ruoff, *Wordsworth and Coleridge: The Making of the Major Lyrics, 1802–4* (New Brunswick, N.J.: Rutgers University Press, 1989), especially the conclusion of chapter 6 (p. 212). Ruoff makes the point that Coleridge has transformed the crisis of his marriage into a vocational one: "'Dejection' methodically suppresses the matter of delight, omitting all scenes of remembered pleasure. It insists that dejection is a chronic problem, just as Wordsworth-Edmund's joy is an enduring gift." In other words, the absence at the heart of the poem is everything that marked its experiential origins.

8. Mary Robinson, *Poetical Works* (London: James & Co., 1824), pp. 58, 38. All references are to this edition of Robinson's works.

9. The same case is made in the early poem to Charles Lloyd of 1796, "Addressed to a Young Man of Fortune, who Abandoned himself to an indolent and causeless Melancholy" (*CP*, pp. 157–58), in which Coleridge recommends *work* as a cure for "sickly dreams," and suggests that the young man take a look at someone who is genuinely miserable as a way of correcting his own delusions of misery. The youthful Coleridge, at least, understood the difference between the extremes of truly motivated unhappiness and those purely imagined ills that lead to a false melancholy.

10. Cf. the "visionary dreariness" of *Prelude* 11.310 which invests the mouldered gibbet in the eye of Wordsworth returning, so to speak, to the scene of the crime.

11. The only other change between the version of the *Morning Post* and that of 1817 is the elimination of line 37 ("A boat becalm'd! a lovely sky-canoe!"), which is now unnecessary since the poem is no longer addressed to Wordsworth, and the reference to "Peter Bell" would be irrelevant. But this change hardly affects the *nature* of the illness which the earlier change takes pains to diagnose more accurately. For all variants in the different stages of the poem, see Stephen Maxfield Parrish, ed., *Coleridge's Dejection: The Earliest Manuscripts and the Earliest Printings* (Ithaca, N.Y.: Cornell University Press, 1988).

12. Harold Bloom, *The Visionary Company: A Reading of English Romantic Poetry* (Garden City, N.Y.: Doubleday, 1961), pp. 216–23. Stuart Curran, *Poetic Form*

and British Romanticism (New York: Oxford University Press, 1986), pp. 75–76, discusses the balanced structure and the absence of strict stanzaic regularity in the poem, citing as "strophe" Coleridge's contemplation of his inertia, and as "antistrophe" the matter of the great storm. His scheme is vitiated, however, by the fact that the supposed antistrophe formally precedes the autobiographical strophic material. A. Harris Fairbanks, "The Form of Coleridge's Dejection Ode," *PMLA*, 90 (1975): 874–84, discusses the problems of the ode's "form," reviewing the history of the critical attempts to deal with its peculiarities of structure and diction. He remarks (pp. 877–78) the sudden transitions as typical of the Pindaric ode, but doesn't go as far as I do to discuss the breaks *within* the grammatical units of each stanza. For a Hegelian reading of the ode based on the principles of Hans Gadamer, see Cyrus Hamlin, "The Hermeneutics of Form: Reading the Romantic Ode," *Boundary 2*, 7.3 (1979): 1–30, which also discusses the "principle of concentric frames" within the poem.

13. M. H. Abrams, "Structure and Style in the Greater Romantic Lyric," in *From Sensibility to Romanticism: Essays Presented to F. A. Pottle,* ed. F. W. Hilles and Harold Bloom (New York: Oxford University Press, 1965), pp. 527–60. See Beverly Fields, *Reality's Dark Dream: Dejection in Coleridge* (Kent, Ohio: Kent State University Press, 1967), for one of the few critics who admire the immediacy and authenticity of the letter form. Most readers prefer the shapeliness of the ode.

14. John Hollander, *Rhyme's Reason: A Guide to English Verse,* rev. enl. ed. (New Haven: Yale University Press, 1989), p. 1, distinguishes between "tropes, or figures of meaning such as metaphor and metonymy, and schemes, or surface patterns of words."

15. See Jerome Christensen, *Coleridge's Blessed Machine Of Language* (Ithaca, N.Y.: Cornell University Press, 1981), esp. p. 27 ("Chiasmus is the blessed machine of Coleridge's language"), and pp. 260–69; and John Hodgson, *Coleridge, Shelley, and Transcendental Inquiry* (Lincoln: University of Nebraska Press, 1989), esp. pp. 4–44, for chiasmus as a master trope in Coleridge. For Hodgson, "the images expressing [the] barrier to transcendental inquiry will necessarily be tropes of uncertainty: Coleridge's are most frequently figurations of infinite regress, disorientation, and blankness" (p. 40). But neither of these critics is especially interested in Coleridge's poetry or in the strictly *rhetorical* use of chiasmus as a poetic device. For a compendious survey of chiasmus as a master trope (albeit in ancient Greek and Hebrew literature), see the encyclopedic work of John Welch, ed., *Chiasmus in Antiquity* (Hildesheim: Gerstenberg, 1981), which demonstrates the multiple possibilities for chiasmus as more than a simple *a b b a* structure, but one that contains hysteron proteron, epanodos, and palistrophe within its arsenal of rhetorical possibilities. For a provocative discussion of Wordsworthian chiasmus (again as a figural rather than a rhetorical device), see Andrez Warminski, "Missed Crossing: Wordsworth's Apocalypses," *Modern Language Notes,* 99 (1984): 983–1006. In a detailed reading of the Boy of Winander episode in *Prelude* 5, Warminski concludes that a word such as "hung" "unhinges the economy of loss and restoration, its symmetrical chiasmic reversals, and the (cognitive) psychological model on which they are based" (p. 995). Justus George Lawler, in his provocative book *Celestial Pantomime: Poetic Structures of Transcendence* (New Haven: Yale University Press, 1979), reads chiasmus "as primarily representative of the intersection of the infinite and the finite, and of man's confusion as the conjunction of both; it is secondarily representative of the intersection of female and male, also with its attendant confu-

sions" (p. 53), but Coleridge gets only a single nod (Christabel as "dreaming fearfully, / Fearfully dreaming").

16. I leave to other critics the task of explaining the relationship between enclosure and mirroring, and the rhetorical use of chiasmus as trope, from a strictly psychoanalytic standpoint. Both Freud's *Beyond the Pleasure Principle* and *The Seminar of Jacques Lacan* (especially book 7) would provide helpful theoretical models for such an investigation, but my primary interest is poetic, that is, formal and generic.

17. In his sensitive reading of the poem, Reeve Parker, *Coleridge's Meditative Art* (Ithaca, N.Y.: Cornell University Press, 1975), p. 185, notes the chiasmus of lines 10–11 but does not discuss its important resonances.

18. One easy way to read these lines, of course, is to take line 9 as a self-contained exclamation, and lines 10–14 as a second, completed sentence. But given the frequency of exclamation points *within* sentences in Romantic poetry as well as the conjunctive "and" that begins line 10, it is a credible possibility that Coleridge wishes the lines to have the heft of a single sentence. Lines 11–14 in "Frost at Midnight" form a similar kind of run-on sentence.

19. This might be considered a version of the rhetorical device known as epanalepsis, by which a line begins and ends with the same word. It is a reduced chiasmus, having eliminated a crucial middle term. Coleridge might have said: "When two unequal minds meet in one house, and in one house two discordant wills."

20. Reeve Parker quotes (p. 203) from an essay by Coleridge in *Blackwood's* of 1821 (from *Collected Works,* ed. W. G. T. Shedd [New York: Harper, 1853], 4:432): "The best and surest nepenthe of solitary pain is opened out . . . in the collation and constructive imagining of the outward shapes and material forces that shall best express the essential form, in its coincidence with the idea, or realize most adequately that power, which is one with its correspondent knowledge, as the revealing body with its indwelling soul." As in art, so in psychology: Coleridge makes everything a story of containment, of the binding perimeter as that which gives form to the indwelling spirit. Ammons, an unabashed Coleridgean organicist, has made of this his constant obsession; see, especially, his book-length poem *Sphere: The Form of a Motion* (New York: Norton, 1974).

21. See Norman Fruman, "Coleridge's Rejection of Nature and the Natural Man," in Gravil, Newlyn, and Roe, pp. 69–78, for a discussion of Coleridge's various uses of these terms.

22. Marshall Suther, *The Dark Night of Samuel Taylor Coleridge* (New York: Columbia University Press, 1960), pp. 134–35. The entire chapter on "Dejection" (pp. 119–51) is worth reviewing.

23. See also Ruoff, who notes that "the habits of 'abstruse research,' which in the Verse Letter had been a strategy for withdrawal from feeling caused by [his] unhappy marriage, now become as much a cause in themselves as a failed anodyne" (p. 176).

24. Parker hears Hamlet's "suicidal dejection" in Coleridge's grief, (p. 172), but this does violence, I think, to the nature of his clinical depression. He is too weary to contemplate, let alone to realize, suicidal thoughts.

25. See the analysis of Paul Magnuson, *Coleridge's Nightmare Poetry* (Charlottesville: University of Virginia Press, 1974), pp. 107–25, for a discussion of the buffetings dramatized in the ode.

26. Michael Cooke, *The Romantic Will* (New Haven: Yale University Press,

1976), takes as its premise the availability, even the universality, of the will as a Romantic phenomenon. Quoting Coleridge's aphorism that will "is the law of our nature," Schopenhauer's claim that "the self-consciousness is intensely, really even exclusively, occupied with willing," and even Boehme's "Every life is essential and based on will," Cooke has constructed an eclectic anatomy of the Romantic will. For him, Coleridge's definition of the imagination, borrowed from Schelling, offers the classic reconciliation between world and the "absolute Self" (see, e.g., "[T]he presence of the will in imagination becomes as patent as the presence of the self" [p. 29]). Cooke's conclusion is one with which much of what I say in this book agrees but also takes issue: "Though suggesting the paramountcy of the will in so many ways, romanticism strikingly avoids the two extremes of the will—its impulse to mere arbitrary definition, or solipsism, and its smothering in the possessiveness of death. Accordingly, we may regard the period as a negotiation between the necessary self and an inevitable world, with the will at once underlying and burdened by every action, and the state of being both assumed and problematically pursued" (p. 222).

27. In a more negative manifestation, spectatorship enters the poem "Fears in Solitude" twice: first in the imagined third-person "humble man," half-sleeping on the ferns and distanced from the "speaker," who turns out at the end to have been all along that indolent person; and second at a political level, in Coleridge's fears for the English conception of war as a spectator sport: "war and bloodshed; animating sports, / The which we pay for as a thing to talk of, / Spectators and not combatants! (ll. 94–96).

28. Parker writes that the poem "*dramatizes* an emotional crisis; it does not simply record, from Coleridge's life, an about-face in psychological speculation" (p. 192). But he also acknowledges that in the opening of stanza 7 "what seems . . . a sudden wrench in the poet's monologue has been a serious obstacle to accepting the final version of 'Dejection' as a coherent poem" (p. 195). Paul Fry, *The Poet's Calling in the English Ode* (New Haven: Yale University Press, 1980), p. 163, says, wrongly I think, that "the storm does not directly affect the poet's consciousness." Recognizing that the storm is "deliberately a pastiche of other poets' poems" (p. 168), Fry denies Coleridge a true exorcism in the final stanzas, beginning with "Hence, viper thoughts."

29. One might recognize as an analogy those moments in *The Prelude* that follow a pattern of concentration, relaxation, and responsiveness to the unexpected. "The Boy of Winander" (5.389–415) comes to mind, as does Wordsworth's automatic recovery from his nervous breakdown: "I shook the habit off / Entirely and for ever" (11.253–54).

30. See, e.g., Magnuson, who makes the common mistake, by ignoring the present perfect verbs, in referring to lines 47–56, that Coleridge "is seeing nature directly for the first time" (p. 28). Mileur is closer to understanding the variety of the poem (although he, too, ignores the temporal distinctions in Coleridge's figurations of nature), in his discussion of Coleridge's "Almighty Spirit" as "an implicit event that escapes the order of nature, escapes the order of figuration, and escapes even the order of self" (pp. 44–45). What Coleridge dramatizes in the poem is the process whereby that which seems to have escaped has in fact been apprehended all along, so perhaps the transcendent "Almighty Spirit," which seems to be of a different figurative order from the natural details, in fact occupies an equivalent "epistemological category coming into being—a category of mediation" (p. 21). Charles Rzepka, *Self as Mind* (Cambridge, Mass.: Harvard University Press, 1986),

p. 129, in a sensitive reading of the poem, makes, I believe, the same mistake of thinking Coleridge's change of mind sudden when he writes that "the world at hand obtrudes on the poet's reverie. . . . [He] awakens from his reveries of self-dispersion to find himself embowered by the very Nature he had enclosed." The one exception to the general critical error is James K. Chandler, "Romantic Allusiveness," *Critical Inquiry*, 8 (1982): 468, in an obiter dictum concerning the poem. See also Anne K. Mellor, "Coleridge's 'This Lime-Tree Bower My Prison,'" *Studies in Romanticism*, 18 (1979): 253–70; A. W. Rudrum, "Coleridge's 'This Lime-Tree Bower My Prison,'" *Southern Review* (Adelaide), 1:2 (1964): 30–42. James Engell, "Imagining into Nature: 'This Lime-Tree Bower My Prison,'" in *Coleridge, Keats, and the Imagination*, ed. J. Robert Barth, S. J., and John L. Mahoney (Columbia: University of Missouri Press, 1990), pp. 81–96, deals elegantly with what Engell labels the essential "Romantic syntax" of the poem.

31. Two other comparably reparatory gestures suggest themselves as analogies to Coleridge's condition here. The first is in Keats's journal letter to his brother and sister-in-law in America, where he suggests that the act of reading a passage of Shakespeare each Sunday at noon will bring them closer together (Keats, *Letters*, 2:5). The second is in Elizabeth Bishop's neo-Romantic "Poem," where an old painting serves as the mediating figure between the poet and a dead great-uncle she never knew but with whom her "vision" has coincided. See my essay "Landscape and Knowledge: The Poetry of Elizabeth Bishop," *Modern Poetry Studies*, 6 (1975): 203–23, for a study of Bishop's updating of Romantic poetic practice. One other poem of Coleridge's deserves mention in this matter. The late "Garden of Boccaccio" (1828) begins with a ten-line description of chronic anomie, characterized by tropes of negation and absence:

> Of late, in one of those most weary hours,
> When life seems emptied of all genial powers,
> A dreary mood, which he who ne'er has known
> May bless his happy lot, I sate alone . . .

To "win relief," Coleridge chiastically attempts to conquer vacancy: "Call'd on the Past for thought of glee or grief. / In vain! bereft alike of grief and glee." His cure comes, unexpected, in the form of a print of Boccaccio's garden, given to him by his landlady, Mrs. Gillman, which has the salutary effect of translating him out of himself and into the the depicted garden: "I see no longer. I myself am there" (l. 65).

32. Parker, pp. 121–38, on "Frost at Midnight," discusses companionable form(s) as a structural as well as a thematic principle in the poem.

33. For a harsher reading of these lines, and of the poem generally, see Tilottama Rajan, "Image and Reality in Coleridge's Lyric Poetry," in *Dark Interpreter: The Discourse of Romanticism* (Ithaca, N.Y.: Cornell University Press, 1980), pp. 204–59, esp. p. 228, on the presumed affirmations within the conversation poems: "[T]hey always seem to claim an experience of epiphany, but to do so only vicariously, through an *alter ego* who is ambiguously Yeatsian mask and Shelleyan epipsyche, therefore ironic and sentimental."

34. Tilottama Rajan, *The Supplement of Reading: Figures of Understanding in Romantic Theory and Practice* (Ithaca, N.Y.: Cornell University Press, 1990), p. 121, discusses the poem, and Coleridge's absence from it, as part of his hermeneutic experiments which become, in his later conversation poems, "a problem of self-

negation." Rajan treats all of the conversation poems as experiences of reading; see "The (Un)Persuaded Reader: Coleridge's Conversation with Hermeneutics," pp. 101–35.

35. Walter Jackson Bate, *Coleridge* (New York: Macmillan, 1968), p. 50, rightly calls Colerdge's blessing a surrender, through which he "can acquire his own vicarious release of heart, his own security and confidence in what he thinks and hopes."

36. The heavily charged prepositions are, perhaps, another legacy of Coleridge to Wordsworth. An equivalently suggestive phrase comes in the blessing at the end of "Dejection": "*To* her may all things live" (l. 135); here the preposition implies inwardness as well as direction, as if Coleridge wishes all things to live *within* Sara, and to grow *toward* her. What Wordsworth developed as a stylistic signature he may have learned from small moments like this one in Coleridge's poetry. See Christopher Ricks, "The Twentieth-Century Wordsworth," in *Twentieth-Century Literature in Retrospect,* ed. Reuben A. Brower, vol. 2 of *Harvard English Studies* (Cambridge, Mass.: Harvard University Press, 1971), pp. 343–63.

37. Friedrich Nietzsche, *The Birth of Tragedy,* in *Basic Writings of Nietzsche,* ed. Walter Kaufmann (New York: Modern Library, 1968), p. 132.

38. Cf. Coleridge's characterization of Spenser's "mind [as] constitutionally tender, delicate, and, in comparison with his three great compeers, I had almost said, *effeminate*" (*BL,* 1:36; on Spenser's "deep moral earnestness," see *Notebooks,* 3:4501). In one of his dark later poems Coleridge even goes so far as to address "man" as "[a] phantom dim of past and future wrought, / Vain sister of the worm" (the 1832 "Self-Knowledge"). Whether this refers to a Blakean emanation, a Jungian anima, a Shelleyan epipsyche, or a mere self-loathing un-manning is entirely unclear.

39. As a counter, however, to the almost constant asssociation of idleness with effeminacy in his poetry, Coleridge adduces the figure of Joan of Arc, in both his drama and his poem "The Destiny of Nations," as an exemplary heroic (i.e., active) partisan.

40. James Engell and W. Jackson Bate suggest in their note to this passage the currency of Coleridge's idea in both native English empiricism and German Romanticism. Imagination as the intermediate force (Kant's theory of the transcendental synthetic) between active reasoning and passive associationism informs K. M. Wheeler, *The Creative Mind in Coleridge's Poetry* (Cambridge, Mass.: Harvard University Press, 1981), which treats "the paradoxical relation of the active-passive impulses on a conscious-unconscious topography" (p. 79) and the ways in which Coleridge's poems demonstrate his theories about the creative mind. According to Wheeler, in "The Eolian Harp," even words such as "stretch" and "behold" (st. 2) give "a model of the creativity of perception itself, and the active role the supposedly passive percipient can play" (p. 80).

41. Parker duplicates the chiasmus of the poem in his comment, "the moon in the old man and the old man in the moon finding in each other a companionable form" (p. 242).

Chapter 4

1. Richard Macksey, "Keats and the Poetics of Extremity," *Modern Language Notes* 94 (1984): 845–84, esp. 872–73, emphasizes the passivity of Autumn's postures and denies her status as a "subject," stressing instead her "objective personified form."

2. I have suggested, in chapter 1, the parameters of melancholy and indolence as they changed between the Middle Ages and the nineteenth century. We might say that good and bad melancholy give way in Keats to good and bad indolence, not from a moral but from an aesthetic standpoint.

3. We may even hear "snoozings" buzzing through the "last oozings" since, according to the historical evidence of the *OED*, "snooze" existed for Keats.

4. Reuben Arthur Brower, *The Fields of Light: An Experiment in Critical Reading* (New York: Oxford University Press, 1951), p. 43.

5. Helen Vendler, *The Odes of John Keats* (Cambridge, Mass.: Harvard University Press, 1983).

6. G. M. Matthews, ed., *Keats: The Critical Heritage* (London: Routledge & Kegan Paul, 1971), p. 1, makes the point that much of the initial critical hostility to Keats's poetry was directed against the conservatism, not to say archaism, of its diction and style, its conscious effort to resort to Elizabethan models. This point is the pendant to Marjorie Levinson's reading of the hostile remarks of people such as Byron as entirely class-conscious; see *Keats's Life of Allegory: The Origins of a Style* (London: Basil Blackwell, 1988), pp. 22–24.

7. Two essays by Paul Fry steer a middle path between the aesthetic view of Helen Vendler and the political stance of Jerome McGann and other critics informed by Marxist ideology. See Paul H. Fry, "History, Existence, and 'To Autumn,'" *Studies in Romanticism*, 25 (1986): 211–19; and "Literature and Our Discontents," *Yale Review*, 73 (1984): 603–16, in which Fry takes issue with both "the totalizing visions of aesthetics and politics alike" (p. 616).

8. In her interesting chapter on Keatsian receptivity, Hermione de Almeida demonstrates Keats's debt for his aesthetics (especially the concept of negative capability) to Romantic medicine as much as to Hazlitt; see *Romantic Medicine and John Keats* (New York: Oxford University Press, 1991), pp. 286–98. Contemporary physical scientists appropriated Lockean ideas concerning active and passive power first adumbrated in the *Essay Concerning Human Understanding*.

9. Geoffrey Hartman, "False Themes and Gentle Minds," in *Beyond Formalism: Literary Esssays, 1958–1970* (New Haven: Yale University Press, 1970), pp. 285, 283, 289.

10. Brigit Gellert Lyons, "Milton's 'Il Penseroso' and the Idea of Time," in *Voices of Melancholy: Studies in Literary Treatments of Melancholy in Renaissance England* (London: Routledge & Kegan Paul, 1971), pp. 149–61. See also Spenser's figure of Phantastes, one of the trio of mental attributes (imagination, memory, and understanding) in *Faerie Queene* 2.9.50–52, a melancholic born under Saturn.

11. References are to John Milton, *Complete Poems and Major Prose*, ed. Merritt Y. Hughes (New York: Odyssey Press, 1957).

12. Steven Knapp, *Personification and the Sublime: Milton to Coleridge* (Cambridge, Mass.: Harvard University Press, 1985), p. 128.

13. All citations are from J. Logie Robertson, ed., *The Complete Poetical Works of James Thomson* (London: Henry Frowde/Oxford University Press, 1908), pp. 251–308.

14. See Dorothy Wordsworth's journal entry for May 9, 1802, a Sunday morning: "The air considerably colder to-day, but the sun shone all day. William worked at *The Leech Gatherer* and other poems for Coleridge. I was oppressed and sick at heart, for he wearied himself to death. After tea he wrote two stanzas in the manner of Thomson's *Castle of Indolence*, and was tired out. Bad news of Coleridge" (*Journals of Dorothy Wordsworth*, ed. Ernest de Selincourt [London: Mcmillian, 1959],

1:145). The conjunction of Thomson; of Wordsworth's "Resolution and Independence," in which figuration, metaphor, and allegorical embodiment are all central; and of the shared fatigue of Dorothy, William, and the absent Coleridge is too potent to be merely coincidental.

15. Robertson's preference here, and his response to Thomson generally, suggest the kind of involvement in "Romantic ideology" that Jerome McGann has identified as constituting the primary scholarly tradition *of* (in both senses) Romanticism. What to another critic would be the hermeneutic problem of trying to understand a phenomenon (in this case a literary work or movement) from an appropriate point outside it is for McGann the ideological dilemma of trying to evaluate Romanticism while having bought into its central premises, as most major literary critics of the past seem to have done. See McGann's seminal study *The Romantic Ideology: A Critical Investigation* (Chicago: University of Chicago Press, 1983).

16. Gray writes rather jovially in a letter of May 1742 to Richard West, attempting to distinguish from black melancholy his own version of "white Melancholy, or rather *Leucocholy* . . . which though it seldom laughs or dances, nor ever amounts to what one calls Joy or Pleasure, yet is a good easy sort of a state, and *ça ne laisse que de s'amuser.* The only fault of it is *insipidity;* which is apt now and then to give a sort of Ennui, which makes one form certain little wishes that signify nothing." *The Letters of Thomas Gray,* ed. D. C. Tovey, 3 vols. (London, 1900–1912), 1:102. For a discussion, heavily influenced by Foucault, of this passage and other attempts to define madness, see Allan Ingram, *The Madhouse of Language: Writing and Reading Madness in the Eighteenth Century* (London: Routledge, 1991), pp. 77–104.

17. William Shenstone, *Poetical Works,* 2 vols. (Edinburgh: J. Robertson, 1773), 1:88–89. Shenstone's letters are also filled with remarks about his own temperamental attraction to indolence, for example, in a 1745 letter to Richard Graves: "I am sensible of the daily progress I make towards insignificance." *The Letters of William Shenstone,* ed. Marjorie Williams (Oxford: Basil Blackwell, 1939), p. 94.

18. See D. W. Jefferson, "The Mid-Eighteenth Century and Its Crisis: The Poetry of Indolence," *English,* 31 (1982): 95–119, for a summary of the fascination with indolence among the pre-Romantics in both their poems and their letters.

19. See *Letters,* 1:224 ("[W]e hate poetry that has a palpable design upon us"); also Shelley's claim in the preface to *Prometheus Unbound* that "didactic poetry is my abhorrence."

20. In Matthews, p. 119. Another, anonymous review (*Champion,* June 8, 1818), *perhaps* by Richard Woodhouse or John Hamilton Reynolds, makes a similar point: "Mr Keats goes out of himself into a world of abstractions:—his passions, feelings, are all as much imaginative as his situations" (Matthews, p. 89).

21. These include Walter Jackson Bate, Douglas Bush, David Perkins, and, more recently, Helen Vendler, whose tracing of the development of Keats's negotiations with linguistic problems maintains an organic bias comparable to that of her predecessors.

22. According to Susan Wolfson, *The Questioning Presence: Wordsworth, Keats, and the Interrogative Mode in Romantic Poetry* (Ithaca, N.Y.: Cornell University Press, 1986), p. 329, throughout the ode "Keats makes the voice of retrospective questioning an almost querulous one, using it as a rhetorical figure in a drama of a poet averse to the challenge of verse. He summons these shadowy figures into the poetic present only to wonder why their presence was not more forceful."

23. This intertwining of soul-making, aesthetics, and democracy has an interest-

ing parallel to, if not exactly an origin in, Shaftesbury's *Characteristics:* to love beauty is "advantageous to social affection, and highly assistant to virtue, which is itself no other than the love of order and beauty in society." Quoted in Terry Eagleton, *The Ideology of the Aesthetic* (Oxford: Basil Blackwell, 1990), p. 35.

24. Margaret Homans, "Keats Reading Women, Women Reading Keats," *Studies in Romanticism,* 29 (1990): 341–70, discusses this letter with regard to Keats's complex and resentful feelings toward the power of (especially elite) women readers. See p. 345: "Keats habitually makes the apparent femininity of his negative capability enhance masculine power and pleasure, in writing as in love."

25. In addition to De Almeida, see Stuart Sperry, *Keats the Poet* (Princeton: Princeton University Press, 1973); and Donald Goellnicht, *The Poet–Physician: Keats and Medical Science* (Pittsburgh: University of Pittsburgh Press, 1984).

26. Henry James, "The Lesson of Balzac," in *Literary Criticism* (New York: Library of America, 1984), p. 130.

27. For similar remarks, see *Letters,* 2:134, 227, and 239.

28. Friedrich Nietzsche, *Beyond Good and Evil,* trans. Walter Kaufmann (New York: Random House, 1966), pp. 25–26.

29. Sir Richard Blackmore, *A Treatise of the Spleen and Vapours: or, Hypocondriacal and Hysterical Affections* (1725); cited in Richard Hunter and Ida Macalpine, eds., *Three Hundred Years of Psychiatry, 1535–1860* (1963; rpt. Hartsdale, N.Y.: Carlisle Publishing, 1982), p. 322.

30. See Goellnicht, p. 204, who refers to William Babbington and James Curry, *Outlines of a Course of Lectures on the Practice of Medicine as Delivered in the Medical School of Guy's Hospital* (London: M'Creery, 1811).

31. John Wilson Crocker's infamous hostile review in the *Quarterly Review* (April 1818) makes a criticism of what might in some other context be considered a virtue for a poet: "He wanders from one subject to another, from association, not of ideas but of sounds" (Matthews, p. 112). Such aural associations are also audible in the letters.

32. Levinson discusses the "vulgarity" of Keats's "fulsome [*sic*] claim to literary ease" (pp. 11–15).

33. Wolfson mentions the double punning as an example of Keatsian "fine saying of things said unintentionally" (p. 304). Her entire analysis makes valuable points about the implicit "questioning" as well as the explicit "questions" throughout Keats's poetry.

34. I have discussed the concept of seasonableness in regard to the "Ode to a Nightingale" in "Keats's 'Coming Muskrose' and Shakespeare's 'Profound Verdure,'" *ELH,* 50 (1983): 347–62.

35. Within the available medical literature, George Cheyne describes the second stage of "vapours" as a condition that moves along a range from "a deep and fixed *Melancholy*" through crying, grief, and anguish, which "generally terminate in *Hypochondriacal* or *Hysterical Fits* (I mean *Convulsive* ones) and *Faintings,* which leave a Drowsiness, *Lethargy,* and extreme Lowness of Spirits for some Time afterwards." George Cheyne, *The English Malady: or, a Treatise of Nervous Diseases of all Kinds . . . With the Author's own Case at Large* (London, 1733), p. 199. "Fit," in other words, seems more appropriate to hysteria than to either the melancholy from which it derives or the torpor to which it leads. Keats compresses the entire physiological–psychological process into a single moment by using the word this way.

36. See Anselm Haverkamp, "Mourning Becomes Melancholia—A Muse De-

constructed: Keats's *Ode on Melancholy,"* *New Literary History,* 21 (1990): 693–706, for an application to Keats's ode of Freud's notion that melancholy is *apparently* causeless. Haverkamp's conclusion—that Keats "nourished the ambivalence at the bottom of his melancholia and followed, in a poetical 'working through,' the repetition compulsion of modern writing" (p. 705)—is consistent with my comparable placing of indolence at the center of the poetry.

37. I cannot determine whether Keats was aware of the work of Anne Finch, but there is a significant connection between his depiction of melancholy and the conclusion of her poem "The Spleen," admired by contemporary physicians for its supposed clinical accuracy. Finch invokes her subject as a "Proteus to abus'd Mankind," capable of aping everything but lacking both a "real cause" and a continuous shape. At the poem's end, as at the end of Keats's ode, the adventurer is caught, the trickster tricked, the would-be hero sacrificed to the here *un*gendered abstraction:

> Not skilful Lower thy Source could find,
> Or thro' the well-dissected Body trace
> The secret, the mysterious ways,
> By which thou dost surprise, and prey upon the Mind.
> Tho' in the Search, too deep for Humane Thought
> With unsuccessful Toil he wrought,
> 'Till thinking Thee to've catch'd, Himself by thee was caught,
> Retain'd thy Pris'ner, thy acknowledg'd Slave,
> And sunk beneath thy Chain to a lamented Grave.

See Anne Finch, *Selected Poems of Anne Finch, Countess of Winchilsea,* ed. Katharine M. Rogers (New York: Frederick Ungar, 1979), pp. 145–49.

Chapter 5

1. All quotations are from Virginia Woolf, *Mrs. Dalloway* (London: Hogarth Press, 1929), pp. 16, 50–56.

2. All quotations are taken from Bernard F. Dick, ed., *Dark Victory* (Madison: University of Wisconsin Press, 1981).

3. A recent version of this somewhat simple view is Roger Sales, *English Literature in History, 1780–1830: Pastoral and Politics* (London: Hutchinson, 1983), part of a series edited by Raymond Williams. For Sales pastoral "offers a political interpretation of both past and present. It is a propagandist reconstruction of history" (p. 17), and "should not be seen in terms of an elegant literary genre. It was a statement of political creed" (p. 28). The case of Shelley certainly disproves such simplistic generalizations because, although he is a gentleman writing pastoral, he nowhere approves the status quo. The persistence of pastoral has been remarked by—of all people—Jacques Lacan, who adopts an attitude compounded of equal doses of Freud and William Empson when he remarks that "the domain of pastoral is never absent from civilization; it never fails to offer itself as a solution to the latter's discontents. . . . Nowadays, it is often masked; it appears for example in the more severe and more pedantic form of the infallibility of proletarian consciousness." See Jacques-Alain Miller, ed., *The Seminar of Jacques Lacan,* bk. 7, *The Ethics of Psychoanalysis, 1959–1960,* trans. Dennis Porter (New York: Norton, 1992), p. 88.

4. Alastair Fowler, *Kinds of Literature: An Introduction to the Theory of Genres and Modes* (Cambridge, Mass.: Harvard University Press, 1982), pp. 253–4. Pas-

toral is, as Fowler goes on to observe, never really pure: it always generates the sense of an ideal tainted or unreachable. For a different view of pastoral, based on Kenneth Burke's concept of scene–agent ratios, the "synecdochic relation . . . between person and place," see Paul Alpers, "What Is Pastoral?" *Critical Inquiry*, 8 (1982): 437–60. Alpers says that the decision to use landscape as the representative anecdote of pastoral (which both Bruno Snell and Renato Poggioli do in their influential texts) derives from Romantic assumptions about aesthetics and poetry. Alpers defines the "representative anecdote" of pastoral as "the lives of shepherds." Shelley is interesting as a pastoralist because all the standard pastoral elements exist in his poetry, but his is a world singularly bereft of shepherds. In the older vocabulary Shelley's pastoral is entirely soft rather than hard. No georgic element intrudes, although, as I point out later in this chapter, the end of *Prometheus Unbound* aestheticizes labor, making that which was formerly onerous into something pleasurable: "Labour and Pain and Grief in life's green grove / Sport like tame beasts—none knew how gentle they could be!" (4.404–5).

5. A brief cue to the direction I shall follow was made in a review of three books dealing with Shelley's purported radical political and philosophical thought. See William Keach, "Radical Shelley?" *Raritan*, 5.2 (1985): 120–29. His question mark is especially significant. Keach reminds us, at the end, that "[r]adical Shelley keeps his distance from the asssumptions and instincts of those he continues to inspire" (p. 129), owing primarily to his complicated feelings about the nature of class. On the subject of Shelley's conservatism, one might consult as well Donald H. Reiman, "Shelley as Agrarian Reactionary," *Keats–Shelley Memorial Bulletin*, 30 (1979): 5–15; Sandra M. Gilbert and Susan Gubar, *The Madwoman in the Attic: The Woman Writer and the Nineteenth-Century Literary Imagination* (New Haven: Yale University Press, 1979), p. 6; and Ross Woodman, *The Apocalyptic Vision in the Poetry of Shelley* (Toronto: University of Toronto Press, 1964). Barbara Charlesworth Gelpi, *Shelley's Goddess: Maternity, Language, Subjectivity* (New York: Oxford University Press, 1992), likens Shelley to Herbert Marcuse, both of them "middle-class intellectuals writing during periods of hegemonic conservatism" (p. 162). If we wish to label Shelley high-bourgeois instead of aristocratic, we must do so with an understanding of the relative differences between the English class system and our own.

6. See William Keach, *Shelley's Style* (New York: Methuen, 1984); and Stuart Curran, *Poetic Form and British Romanticism* (New York: Oxford University Press, 1986), passim, for the fullest discussions of Shelley as stylist. As an anecdotal aside, I might mention an incident of some years back in the Harvard English department. We graduate students were asked to write a paper comparing any sonnet of Sidney's to one of Shakespeare's. One of us, who later left *sans* degree to assume his seat in the House of Lords, chose "Come Sleep, O Sleep, the Certain Knot of Peace," and "Weary with Toil, I Haste Me to My Bed," his major *aperçu* being that Sidney could never have begun a poem "Weary with toil," but that for a middle-class writer such as Shakespeare such a trope was both justifiable and natural. We were amused at what we regarded as such a nonliterary judgment; in retrospect I realize that the young aristocrat was probably correct.

7. Matthew Arnold, *Essays in Criticism, Second Series* (1888; rpt. London: Macmillan, 1905), p. 252.

8. Stuart Curran makes a similar point by differentiating Shelley from Wordsworth: the former "is not engaged by the presence of nature per se. To him in his philosophical idealisms it is a neutral grounding for what does greatly con-

cern him, the mind's internal adjustments, its translation of the objects of perception into mental points of reference." Stuart Curran, "Shelley's Pisan Pastorals," in *Paradise of Exiles: Shelley and Byron in Pisa,* ed. Mario Curreli and Anthony L. Johnson (Salzburg: Institut für Anglistik und Amerikanistik, 1988), p. 19. I would argue, beyond Curran, that Shelley's pastoral, far from being an imaginative reverie, is constituted by his sense of aristocratic entitlement, and is a highly material one.

9. Percy Bysshe Shelley, *Letters,* ed. Frederick L. Jones (Oxford: Clarendon Press, 1964), 2:71n. Shelley made the claim according to Thomas Love Peacock.

10. In this regard it is helpful to think of Shelley in the tradition of Romantic pastoral formulated by Schiller in his condemnation of the idyll: "They place that purpose *behind* us, *toward* which they should, however, lead us, and hence they imbue us with a sad feeling of loss, not with joyous feelings of hope." Friedrich Schiller, *Naive and Sentimental Poetry,* trans. Julias Elias (New York: Frederick Ungar, 1966), p. 149. Shelley's pastoral is always of the future, and by rights might be labeled utopian rather than nostalgic.

11. Earl A. Wasserman, *Shelley: A Critical Reading* (Baltimore: Johns Hopkins University Press, 1971): "[The poem] redirects the same ideological and psychoreligious pattern to a wholly world-oriented view in order to ask what it reveals about life, rather than about divinity and immortality, as though it were the *Hymn* seen from the other side" (p. 198).

12. Donald Davie, "Shelley's Urbanity," in *Purity of Diction in English Verse* (London: Chatto & Windus, 1952), pp. 133–59.

13. Donald H. Reiman, "Structure, Symbol, and Theme in 'Lines Written Among the Euganean Hills,'" reprinted in *Shelley's Poetry and Prose,* ed. Donald H. Reiman and Sharon B. Powers (New York: Norton, 1977), pp. 579–96, provides the clearest analysis of the structure and style of the poem, but curiously ignores the difficult peculiarities of the poem's ending, which concern me here.

14. M. H. Abrams, "Structure and Style in the Greater Romantic Lyric," in *From Sensibility to Romanticism: Essays Presented to F. A. Pottle,* ed. F. W. Hilles and Harold Bloom (New York: Oxford University Press, 1965), pp. 527–60; see also Earl Wasserman, "The English Romantics: The Grounds of Knowledge," *Studies in Romanticism,* 4 (1964): 17–34.

15. According to Neville Rogers, *Shelley at Work: A Critical Inquiry,* 2nd ed. (Oxford: Clarendon Press, 1967), p. 246, "Epipsychidion" began with its ending, the first part Shelley composed. This gives a new twist to my sense of *termini a quo* and *ad quem.*

16. William A. Ulmer, *Shelleyan Eros: The Rhetoric of Romantic Love* (Princeton: Princeton University Press, 1990), pp. 131–55 ("Italian Platonics"), discusses the tower as a version of Wordsworth's Ruined Cottage, and as a literary palimpsest. Ulmer concludes that "by extolling a golden age, *Epipsychidion* glances back to classical pastoral. But the poem dislocates its classical models by supplementing nature with civilization" (p. 146). I prefer to think of such supplementarity as a principle inhererent in all versions of sophisticated pastoral beginning with Virgil.

17. The various minglings depicted in the poem owe something to Shelley's delighted feelings about Italy, what it was and what it represented. Among his earliest recorded impressions (April 20, 1818, to Peacock) is his observation that "the union of culture and the untameable profusion and loveliness of nature is here so close that the line where they are divided can hardly be discovered" (*Letters,* 2:7). Shelley's editor suggests that the end of the "Epipsychidion" (ll. 483–512) is

probably based on Shelley's description of the Baths of Caracalla (March 23, 1819) in *Letters,* 2:84.

18. F. R. Leavis long ago pointed out the difficulties in Shelley's syntax and the vagueness of his pronominal antecedents; see "Shelley," in *Revaluation: Tradition and Development in English Poetry* (1936; rpt. New York: Norton, 1963), pp. 203–40. My point here is not to second Shelley's hostile critics but to attach his style (which they might label lazily indolent) to his philosophical program of "possession." Wasserman, *Shelley,* p. 449, stresses the "identity of the poet and Emily not only with each other but also with their island paradise" (ll. 549–52) and their regression to an "original human state" as the island returns to a golden age. His philosophical bias encourages him to stress that "the most intimate relationship they can attain in life is only the mutuality of possessing and being possessed by each other and their island circumference of bliss, while yet remaining distinct" (p. 456).

19. Jean Hall, *The Transforming Image: A Study of Shelley's Major Poetry* (Urbana: University of Illinois Press, 1980), p. 12, discusses the "sense of incompleteness" generated by the envoi. This emerges as part of a recurring pattern within the larger context of Shelley's poetry. Newman Ivey White, *Shelley* (New York: Knopf, 1940), 2:268, also discusses the inconsistencies of the ending; and Stuart Sperry, *Shelley's Major Verse: The Narrative and Dramatic Poetry* (Cambridge, Mass.: Harvard University Press, 1988), p. 175, mentions the sexism inherent in Shelley's harem.

20. Although Wasserman, *Shelley,* p. 420n., connects the incest motif in "Epipsychidion" and throughout Shelley's works generally with the Song of Songs, his translation of the Homeric hymns, and "the mythic condition of a Golden Age, a paradisiacal state," it is important to note that in Virgil and elsewhere incest exists as a possibility only among the gods, never among humans even in paradise. Surely the incest motif must be one of Shelley's most extreme aristocratic appropriations of pastoral. Nathaniel Brown, *Sexuality and Feminism in Shelley* (Cambridge, Mass.: Harvard University Press, 1979), has the fullest treatment of incest, and of idealized, fully passionate but nonerotic relationships—with both men and women—in Shelley.

21. For the contradictions between Shelley's doctrine of free love and the totality of Emily-as-sun, see James Rieger, *The Mutiny Within: The Heresies of Percy Bysshe Shelley* (New York: Braziller, 1967), pp. 201–2.

22. Irving Babbitt, *Rousseau and Romanticism* (Boston: Houghton Mifflin, 1919), pp. 220–39.

23. W. B. Yeats, *"Prometheus Unbound"* (1932) in *Essays and Introductions* (London: Macmillan, 1961), p. 424.

24. W. B. Yeats, "Poetry and Tradition" (1907), in *Essays and Introductions,* p. 251.

25. W. B. Yeats, "The Philosophy of Shelley's Poetry" (1900), in *Essays and Introductions,* p. 95.

26. Stephen treated Shelley as a figure from the distant past rather than, as Yeats did, a virtual contemporary. For Stephen, Shelley was a mere dabbler in utopian fantasies, and *Prometheus Unbound* embodied a millennial concept "that man is to be made perfect by the complete dissolution of all the traditional ties by which the race is at present held together. . . . In the coming world everybody is to say exactly what he thinks." Stephen misunderstood Shelley's pastoral worlds as fairylands: "He is happiest when he can get away from the world altogether into a vague

region, having no particular relation to time or space; to the valleys haunted by the nymphs in the *Prometheus;* or the mystic island in the *Epipsychidion,* where all sights and sounds are as the background of a happy dream, fitting symbols of sentiments too impalpable to be fairly grasped in language; or that 'calm and blooming cave' of the lines in the Euganean hills." See Leslie Stephen, *Hours in a Library,* 4 vols. (London: Smith, Elder & Co., Duckworth, 1907), 3:379 and 404–05.

27. Harry Berger, Jr., *Second World and Green World: Studies in Renaissance Fiction-Making* (Berkeley: University of California Press, 1988), p. 251.

28. For a strong reading of the role of the fourth act as "aria" and of the impelling revocation of Prometheus' curse at line 59, see Tilottama Rajan, "Deconstruction or Reconstruction: Reading Shelley's *Prometheus Unbound,*" in *The Supplement of Reading: Figures of Understanding in Romantic Theory and Practice* (Ithaca, N.Y.: Cornell University Press, 1990), pp. 298–322. Rajan, in her earlier treatment of Shelley in *Dark Interpreter: The Discourse of Romanticism* (Ithaca, N.Y.: Cornell University Press, 1980), sees his career as "an alternation between idealism and skepticism" (p. 83) which invites the kind of deconstructive readings she favors. Other recent critics have found a new climax in the play. Stuart Curran, *Shelley's Annus Mirabilis* (San Marino, Calif.: Huntington Library, 1975), p. 38, locates it during Asia's meeting with Demogorgon (2.4); in her lengthy, persuasive feminist commentary, Gelpi (pp. 137–266) realigns Shelley's pastoral experiments specifically with the descent of the Mother Goddess to rescue a lost son or lover.

29. Famous cases for Shelley's skepticism have been made by C. E. Pulos, *The Deep Truth: A Study of Shelley's Skepticism* (Lincoln: University of Nebraska Press, 1954); and Harold Bloom, *Shelley's Mythmaking* (New Haven: Yale University Press, 1959). More recent approaches have been taken by the deconstructive Paul De Man, "Shelley Disfigured," in *Deconstruction and Romanticism,* ed. Harold Bloom (New York: Continuum, 1979), pp. 39–73; and by Terence Allan Hoagwood, in *Skepticism and Ideology: Shelley's Political Prose and Its Philosophical Context from Bacon to Marx* (Iowa City: University of Iowa Press, 1988), who examines the prose but not the poetry. See also Andrew M. Cooper, *Doubt and Identity in Romantic Poetry* (New Haven: Yale University Press, 1988), esp. pp. 7–34, 165–84. No surer antiapocalyptic note is sounded in Shelley than the concluding lyric in *Hellas* ("The world's great age begins anew"), which treats the cycles of history with an unstated sense that every golden age must succumb to the ravages of subsequent falls. That sense is made manifest in the pathetic conclusion, surely an anticipation of all sorts of fin-de-siècle weariness in avatars as diverse as the early Yeats and the fictional Stephen Dedalus. Shelley proclaims an end to history by treating it as a Gordian knot that requires an Alexander to undo it:

> O cease! must hate and death return?
>   Cease! must men kill and die?
> Cease! drain not to its dregs the urn
>   Of bitter prophecy.
> The world is weary of the past,
> O might it die or rest at last!

The oppressiveness of the past may potentially repeat itself in the future; finality can be expressed only by hopeful imperatives ("Cease!") and optatives ("O might it die").

30. For aspects of Virgilian imagery, see W. R. Johnson, *Darkness Visible: A Study of Vergil's Aeneid* (Berkeley: University of California Press, 1976); Bernard

Knox, "The Serpent and the Flame: The Imagery of the Second Book of the *Aeneid*," in *Virgil: A Collection of Critical Essays*, ed. Steele Commager (Englewood Cliffs, N.J.: Prentice-Hall, 1966), pp. 124–42; Victor Pöschl, *The Art of Virgil: Image and Symbol in the Aeneid*, trans. Gerda Seligson (Ann Arbor: University of Michigan Press, 1962); and Michael C. J. Putnam, *The Poetry of the Aeneid* (Cambridge, Mass.: Harvard University Press, 1965).

31. Jerrold E. Hogle, *Shelley's Process: Radical Transference and the Development of His Major Works* (New York: Oxford University Press, 1988), pp. 202–4, also includes Plato's Cave, Homer's Cave of the Nymphs, Zoroaster, the Cumaean Sibyl, and Shelley's own "still cave" of Poesy in "Mont Blanc" among the sources for this scene. Hogle calls the cave a "serene but teeming clearinghouse of figural possibilities." His extended analysis of *Prometheus Unbound*, especially pp. 167–205, deserves attention.

32. Oscar Wilde, "The Soul of Man Under Socialism," in *Complete Works*, ed. Robert Ross (New York: Bigelow, Brown, 1905), 4:298–99.

33. Neville Rogers continues the interpretation of Shelley as Platonist when he remarks: "Men, he believed with Rousseau, Montesquieu, and others, are naturally virtuous and happy but have been corrupted by the evils resulting from false sophistication and false civilization" (p. 27).

34. Taking a cue from Paul Cantor, I wonder whether Shelley's aristocratic pastoral owes a debt to Rousseau's *Reveries of the Solitary Walker*, especially since this work, its author's last, implies that only a select few can profit from the escape from society that Rousseau himself enjoys. The dreamer–walker has the best of the natural and socially progressive situations. Rousseau's own self-aggrandizing image in this book differs from his theories in *The Social Contract* concerning the problems of man in society. See Paul Cantor, "A Discourse on Eden," in *Creature and Creator: Myth-Making and English Romanticism* (Cambridge: Cambridge University Press, 1984), pp. 1–25, on Rousseau, and "The Prelude to Apocalypse" (pp. 77–102), on *Prometheus Unbound*. Cantor labels *Prometheus* an "anti-mythic myth" because Shelley employs myth "but distrusts its power" (p. 94); his use of pastoral, I suggest, is equally peculiar, but not in a negative way. Gelpi, who calls Prometheus and the Oceanides a quartet imagined "as stay-at-homes in a single cave or as leisured gentry with the diversion of travel between two" (p. 245), strikes the right tone, and makes the life of the new order sound remarkably like that of Judith Traherne and her noble doctor–husband in *Dark Victory*. Once more, breeding tells.

35. Curran, *Poetic Form and British Romanticism*, p. 116, calls Shelley's "the subtlest and most extensive reinterpretation of pastoral after Wordsworth's." In his twelve pages on Shelley (pp. 116–27), however, he does little with *Adonais* other than labeling it "a poem of almost abstracted generic purity" (p. 124), giving more attention to "Rosalind and Helen," which he admires, and to "Julian and Maddalo," as examples of "the singing contest [as] ultimately one act of humane fellowship in sympathy with and linking life and art" (p. 123).

36. The obvious Virgilian echoes in Shelley occur in the last song from *Hellas* ("The world's great age begins anew"), whose premise reminds us of Eclogue 4; in the epigraph to "Julian and Maddalo" from Eclogue 10 (the Maniac is like Virgil's love-torn Gallus); and in the dialogue of the two fauns in *Prometheus Unbound* 2.2. Wasserman, *Shelley*, pp. 310–23, discusses the additional importance of the second and fourth Georgics, and of Anchises' speech to his son in *Aeneid* 6.724–27.

37. Michael C. J. Putnam, *Virgil's Pastoral Art* (Princeton: Princeton University

Press, 1970), pp. 342–94, in his extended commentary on the tenth Eclogue, says that Virgil accepts "the final antagonism that exists between 'pastoral' (both as a poetic style and as a mode of life) and the realities of the Roman social and creative world around him" (p. 379). Paul Alpers, *The Singer of the Eclogues: A Study of Virgilian Pastoral* (Berkeley: University of California Press, 1979), pp. 222–40 (on the last Eclogue), argues against more conventional critics, such as Putnam, who think of pastoral as a reflection of Arcadian dolce far niente; instead he thinks of pastoral "not in terms of wish fulfillment but in terms of human needs and relations" (p. 225). Alpers's commentary on Eclogue 10 makes relevant reading for anyone interested in the "pastoral" peculiarities of *Adonais*. I think, especially, of his analysis of the way Virgil defers his own presentation: "[T]he poet who represents himself as a shepherd tests that project by representing (himself as?) another poet who represents himself as a shepherd" (p. 228; just as Virgil *is*, in some sense, Gallus, so is Shelley Keats); his sense of the two equivalent versions of pastoral, "the social and the egotistical" (p. 229); and, most important, his sense of the strength rather than the fragility of pastoral: "Pastoral, or any form of literary questioning, is truthful only if it does not presume on its own stability" (p. 237). For a discussion of the relationship of Eclogue 10 to *Alastor*, see Richard Cronin, *Shelley's Poetic Thoughts* (New York: St. Martin's Press, 1981), pp. 84–88.

38. I think of Richard Poirier's classic work *The Performing Self* (New York: Oxford University Press, 1971) in this regard. For example: "[B]y performance I mean, in part, any self-discovering, self-watching, self-pleasuring response to the pressures and difficulties I've been describing" (p. xiii); and "Performance may, in its self-assertiveness, be radical in impulse, but it is also conservative in its recognitions that the self is of necessity, if unwillingly, inclusive of all kinds of versions, absorbed from whatever source, of what the self might be" (p. xiv). I take these assertions as approximate truths regarding Shelley's self-performing, self-defining stylistic gestures.

39. John W. Draper, *The Funeral Elegy and the Rise of English Romanticism* (New York: New York University Press, 1929), deals mostly with broadsides and graveyard poetry but extensively surveys the field of elegy from the Restoration through the end of the eighteenth century. He has the dubious distinction of saying that "*Lycidas,* composed in the tradition of Renaissance pastoralism, with its characteristically Renaissance panegyric on Fame and its ecclesiastical satire in the tradition established by Petrarch, has nothing to contribute to the present study" (p. 71), a claim that certainly flies in the face of the more recent estimates of "Lycidas" by critics of Romanticism. Draper cites, inter alia, John Potenger's *Pastoral Reflections on Death* (1691) and Nahum Tate's couplet poem, *Pastoral Elegy in the Memory of of the Duke of Ormond* (1688), as examples of post-Miltonic pastoral elegies (pp. 192–93). In addition, there are two elegies by John Oldham—a version of Moschus' elegy for Bion, in memory of the Earl of Rochester, and an imitation of Bion's "Lamentation for Adonis"—both written in heroic couplets; see *The Poems of John Oldham,* ed. Harold F. Brooks and Roman Selden (Oxford: Clarendon, 1987), pp. 127–37.

40. See Donald H. Reiman, ed., *The Romantics Reviewed,* pt. C (New York: Garland, 1972), pp. 147–51, 510–13, 531–32.

41. Eric Smith, *By Mourning Tongues: Studies in English Elegy* (Ipswich, Eng.: Boydell Press, 1977), p. 68. Smith says that Shelley's self-presentation "implies a gross and nauseating self-pity for which no justification is given," but he seems

bothered equally by the poet's self-pity and his distanced aloofness. Readers have often been unsure how to place themselves vis-à-vis the autobiographical subject in Shelley's lyrics.

42. Peter Sacks, *The English Elegy: Studies in the Genre from Spenser to Yeats* (Baltimore: Johns Hopkins University Press, 1985), pp. 138–65, in the fullest recent treatment of the poem, mentions only in passing the matter of Shelley's theatricality, relegating it to a footnote (p. 347, n. 16). I am indebted to Sacks's analysis and appreciation of the poem, especially to his astute remarks on Shelley's various uses of the Spenserian stanza, and the way the alexandrines "mount beyond themselves" (p. 151) in the ampler affirmations of the poem's second half.

43. Reiman and Powers, p. 478. Note also Shelley's subsequent remark: "We are on the verge where words abandon us." The primary danger for a person is being abandoned *by* language, not failing to find the right words. Both Gelpi (p. 187) and Hogle (p. 13) make comparable points about the multiplicity of selfhood in Shelley. The latter, although he includes ethics, politics, style, metaphysics, and epistemology in his dense and thorough reading of Shelley's major poetry, is less interested in the role of aesthetics in Shelley's philosophy.

44. See Harold Bloom, "The Internalization of Quest Romance," in *The Ringers in the Tower* (Chicago: University of Chicago Press, 1971), pp. 13–36. Lore Metzger, *One Foot in Eden: Modes of Pastoral in Romantic Poetry* (Chapel Hill: University of North Carolina Press, 1986), pp. 59–78, discusses *Adonais* in relation to pastoral tradition, and considers the progress of the poem as "a series of resting places in the forms of earthly paradises, a series that culminates in the promise of eternal paradise" (pp. 74–75). Metzger undervalues, I think, the demi-paradises of "Epipsychidion," and *Prometheus Unbound,* claiming that "Shelley never embodied in his mature poetry a physical rather than a metaphysical model for creating a modern paradise out of the 'wrecks' of Eden" (p. 78).

Chapter 6

1. S. Weir Mitchell, *The Mother and Other Poems* (Boston: Houghton Mifflin, 1893), p. 59.

2. S. Weir Mitchell, "Evening by the Sea," ibid., p. 58. There is a larger issue here as well: the relationship of poets such as Whitman to the medical, moral, and physiological discourses of indolence throughout the first half of the century. Whitman knew the work of the British physician George Moore, whose anti-phrenological tract *The Power of the Soul over the Body Considered in Relation to Health and Morals* (1845; rpt. New York: Harper and Brothers, 1848) distinguishes, as Montaigne had done, between the need for rest and an excessive reliance on it. Whereas indolence is salutary in moderation, "healthy will is necessarily connected with bodily activity. This indolent vacuity, however, may become habitual, and then a legion of evils of a worse kind crowd in upon the soul, for irritability takes the place of natural action when the body is not duly employed" (p. 199).

3. Ralph Waldo Emerson, *Complete Works,* (Boston: Houghton Mifflin, 1904), 9:250–51.

4. For all its prominence in our collective memory, "loafing" and its variants appear minimally in *Leaves of Grass*: five times in "Song of Myself" (1.4, 1.5, 5.3, 15.9, 33.2), once each in "A Song of Occupations" and "To Think of Time." See Harold Edwin Eby, *A Concordance of Walt Whitman's "Leaves of Grass" and Selected Prose Writings* (Seattle: University of Washington Press, 1949). According to both

the *OED* and *A Dictionary of American English,* ed. Sir William A. Craigie (Chicago: University of Chicago Press, 1942), the origin of the word is unknown, but it made its first appearances in the 1830s (in *Harvardiana*). Whitman was the first to use the verb as a noun: "The farmer stops by the bars as he walks on a First-day loafe and looks at the oats and rye." The *OED* cites *Martin Chuzzlewit,* significantly Dickens's American novel, as a source; another interesting one is an article in the *Boston Journal* on the subject of specifically *literary* effort and its opposite: "Tennyson does the greater part of his literary work . . . between breakfast and lunch, and loafs the rest of the day."

5. George Santayana, "The Poetry of Barbarism," in *Interpretations of Poetry and Religion* (New York: Charles Scribner's Sons, 1900), pp. 177, 180.

6. The strongest recent case for Whitman's debts to the Romantics has been made by Diane Wood Middlebrook, in *Walt Whitman and Wallace Stevens* (Ithaca, N.Y.: Cornell University Press, 1974), who places Whitman's "Real Me" within the tradition of Coleridgean notions of the artist. Middlebrook says, rightly, that "the image of the loafing poet is central to the Romantic ideology of the poem"; she finds a parallel in "Frost at Midnight" for Whitman's "describing himself in a condition of unimaginativeness. . . . He is waiting for something and killing time with a little talk about himself" (p. 36). In addition, Middlebrook notes that "in Stevens, as in Whitman, the figure on whom imagination descends is characteristically a lounger—prone, or otherwise at his ease in a sensuous setting" (p. 37).

7. Emory Holloway, ed., *The Uncollected Poetry and Prose of Walt Whitman,* 2 vols. (Garden City, N.Y.: Doubleday, 1921), 1.44–46. Whitman was certainly posing in this piece. Much of his early journalism, such as the articles he wrote at the *Long Island Evening Star,* concerns the moral improvement of the young. He could speak (from experience?) equally well on behalf of loafing and against its pernicious influence.

8. Philip Callow, *From Noon to Starry Night: A Life of Walt Whitman* (Chicago: Ivan R. Dee, 1992), pp. 113, 129. Observations of this kind go back to Mark Van Doren's discussion of Whitman's *erethisia*—his chronic sensory excitement and susceptibility to touch—and his large, languorous body, as well as an adolescence that "seem[ed] almost wholly characterized by indolence and impressionability." See John Kinnaird, "*Leaves of Grass* and the American Paradox," in *Whitman: A Collection of Critical Essays* ed. Roy Harvey Pearce (Englewood Cliffs, N.J.: Prentice-Hall, 1962), p. 25.

9. Michael Moon, *Disseminating Whitman: Revision and Corporeality in Leaves of Grass* (Cambridge, Mass.: Harvard University Press, 1991), states the case for the ways in which "Whitman uses self-censorship strategically, making it a means of extending rather than contracting the range of his writing's meanings" (p. 45), and by which he evades traditional means of troping desires in order to render his own homoerotic ones more effectively.

10. For a discussion of Wordsworthian encounters, see Frederick Garber, *Wordsworth and the Poetry of Encounter* (Urbana: University of Illinois Press, 1971); also Willard Spiegelman, *Wordsworth's Heroes* (Berkeley: University of California Press, 1985).

11. Whitman read R. M. Milnes's essay on Keats in the *North British Review,* and in response to Keats's claim that the poet is the least poetical of creatures, he suggested: "The great poet absorbs the identity of others, and the experience of others, and they are definitely in him or from him; but he perceives them all through the powerful press of himself." In another article he scribbled "Materialism

as the foundation of poetry" (quoted in Callow, pp. 132–33). Among recent scholars, Diane Middlebrook (pp. 41–42) best demonstrates how Whitman shared the receptive, gestating, "feminine" imagination that Lionel Trilling long ago claimed as one Keats's strengths.

12. D. H. Lawrence, *Studies in Classic American Literature* (New York: Viking, 1964), p. 170.

13. Alan Helms, "'Hints . . . Faint Clews and Indirections': Whitman's Homosexual Disguises," in *Walt Whitman: Here and Now,* ed. Joann P. Krieg (Westport, Conn.: Greenwood Press, 1985), pp. 61–67.

14. Richard Poirier has made the point, in several contexts, that American pastoral is both democratic and conversational, although the latter can be said to be a direct inheritance from, rather than a swerving away from, the language of Virgil's Eclogues; see, especially, chapter 2, "The Transformation of Work," in *Poetry and Pragmatism* (Cambridge, Mass.: Harvard University Press, 1992), pp. 79–125. For an extended discussion of Frost as pastoralist, see John F. Lynen, *The Pastoral Art of Robert Frost* (New Haven: Yale University Press, 1960).

15. Henry David Thoreau, "Economy," in *Walden* (New York: Library of America, 1985), p. 329. Cf. Thoreau's journal entry of April 29, 1852: "The art of life, of a poet's life, is, not having anything to do, to do something," in *The Journal of Henry D. Thoreau,* ed. Bradford Torrey and Francis H. Allen (New York: Dover, 1962), 1:394.

16. It would be disingenuous to use this word now without some nod in the direction of Jacques Derrida's conception of the supplement, see *Of Grammatology,* trans. Gayatri Chakravorty Spivak (Baltimore: Johns Hopkins University Press, 1976), pp. 144–45. Derrida distinguishes between a "supplement," as that which either replaces or adds, and a "complement." In English as in French, the supplement is "an exterior addition," like the coat of paint in Frost's poem "The Investment." I use the word as a means to justify the category of "the aesthetic," which in either case (as complement or supplement) has an ambiguous connection to the base that supports it. The supplement, like Frost's coat of paint, has the additional function of protecting, rather than merely ornamenting, the thing beneath it.

17. Michael Pollan, *Second Nature: A Gardener's Education* (New York: Dell, 1991), pp. 50, 271.

18. In my book *The Didactic Muse: Scenes of Instruction in Contemporary American Poetry* (Princeton: Princeton University Press, 1989), I examine a variety of poets who embody, though in thoroughly different ways, a didactic impulse.

19. Frank Lentricchia, *Robert Frost: Modern Poetics and the Landscapes of Self* (Durham, N.C.: Duke University Press, 1975); and Richard Poirier, *Robert Frost: The Work of Knowing* (New York: Oxford University Press, 1977). Lentricchia's final chapter, "The Scope and Limits of Supreme Fiction" (pp. 139–72), summarizes Frost's place in post-Kantian aesthetics. One detects, however, a slightly puritanical streak in Lentricchia's summary of Frost on play: "All freedom from the excruciation of existence is purely aesthetic achievement" (p. 149). Poirier points us toward the necessity and labor, as well as the fun, of such "pure" aesthetic achievement.

20. See, in this regard, the witty denial of this basic principle of Aristotelian logic in Howard Nemerov's "Metaphysical Automobile":

> You can't resolve a contradiction by
> Getting between the warring opposites.

> The idea of a car either has a dent
> In its left front fender or it downright don't,
> There's no third way. For on the roads of thought
> You're either nominalist or realist,
> The only question universals ask
> Is is you is or is you ain't my baby?

And yet:

> So straight
> Flat roads of logic lie about a globe
> On which the shortest way between two points
> Happens to be a curve. And so do song
> And story, winding crank and widdershins,
> Still get there first, and poetry remains
> Eccentric and odd and riddling and right,
> Eternal return of the excluded middle.

The Collected Poems of Howard Nemerov (Chicago: University of Chicago Press, 1977), pp. 452–53.

21. Roger Gilbert, *Walks in the World: Representation and Experience in Modern American Poetry* (Princeton: Princeton University Press, 1991), p. 58, argues against most critics of the poem by claiming that "useful objects are abandoned because the person to whom they are of use no longer exists." He thinks the woodcutter has died, and that Frost presents the woodpile as a "small-scale version of the statue in Shelley's 'Ozymandias'" (p. 59). Gilbert's point is unprovable: the man has gone and we can know nothing about him. And since the woodpile is neither sculpted, representational, nor legible, we cannot take it as a speaking monument.

22. Elizabeth Bishop, *The Complete Poems, 1927–79* (New York: Farrar Straus Giroux, 1983), pp. 127–28.

23. Anne Stevenson, "Letters from Elizabeth Bishop," *Times Literary Supplement,* March 7, 1980, pp. 261–62.

24. James Merrill, *From the First Nine: Poems, 1946–76* (New York: Atheneum, 1982), p. 291.

25. James Merrill, *The Changing Light at Sandover* (New York: Atheneum, 1982), p. 38.

Appendix A

1. Judith Chernaik, *The Lyrics of Shelley* (Cleveland: Press of Case Western Reserve, 1972); Richard Cronin, *Shelley's Poetic Thoughts* (New York: St. Martin's Press, 1981), pp. 242–49, on "With a Guitar. To Jane," and its debt to Herrick; Donald Davie, *Purity of Diction in English Poetry* (London: Chatto & Windus, 1952), pp. 133–59; G. M. Matthews, "Shelley's Lyrics," in *The Morality of Art,* ed. D. W. Jefferson (London: Routledge & Kegan Paul, 1969), pp. 195–209; William Keach, "Shelley's Last Lyrics," in *Shelley's Style* (New York: Methuen, 1984), pp. 201–34.

2. The phrase is from Byron's description of his own poetry, in a letter to John Murray, August 23, 1821. See *Byron's Letters and Journals,* ed. Leslie A. Marchand (Cambridge, Mass.: Harvard University Press, 1978), 8:186–87; it has been appropriated as the title of Alan Richardson, *A Mental Theater: Poetic Drama and*

Consciousness in the Romantic Age (University Park: Pennsylvania State University Press, 1988); see, especially, pp. 124–53 on *Prometheus Unbound* and the relation to a "mental theater" of the intensely lyrical act 4.

3. Helen Vendler, "Lionel Trilling and the *Immortality Ode,*" *Salmagundi,* 41 (1978): 66–86, posits the capacity for metaphor as the major difference between children and adults.

Index

Abrams, M. H., 45, 64, 74, 76, 116
Absence
  Coleridge's obsession with, 74, 76
  in Keats's poetry, 84
Acedia, Accidie
  Coleridge's, 63
  concept of, 7–9
  metamorphosis of, 10
  as urban disease, 14
"Adam's Curse" (Yeats), 24
Adolescence, and poetic vocation, 56
Adonais (Shelley), 111, 130–41, 162,
    167
  anticipation of Shelley's death in, 162
  last lines of, 140
  pastoral frame of, 137
Aeneid, The (Virgil), 124
"Aesthetic, the," 4
  in Frost's poetry, 150
  indolence and, 157
Aestheticism
  Romantic, 153
  self-indulgent, 26
Aesthetic Letters (Schiller), 28
Aesthetics
  ethical conduct and, 52
  experience of, 16–17
  Nietzsche on, 77
  origins of, 28
  of watching, 70
Agriculture, culture and, 53
"Alastor" (Shelley), 133

Alexandrian monastics, 8
Allegory
  in Keats's poetry, 85
  in Merrill's poetry, 160
  pseudo-Spenserian, 132
  in Shelley's poetry, 127, 128,
    135–36
  in Thomson's poetry, 88–89
Alliteration
  in Whitman's poetry, 146
  Wordsworth's use of, 55
Almeida, Hermione de, 98
American Gardener, The (Lacy), 151
Ammons, A. R., 67
"Among the Multitude" (Whitman), 149
Anacoluthon, 69
"Rime of the Ancient Mariner, The"
    (Coleridge), 64, 71
"An Irish Airman Foresees His Death"
    (Yeats), 104
Annexes (Whitman), 145, 146
Apatheia, 7, 90
Apathy
  in Keats's poetry, 94
  Robinson's, 61–62
"Apple-Picking, After" (Frost), 150
Aristocracy
  and pastoral, 110
  and pastoral poetry, 123
  Shelley's view of, 109–10
Aristotle, 28, 152
Arnold, Matthew, 111

213

Cooke, Michael, 194–95 n.26
Critique of Aesthetic Judgement (Kant), 18
Cronin, Richard, 161
"Crossing Brooklyn Ferry" (Whitman),
  149

Dante
  and concept of sloth, 8
  sonnet to Cavalcanti of, 115
Dark Victory (Robinson), 109, 110,
  166
Davie, Donald, 27, 112, 161
Davies, Hugh Sykes, 5
Davis, Bette, 109
Death
  perfect pastoral of, 141
  Shelley's, 162
  in Whitman's poetry, 146
Defence of Poetry, A (Shelley), 167
Dejection, Coleridgean, 69, 72, 161
"Dejection: An Ode" (Coleridge), 60, 62,
  92, 148
  active and passive poles in, 78
  analysis of, 70
  conclusion of, 71
  form of, 67
  negation in, 70, 81
  seventh stanza of, 77
  sixth stanza of, 69
  tension in, 66
  use of trope in, 65
Derrida, Jacques, 186 n.18, 210 n.16
Dialogue, in *Lyrical Ballads,* 28
Didacticism, in Romantic poetry, 90,
  91
Dowden, Edward, 111
Drum-Taps (Whitman), 150
Dunciad, The (Pope), 79–80

Eagleton, Terry, 50, 98
Economics, of leisure industry, 11
Elias, Norbert, 11
Eliot, George (Mary Ann Evans), 6–7, 28,
  82
Emerson, Ralph Waldo, 143, 151, 157,
  160
Empson, William, 30
"End of March, The" (Bishop), 158
Endymion (Keats), 24, 101, 153
"Eolian Harp, The" (Coleridge), 65, 78,
  148
"Epipsychidion" (Shelley), 111, 116–23,
  127, 128, 133, 137, 139, 141, 148,
  162, 163, 166, 167
"Epistle to John Hamilton Reynolds"
  (Keats), 101
Eroticism
  Marlovian, 86
  in Shelley's poetry, 119–20, 122
"Eve of St. Agnes, The" (Keats), 88, 132
"Experience" (Emerson), 160

"Expostulation and Reply" (Wordsworth),
  29–30, 35, 143

Faerie Queene, The (Spenser), 9
"Fair Stars Were Twinkling, The" (Shel-
  ley), 161
"Fall of Hyperion" (Keats), 116
Fatigue, pleasures of, 6. *See also* Indolence
"Fears in Solitude" (Coleridge), 77
Felix Farley's Bristol Journal, 68
Feminism, and writing of literary history,
  5
Fielding, Henry, 45
"Filling Station" (Bishop), 157–58
Fitzgerald, Geraldine, 109
Foucault, Michel, 14
"Fountain, The" (Wordsworth), 30–31, 33
Fourier, Charles, 144
"Four Seasons Fill the Measure of the
  Year" (Keats), 103–4
Fowler, Alastair, 110
Fox, Ruth, 9, 10
Freedom
  in Frost's poetry, 154
  in Milton's rhetoric, 87
  in sense of leisure, 18
  Shelley's vision of, 121
Freud, Sigmund, 15
Frost, Robert, 4, 142
  accident in poetry of, 155–56
  and aristocratic pastoral, 152
  binaries in poetry of, 157
  extravagance in poetry of, 153
  feeling for abandonment of, 155
  human forgetfulness in poetry of, 155
  indolence in poetry of, 150, 152, 154,
    157
  influence of Whitman on, 150
  nature in poetry of, 154, 156
  ornament in poetry of, 153, 155
  purpose in poetry of, 155–56
  work in poetry of, 152
"Frost at Midnight" (Coleridge), 71, 74–
  76, 77, 78, 81, 158
Fuller, Margaret, 144

"Garden of Boccaccio" (Coleridge),
  196 n.31
Gardens, in American poetry, 151–52. *See
  also* Landscape
Generalizations, passive, 38
Geography III (Bishop), 159
"Gipsies" (Wordsworth), 33
Godwin, William, 59
Goellnicht, Donald, 98, 99, 101
Goethe, Johann Wolfgang von, 8
"Good-Bye My Fancy" (Whitman), 145,
  146
Grasmere Fair, 23
Gray, Thomas, 91
Greeley, Horace, 144